Reappraisals

Also by Peter Uwe Hohendahl

*Building a National Literature: The Case of Germany,
1830–1870*
(translated by Renate Baron Franciscono)

The Institution of Criticism

Reappraisals

Shifting Alignments in Postwar Critical Theory

Peter Uwe Hohendahl

Cornell University Press
Ithaca and London

First published 1991 by Cornell University Press.

International Standard Book Number 0-8014-2455-0 (cloth)
International Standard Book Number 0-8014-9706-X (paper)
Library of Congress Catalog Card Number 91-10217

Printed in the United States of America

Librarians: Library of Congress cataloging information appears on the last page of the book.

⊗ The paper in this book meets the minimum requirements of the American National Standard for Information Sciences— Permanence of Paper for Printed Library Materials, ANSI Z39.48-1984.

Contents

Preface

The title of this book calls attention to significant shifts in the debate about and the use of Critical Theory. Since about 1980, not only the parameters but also the character of the discussion have changed. Before that, by and large, the Frankfurt School and Critical Theory were perceived as part of the larger project of Western Marxism—as a revisionist version of the Marxist tradition in which Hegel's dialectic strongly resurfaced, breaking up the scientific orientation of the Second International and the neoorthodoxy of the Third International. While the evaluation of the Frankfurt School ranged from outspoken hostility to emphatic praise, there was a consensus about the locus of the Frankfurt School within the Marxist tradition.

Recently, however, the boundaries of this tradition have become more fluid. The interface and exchange with other traditions have changed our understanding of both Western Marxism and Critical Theory. The essays collected in this volume reflect as well as respond to these shifts. They attempt to reconsider the Frankfurt School from the vantage point of the contemporary debate in Europe and the United States. Although they were originally written under varied circumstances and with different purposes in mind, they share a common theme: the development of Critical Theory, in particular its history after the Second World War.

More than is usual, I have emphasized the connection with the early Lukács, a link the members of the Frankfurt School never fully acknowledged. Mediated through Lukács's prewar writings, the German romantic tradition, sometimes in its neo-romantic gestalt, left its traces on the Frankfurt School. Of crucial importance for the contemporary debate is the transition from the first to the second generation of Critical Theory, which must not be understood as a mere temporal sequence. Rather, I suggest in these essays that this transition is a complex and intertwined reconfiguration. Sometimes advances occur in the form of a return to older positions, sometimes expected directions change because of confrontations with competing theoretical traditions. For this reason, the essays cannot be organized as a linear historical evolution. Moreover, national theoretical developments rarely coincide. I try to show that the German and the American perspectives vis-à-vis Critical Theory have differed significantly during the last two decades.

With the exception of the Introduction and the final one, the chapters of this book have all appeared in journals and special collections before. An earlier version of Chapter 1 appeared in German in *Geschichtlichkeit und Aktualität*, ed. Klaus-Dieter Müller, Gerhard Pasternack, Wulf Segebrecht, and Ludwig Stockinger (Tübingen: Max Niemeyer Verlag, 1988). Chapter 2 first appeared in *New German Critique* 42 (Fall 1987). Chapter 3 came out in *The German Quarterly* 54 (1981). Chapter 4 is a revised version of an essay that appeared in *New German Critique* 35 (Spring/Summer 1985). An earlier version of Chapter 5 was published in *Telos* 69 (Fall 1986), and a version of Chapter 6 appeared in *Deutsche Literatur in der Bundesrepublik seit 1965, Untersuchungen und Berichte*, ed. Paul Michael Lüzeler and Egon Schwarz (Königstein: Athenäum Publishing House, 1980). I am grateful to the editors of the journals and essay collections for the permission to reprint. Excellent draft translations of Chapters 1 and 6 were provided by Karen Kenkel and Brian Urquhart.

Preface

In the final preparation of the manuscript I was assisted by Andreas Kriefall and Jeffrey Schneider, whose tireless efforts I greatly appreciate. Finally, I thank Gisela Podleski for typing parts of the manuscript.

PETER UWE HOHENDAHL

Ithaca, New York

Reappraisals

Introduction:
Marx, the Frankfurt School,
and West German History

Before 1970 the term "Critical Theory," if used at all in this country, referred to the works of the Frankfurt School, that is, to the writings of Max Horkheimer and Theodor W. Adorno, Herbert Marcuse, and Leo Lowenthal. More recently, the name of Jürgen Habermas has been added to this group, although opinions are divided as to whether his work, especially his more recent theory, can be subsumed under the old term. Yet this uncertainty should be seen as a positive sign, namely as an indication that Critical Theory is alive, responding to new and different cultural and political situations. In Germany the second generation of the Frankfurt School, of which Habermas is the most prominent representative, began to develop its own and different mode of theory after the death of Adorno and the climax of the student revolution in 1969. Although there was less of an obvious turning point than in France—where the defeat of the student revolution in May 1968 also shook the foundations of the Communist party and Marxist theory—in West Germany Critical Theory entered a new phase about 1970, in which ultimately the links to the Marxist paradigm became weaker and the attachment to the Marxian text a question of critical interpretation rather than a matter of faith. Of course, a similar argument can be made for the first generation of the Frankfurt School; at no time can its members be described as orthodox Marxists. Even during the 1930s, when they still used traditional Marxist concepts, they were selective in their application of the Marxist paradigm. Still, they could always reaffirm the element of truth in Marxist theory. Not only does the culture-industry chapter of *Dialectic of Enlightenment* (1947) articulate basic Marxist concepts, but also in Adorno's latest writings, for instance in *Aesthetic Theory*, the presence of Marx is strongly felt. For the next generation this presence is less certain; the revisions are so far-reaching that Marx—as in the writings of Jürgen Habermas—becomes just one theorist among others. Even when a Marxist position is more clearly affirmed, for example in the writings of Oskar Negt and Alexander Kluge, this recuperation does not simply continue an orthodox position; rather, it opens a critical and sometimes polemical dialogue with other strands of Critical Theory.

The American situation is not altogether different.[1] During the 1970s the understanding of Critical Theory was beginning to change, both from within and from the outside. In this country it was of course more the voices of Herbert Marcuse and Leo Lowenthal that dominated the discourse of the 1960s and influenced the New Left. While it would be difficult to give a specific date for this change, both the scope and the emphasis of Critical Theory shifted during the 1970s, but not necessarily in the same direction as in West Germany. On the one hand, partly through the increasing impact of Habermas's work in the English-speaking world, there is an apparent parallel to the West German situation, that is, a reformulation of Critical Theory in terms of linguistic and pragmatic theory;[2] on the other hand, there is also an equally strong attempt to connect the thought of the old Frankfurt School with poststructuralist theory. As Catherine Gallagher observes in a recent essay, the agenda of the New Historicism can be traced back, at least in

1. See Perry Anderson, *In the Tracks of Historical Materialism* (Chicago, 1984).

2. See *Habermas and Modernity*, ed. Richard J. Bernstein (Cambridge, Mass., 1985).

part, to the New Left.³ Thus it would be plausible to define the New Historicism as a radical revision of revisionist (Marcusian) Marxism. Obviously, in this metamorphosis, the model of the classical Critical Theory is hardly discernible anymore; it has become an atmospheric presence. For this reason the term "Critical Theory" has taken on a broader meaning in this country: it includes the Frankfurt School but also different strands of oppositional theory.

In contrast, the West German usage has been much more restricted, since poststructuralist models have been introduced in opposition to the Frankfurt School. Habermas's critical response to French theory (beginning in 1980) would only be the most obvious case in point. As long as the cohesion of the "school" dominated the German situation, the possibility of an integration of Critical Theory and poststructuralist paradigms was clearly remote. In this respect the American situation has been much more ambiguous: while the debate between Habermasians and poststructuralists has been mostly polemical, with a strong sense of defending one's own ground, the appropriation of Benjamin's and Adorno's work by American critics has been less restricted to a particular camp. Benjamin in particular has been claimed for a variety of agendas ranging from Marxism to deconstruction.⁴ As a result, the boundaries of "Critical Theory" have become less clear during the last decade. Moreover, German and American theoretical discourse, in spite of a considerable amount of theoretical exchange, drifted apart during the 1970s and only recently, after the appropriation of poststructuralism in West Germany, can we speak of comparable configurations again.

The broad use of the term "Critical Theory" today reflects a trend toward blending paradigms and models with less regard for traditional boundaries and conceptional logic and more em-

3. Catherine Gallagher, "Marxism and the New Historicism," in *The New Historicism*, ed. H. Aram Veeser (New York, 1988), 37–48.

4. See Michael W. Jennings, *Dialectical Images* (Ithaca, 1987), 1–14.

phasis on the situational aspect of theories, that is, their embeddedness in specific cultural practices. Hence the question What is the meaning and relevance of Critical Theory today? has to be answered in local terms. The response in Germany will differ from that in the United States. In West Germany, Critical Theory, after the disintegration of the Institut für Sozialforschung (Institute for Social Research) in 1969, has positioned itself in opposition to functionalist social theory (for instance, Niklas Luhmann), on the one hand, and a Foucauldian approach, on the other. Even those critics who did not follow the so-called linguistic turn in Habermas's writings and stayed closer to the older Frankfurt School kept a distance, by and large, from poststructuralist theory—Karl Heinz Bohrer's work might be mentioned here—while the supporters of French theory (Michel Foucault) for the most part were no longer familiar with or interested in the tradition of Critical Theory.[5] The exception may be Samuel Weber, a student of Paul de Man and collaborator of Peter Szondi, who introduced Jacques Lacan to a German academic audience in 1978.[6] Weber prepared the transition from Critical Theory to post-Freudian psychoanalysis, while Szondi himself, developing a hermeneutical model in his later work, refused to participate in this trend. More typical, however, is the break with former allegiances and the ensuing formation of a new identity, as we find it in the writings of Helga Gallas, who started out as a Marxist and later embraced poststructuralist theory.[7]

5. Karl Heinz Bohrer (born in 1935) has been a journalist and literary critic and a professor of German at the University of Bielefeld; in 1983 he became editor of the important magazine *Merkur*; see his books *Plötzlichkeit: Zum Augenblick des ästhetischen Scheins* (Frankfurt, 1981), and *Die Entwicklung der ästhetischen Subjektivität* (Frankfurt, 1987).

6. Samuel M. Weber, *Rückkehr zu Freud. Jacques Lacans Ent-stellung der Psychoanalyse* (Frankfurt, 1978).

7. See Helga Gallas, *Marxistische Literaturtheorie: Kontroversen im Bund proletarisch-revolutionärer Schriftsteller* (Neuwied, 1971), and her *Das Textbegehren des "Michael Kolhaas": Die Sprache des Unbewussten und der Sinn der Literatur* (Reinbek, 1981).

What makes the map of contemporary West German criticism and theory difficult to read for outside observers is not so much its ambiguous pluralism, where several models compete for hegemony, but its warped temporal structure, that is, a sometimes odd reversal of the "normal" development of theory and criticism. Instead of moving in a smooth progression from traditional Marxism to revisionist models of various kinds in postwar Germany, the classics of Marxist theory had to be recuperated at various stages. This phenomenon is closely related to the impact of National Socialism in Germany, which was clearly not limited to the years 1933–1945. In more than one way it also determined the critical discourse after 1945. First of all, between 1945 and 1949 it was not for the Germans to decide what critical discourses were acceptable. Just as the Allies could not agree on the political future of Germany, they disagreed about its ideological formation. While the Soviets obviously favored orthodox Marxism in their zone, the Western Allies were less tolerant of Marxist traditions and communist organizations. Unlike Italy or France, West Germany never had a communist mass movement. In fact, the Communist party (KPD) was outlawed in 1956. By that time the political consensus of the young Republic included a strong anticommunist bias that resulted in a virtual ban of Marxist theory as it was developed in East Germany (GDR). At West German universities Marxist theory had no place, at least not during the 1950s. The notable exception was the Frankfurt School, primarily because its members returned to Germany from the United States (as American citizens) and carefully avoided traditional communist rhetoric.

Much of the contemporary German theoretical discussion on the Left, therefore, has to be understood against the background of the history of the Frankfurt School after World War II. Adorno's and Horkheimer's return to Frankfurt and the ensuing reopening of the Institute for Social Research was overshadowed by two concerns: a legitimate apprehension about anti-Semitism in postwar Germany and considerable anxiety about the position of Critical Theory vis-à-vis orthodox Marxism. The latter concern was motivated by internal as well as external circumstances. Already in the United States, Adorno and Horkheimer had learned to disguise their position by an avoidance of Marxist terminology. Yielding to the ideological pressure within the American political discourse after the war, they had purged *Dialectic of Enlightenment* of its Marxist terminology before its publication in 1947. Obviously, this pressure continued in West Germany, where the power of the United States was felt very strongly, and both Horkheimer and Adorno, who relied on their "American" identity, had to take this bias into consideration. Moreover, for the survival of the institute within the West German configuration, a clear distance toward orthodox Marxism was advisable. Adorno's critique of Lukács and Brecht—both very prominent figures in East Germany— has to be seen in this light.

The presence of orthodox Marxism in a hegemonic position in East Germany clearly influenced the trajectory of Critical Theory. One must not forget, however, that the metamorphosis of Critical Theory had occurred already during the early 1940s, long before Adorno and Horkheimer took up their positions in Frankfurt again. As Helmut Dubiel has shown, the essays published in the *Zeitschrift* between 1938 and 1944 indicate a growing rift between the Marxist paradigm and Critical Theory—not only in terms of its relationship to the Soviet Union under Stalin as well as the official communist explanation of fascism, but also in regard to more fundamental assumptions about the evolution of advanced capitalism and its political organization.[8] For the authors of *Dialectic of Enlightenment*, German fascism, Stalinism in Russia, and the American culture industry became part of a larger negative configuration of modernity, a configuration for which the explanatory power of

8. See Helmut Dubiel, *Wissenschaftsorganisation und politische Erfahrung: Studien zur frühen Kritischen Theorie* (Frankfurt, 1978).

traditional Marxism was inadequate. Hence neither Horkheimer nor Adorno was interested in reprinting the essays of the group published during the 1930s. Horkheimer, it seems, even objected to the republication of *Dialectic of Enlightenment* when the need arose in West Germany during the 1960s. In other words, the early writings of the Frankfurt School were not part of the postwar theoretical discourse. As Habermas has observed, the senior figures kept most of the history of Critical Theory out of sight, emphasizing philosophical and cultural questions instead.[9]

Clearly, this version of Critical Theory did fit much better into the Federal Republic than the radical beginnings of the 1930s. Still, the Frankfurt School of the 1950s enjoyed a rather ambivalent position, in certain ways (ideologically) Adorno and Horkheimer were on the margins, their cultural and social criticism undermined the conservative intellectual consensus of the Federal Republic. On the other hand, in terms of their personal influence, they represented the center. This is particularly true for Horkheimer, who served as the *Rektor* of Frankfurt University for a number of years. This ambiguity also very much shaped the reception of Critical Theory in Germany. Especially during the late 1960s, the radical student movement not only appropriated and politicized Critical Theory, they also confronted the members of the Frankfurt School as pillars of the establishment. Symptomatic of this incongruity was the bitter dispute between Adorno and the New Left over the political meaning of Walter Benjamin's work, which Adorno had helped to restore through his 1955 edition.[10] At the same time, Adorno and his disciple Rolf Tiedemann carefully restricted the

9. Jürgen Habermas, "The Dialectics of Rationalization," an interview with Axel Honneth, Eberhard Knödel-Bunte, and Arno Widmann, in *Telos* 49 (1981): 5–31; see esp. 5–6.

10. Walter Benjamin, *Schriften*, 2 vols., ed. Theodor W. Adorno and Gretel Adorno (Frankfurt, 1955); Theodor W. Adorno provided the introduction.

reading of Benjamin's writings to the orthodoxy of the Frankfurt School.[11] In this context, Benjamin's commitment to a communist position during the 1930s, as it surfaces in a number of essays and reviews, was eliminated wherever possible or rejected. Adorno referred back to (and even published) his old letters in which he had argued against the *Passagen* project (Benjamin's study of nineteenth-century culture in Paris) by criticizing its lack of mediations between material factors and literary texts.[12] The New Left, with some support from East German scholars, on the other hand, pointed out that the Frankfurt School, especially Horkheimer and Adorno, had more or less censored Benjamin's essays before they were allowed to appear in the *Zeitschrift*.[13]

In the heated debate between the Frankfurt School and the New Left it was of course not really the philological question that mattered but the political issue, that is, the repression of the Marxist tradition in the new institute in Frankfurt. This concern was shared by some of its younger members, among them Jürgen Habermas and Oskar Negt. They felt that the theory of the Frankfurt School had been truncated after its return to Frankfurt and therefore made a conscious attempt to retrieve the earlier phases of Critical Theory with its stronger emphasis on Marxian concepts and categories. The result was a curious reversal of the theoretical discourse in West Germany. While in France the events of May 1968 led to increasing skepticism toward the Communist party and its dogma, in

11. Rolf Tiedemann, *Studien zur Philosophie Walter Benjamins*, introduction by Theodor W. Adorno (Frankfurt, 1965).

12. Adorno included his own response to Benjamin in the German edition of Benjamin's letters: Walter Benjamin, *Briefe*, ed. Gershom Scholem and Theodor W. Adorno, 2 vols. (Frankfurt, 1966), 671–83.

13. Crucial for the debate are *alternative* 56/57 (Oct./Dec. 1967) and 59/60 (Apr./June 1968), two special Benjamin issues with contributions by Hildegard Brenner, Helga Gallas, and Rosemarie Heise. See also the East German edition of *Das Paris des Second Empire von Baudelaire*, ed. Rosemarie Heise (Berlin, 1971).

West Germany a similar situation led to a radical recuperation of Marx and Lenin based on a strong call for political praxis.

Habermas's essay collection *Theory and Practice* (1963) is symptomatic of this new tendency in two respects. First, Habermas openly discussed problems of social change; second, he left no doubt about his own revisionist position vis-à-vis the Marxist doctrine. Unlike Adorno and Horkheimer, who never fully articulated their position vis-à-vis orthodox Marxism, Habermas, through a renewed reading of the classical texts from Hobbes to Marx, attempted to redefine the project of Critical Theory. Partly by drawing on the later work of Herbert Marcuse, he tried to overcome what he was to coin the "pessimism" of the postwar Frankfurt School, its lack of interest in structural change. Especially in 1969, when Willi Brandt and the Social Democrats formed the West German government (together with the Free Democrats), radical reform seemed to be possible. The West German society appeared to be much more open and flexible than Adorno's theory was prepared to admit.

By the end of the 1960s, Critical Theory found itself in a curious and defensive position. Naturally, conservatives and moderate liberals made Critical Theory responsible for the student movement, calling openly for the state to subdue student unrest. On the other side, Critical Theory faced the increasing opposition of orthodox Marxism in its various forms. Finally, the tension within the Frankfurt School, among the older and the younger generation as well as between internal camps, clearly increased to the point where communication and exchange of ideas became strained—especially under the pressure from the student movement. Although certainly more "political" than Adorno, Habermas also came under attack for his lecture "Die Scheinrevolution und ihre Kinder" (The pseudo-revolution and its children), given June 1, 1968, at the VDS Congress in Frankfurt.[14] Habermas's critique of the students'

14. The VDS (Verband Demokratischer Studenten [Union of Democratic

protest rituals (what he called "Left fascism") was angrily rejected by the New Left. But the disagreement was not limited to political strategy, it was the foundations of Critical Theory that were at stake at this crucial turning point. As much as the members of the second generation disagreed about the failure of classical Critical Theory, that is, its grounding and its political function, they shared a sense that Adorno's late theory had reached an endpoint. Typical for this attitude was the early reception of *Aesthetic Theory* (1970): the positive reviews were written by conservative or moderate critics while the New Left kept a noticeable distance from Adorno's posthumous opus. Adorno's attempt to preserve Critical Theory through an aesthetic discourse met with disbelief and hostile criticism.

The charge of undue "pessimism" resurfaced in the debate of the 1980s. When Habermas criticized Horkheimer and Adorno for their use of dialectical reason—first in his *Theory of Communicative Action* (1981) and later in the essay "The Entwinement of Myth and Enlightenment" (1982)—he clearly focused on the question of rationality in the critique of rationalism.[15] During the late 1960s and early 1970s, the New Left was primarily concerned about Adorno's lack of commitment, that is, his conviction that the late capitalist society could not be overthrown without repeating the mechanisms of social domination and repression. Indeed, for Adorno's postwar theory—particularly in *Negative Dialectics* and *Aesthetic Theory*—the notion of a unified historical process served only as a springboard for the critique of historical progress. Neither Habermas nor the poet and critic Hans Magnus Enzensberger

---

Students]) was an important leftist political group formed by students in West Germany at this time.

15. Jürgen Habermas's essay "The Entwinement of Myth and Enlightenment" has appeared twice in English: in *New German Critique* 26 (1982): 13–30, and in his book *The Philosophical Discourse of Modernity*, trans. Frederick Lawrence (Cambridge, Mass., 1987), 106–30. His other important critique of Horkheimer and Adorno can be found in *The Theory of Communicative Action*, vol. 1: *Reason and the Rationalization of Society*, trans. Thomas McCarthy (Boston, 1984), 366–99.

or Oskar Negt was prepared to accept Adorno's radical critique of the enlightenment.[16] This political decision forced the next generation of theorists to redefine the structure and goal of Critical Theory.

From the typical point of view of Western Europe and the United States, it was first and foremost the work of Jürgen Habermas that articulated the post-Adornian form of Critical Theory. In *Strukturwandel der Oeffentlichkeit* (Structural transformation of the public sphere, 1962), and more forcefully in *Knowledge and Human Interests* (1969), he had already modified the project of the older generation in two ways: by reevaluating the Enlightenment tradition and valorizing European modernity and through his decision to focus on the question of grounding by showing that all forms of knowledge are based on an anthropological definition of needs and interests. The conventional view that these texts established the new form of Critical Theory, however, has to be modified for two reasons. First of all, Habermas's early books do not yet mark the decisive break with the older Frankfurt School. In the development of Habermas's work, especially in its post-Adornian gestalt, the crucial break has to be located in the early 1970s, prepared by Habermas's debate with Niklas Luhmann's systems theory: it is only with the approach to social theory as it is articulated in *Legitimation Crisis* (1973) that Habermas's method is no longer compatible with the model of the classical Frankfurt School.[17] Second, the typical approach, by favoring Habermas, tends to overlook the fact that there are also theorists who follow a different path.

In this respect, the work of Negt and Kluge and also the

16. Hans Magnus Enzensberger (born in 1929) began to write political poetry in the late 1950s and later was coeditor of the influential leftist journal *Das Kursbuch*; his essays on the avant-garde and modern media reflect the influence of Adorno as well as Brecht.

17. See Jürgen Habermas and Niklas Luhmann, *Theorie der Gesellschaft oder Sozialtechnologie—Was leistet die Systemforschung?* (Frankfurt, 1971).

writings of Alfred Schmidt and Albrecht Wellmer have to be mentioned; they remained closer to the older paradigm, though with a stronger interest in retrieving the Marxist and socialist tradition.[18] While Habermas faced Western theory—establishing his own model by working through the theories of Emile Durkheim, George Mead, and Talcott Parsons, and returning to Marx only at the end of the second volume of *The Theory of Communicative Action*—Negt and Kluge in *Oeffentlichkeit und Erfahrung* (The public sphere and experience, 1972) defined their project in terms of Marxist concepts of class and class antagonism. Their reconstruction of a proletarian public sphere, as separate from the classical liberal public sphere analyzed by Habermas in *Strukturwandel*, was politically committed to a socialist project in which the concept of the proletariat was vigorously reintroduced as a major challenge to the social structure of the Federal Republic. In 1972 Negt and Kluge placed in the foreground exactly those aspects of the public sphere that Habermas had barely touched in 1962.

Also, in contrast to Habermas, the authors of *Oeffentlichkeit und Erfahrung* deconstructed the notion of a unified public sphere as the site of ideological and political struggle, underscoring instead the multiplicity and heterogeneity of public spaces. These struggles and conflicts (conceived in terms of class antagonisms) cannot be subsumed, as Habermas argued

18. The social theorist Oskar Negt (born in 1934), a student of Adorno and Horkheimer, and the writer and filmmaker Alexander Kluge (born in 1932) collaborated on a number of important projects. Negt holds a position at the University of Hannover; Kluge began his literary career with *Lebensläufe* (1962) and *Schlachtbeschreibung* (1964). At the same time he became one of the significant representatives of the New German Cinema. Alfred Schmidt (born in 1931), a student of Horkheimer and Adorno, became a professor of social philosophy in 1972. Among his works are *Geschichte und Struktur* (1974) and *Zur Idee der kritischen Theorie* (1974). Albrecht Wellmer is presently professor of philosophy at the University of Constance. Together with Peter Bürger he reinforced the aesthetic dimension of Critical Theory. See especially his book *Zur Dialektik von Moderne und Postmoderne: Vernunftkritik nach Adorno* (Frankfurt, 1985).

in 1962, under the concept of a single, self-contained *Oeffentlichkeit* (public sphere), a space where solutions can be worked out through rational arguments. Much more than Habermas, and certainly also as a reflection of the radical political climate of the early 1970s in West Germany, Negt and Kluge emphasized the *fictional* character of the public sphere, its strategic function for the rising bourgeoisie. They argued explicitly against the formal characteristic of the liberal model that Habermas not only analyzed but also tried to revitalize during the later Konrad Adenauer years. Consequently, they insisted on a materialist grounding of the public sphere by reconnecting the formal structure to its *Produktionsstruktur*, that is, by embedding the model in the actual social experiences of the participating agents.[19] Through this procedure, Negt and Kluge, with an obvious polemical turn against Habermas, wanted to explicate the dialectic between the critical value of the public sphere and its dependence on the actual social relations, a discrepancy that, according to Negt and Kluge, Habermas was unable to solve.

Clearly, Negt and Kluge defended Critical Theory in terms that Habermas had given up after 1969. In a certain way, they restated the hidden orthodoxy of the Frankfurt School, at least in the sense that social history has to be understood as the history of class conflicts (bourgeoisie and proletariat), a social history that is embedded in the actual relations of production. Of course, Adorno would have rejected out of hand the strong belief in the proletariat as a central political agent of political history. He never returned to this position after *Dialectic of Enlightenment*, but there are latent structural similarities—for instance, a general acceptance of the Marxian categories of forces of production and relations of production as well as their dialectical mediation. For this reason Negt and Kluge tended

---

19. Oskar Negt and Alexander Kluge, *Oeffentlichkeit und Erfahrung: Zur Organisationsanalyse von bürgerlicher und proletarischer Oeffentlichkeit* (Frankfurt, 1971), 17.

to understand the public sphere as an epiphenomenon produced by the forces of production (whereas Habermas insisted more on its relative autonomy).

Although Negt and Kluge reinforced a class model, they did not seek an alliance with orthodox Marxist theory as it was produced and disseminated in East Germany. While a part of the New Left moved toward a more orthodox articulation of their opposition and therefore sought alliances with advanced theory in the GDR, Negt and Kluge clearly resisted this trend, mostly for political reasons. The orientation of the Frankfurt School and its theory excluded any rapprochement with orthodox Marxism and its political organizations. The politics of the second generation significantly differed from that of their teachers, especially after 1965, yet their positions only modified or radicalized the stance of the first generation and did not cancel their link with the project of Western Marxism. This became already very apparent in the debate between Habermas (who stood in for the institute) and the New Left.

In 1968, Negt, writing in response to Habermas's critique of the New Left, argued in favor of a revolutionary solution and against the resolution of social as well as ideological conflicts through public debate. He countered the Habermasian argument that the students misunderstood the historical situation and therefore ended up in subjectivist voluntarism by underscoring Habermas's own subjectivism, his unwillingness to recognize the contradictions and the ensuing instability of the West German society. It is interesting to note that Negt at this point invoked the theories of the young Lukács and of Karl Korsch in order to demonstrate the need for revolutionary action. But Negt's critique of Habermas also turned into a critique of the Leninist party and its worn-out political strategies. What Negt suggested as an appropriate response to the repression of state institutions (like universities) were decentralized, spontaneous actions. That is to say, the emphasis was placed on a praxis more suited to subvert the system. What Habermas, not unlike Adorno, perceived as "Putschismus," as pseudo-revolutionary and essentially self-serving posturing, the New Left understood as an attempt to overcome the defensive position of the Frankfurt School, on the one hand, and the rigid response of the Communist party, on the other.

In West Germany, as a result of these tensions, the at least partial identity of Critical Theory and the New Left had already lost its momentum during the early 1970s (at a time when this alliance was still much stronger in the United States). With the rise of repressive state measures after 1972 (*Berufsverbot*) and the radicalization of the protest movement (terrorism), the revised project of Critical Theory, as it was articulated in Adorno's later work, appeared less relevant, since it did not offer a clearly formulated political strategy. It was the political issue, namely the actions of the APO (the extra-parliamentary opposition), that divided the second generation of the Frankfurt School and propelled its factions into different theoretical directions. While Jürgen Habermas's formulation of the project is well known in the West, other strands of Critical Theory were only marginally received outside Germany. The names of Michael Theunissen, Herbert Schnädelbach, and Karl Heinz Bohrer, even those of Albrecht Wellmer and Peter Bürger, have no major resonance in this country.[20] As a result, the present debate about the status of Critical Theory in America is strangely incomplete, since it works with the premise that today Critical Theory is identical with Habermasian theory. Within the German context, however, Habermas's theory represents one possible response to the crisis of the early 1970s. The vitality of Critical Theory, the fact that it survived the closing of the institute is due precisely to this heterogeneity

20. Michael Theunissen (born in 1932), is presently professor of philosophy at the Free University of Berlin; among his works are *Hegels Lehre vom absoluten Geist als theologisch-politischer Traktat* (1970) and *Sein und Schein* (1980). Herbert Schädelbach (born in 1936) received appointments in philosophy at the Universities of Frankfurt and Hamburg; among his works are *Geschichtsphilosophie nach Hegel* (1974) and *Rationalität* (1984).

and the lack of a unified system. By the same token, the relationship of the younger theorists to Horkheimer and Adorno varied greatly, ranging from a systematic critique in the more recent writings of Habermas and his students to various attempts to regenerate Adorno's theory, especially his aesthetic theory.

The impact of the Frankfurt School on contemporary theoretical discourses in Germany comes in various forms and shapes. In a recent essay, Habermas argues that it is precisely the multifaceted character of Critical Theory that has allowed for new and innovative combinations with different models and discourses, among them the hermeneutic tradition, analytical philosophy, systems theory, and structuralism.[21] The most apparent continuity can be traced through the tradition of Western Marxism—for instance, in the writings of Negt and Kluge. In *Geschichte und Eigensinn* (History and self-will, 1981), they return to fundamental Marxist concepts even more rigorously than in *Oeffentlichkeit und Erfahrung*—in particular to the category of labor as the most basic relationship between humans and reality—without, however, ever reducing theory to economic theory. At the same time, there is no attempt to follow Adorno's paradigm of negative dialectics. If one can speak of indebtedness at all, the indebtedness of *Geschichte und Eigensinn* to Adorno articulates itself as a materialist approach for which Adorno's analysis of music is the model.[22] In this case and others, the explicit return of the analysis to Marx's *Capital*—certainly the exception rather than the rule within Critical Theory—serves as a constant reminder that the potential of Marxian theory has not yet been exhausted. This is a position that would not be shared by Claus Offe or Habermas, both of whom have emphasized their historical dis-

21. Jürgen Habermas, "Drei Thesen zur Wirkungsgeschichte der Frankfurter Schule," in *Die Frankfurter Schule und die Folgen*, ed. Axel Honneth and Albrecht Wellmer (Berlin, 1986), 8–12.
22. Oskar Negt and Alexander Kluge, *Geschichte und Eigensinn* (Frankfurt, 1981), 82.

tance from Marx.[23] For them, Marx's impact is mediated at least twice before he enters the discussion of the 1970s: first, through Lukács and Korsch; second, through Horkheimer, Adorno, and Marcuse.

According to Habermas, one can distinguish four areas in which Critical Theory partakes in the contemporary theoretical discourse: (1) an epistemological critique based on *Negative Dialectic*, (2) the project of aesthetic theory and literary criticism, as it was articulated by Benjamin and Adorno, (3) social theory, and (4) concrete interpretation through close reading.[24] What this rather mechanical enumeration does not address is the theoretical metamorphosis of the Frankfurt School during the 1970s and 1980s. Habermas's own remarks underline continuities more than breaks and discontinuities. One of the significant cases of a paradigm shift would be his own work, beginning with his appointment in 1970 as director of the Max Planck Institute, but radical challenges are also visible in the field of aesthetic criticism and social theory. Whether the various discourses in these areas can still be called Western Marxism becomes an open question. In fact, the writings of Negt and Kluge, with their strong and explicit affirmation of the Marxist tradition, are anything but typical for the approach of Critical Theory during the 1970s and 1980s. Their position appears to be marginal compared with Jürgen Habermas and his disciples (Axel Honneth, Hauke Brunkhorst) and a post-Adornian group (Karl Heinz Bohrer, Burghardt Lindner, Albrecht Wellmer, W. Martin Lüdke), which has tried to reopen a critical dialogue with *Negative Dialectic* and *Aesthetic Theory*—a dialogue that was to some extent also encouraged by the impact of poststructuralist theory. The focus of this dialogue is not on restoring Adorno's "doctrine" or even

23. Claus Offe, presently professor of sociology at the University of Bielefeld, is best known in the United States for his *Contradictions of the Welfare State* (1984) and *Disorganized Capitalism: Contemporary Transformations of Work and Politics* (1985).
24. Habermas, "Drei Thesen," 11–12.

his much-debated pessimism but, rather, on epistemological and ontological questions that Adorno, sometimes only obliquely, addressed in his late writings. His critique of Heidegger's ontology would be a case in point. Similarly, his analysis of the avant-garde served as springboard for the extended discussion of modernism and postmodernism between Peter Bürger on the one hand, and Burghardt Lindner and W. Martin Lüdke on the other.[25]

As early as 1974, Bürger had argued in *Theory of the Avant-Garde* that Adorno's philosophy of art was rooted in the historical avant-garde and could therefore no longer be appropriated dogmatically. Similarly, Albrecht Wellmer underscores an inevitable distancing from Adorno's philosophy when he writes (in 1986):

Die These vom Verblendungszusammenhang der modernen Welt ist zwar in vieler Hinsicht aus den konkreten geschichtlichen Phänomenen herausgelesen, sie ist aber—und darin liegt ihre philosophische Schwäche—bei Adorno zugleich in einer Theorie des Begriffs begründet, durch deren Optik sie als a priori wahr erscheint. A priori deshalb, weil aus der Sicht Adornos das Andere dieses Verblendungszusammenhangs das Andere der diskursiven Rationalität sein müsste, und daher das Andere der Geschichte: Nur von einem messianischen Fluchtpunkt her lässt die Analyse der *wirklichen* Vernunft noch als Kritik der *falschen* sich verstehen.

[The thesis of the total obfuscation of the modern world can of course in many respects be read out of concrete historical phenomena, but—and herein lies its philosophical weakness—in Adorno it is grounded in a theory of the concept, through which it appears as true a priori. A priori because, from Adorno's per-

25. The literary critics Burghardt Lindner (born in 1943) and W. Martin Lüdke (born in 1943) represent the third generation of Critical Theory. Both teach literature at the University of Frankfurt. See esp. *"Theorie der Avantgarde": Antworten auf Peter Bürgers Bestimmung von Kunst und bürgerlicher Gesellschaft*, ed. W. Martin Lüdke (Frankfurt, 1976).

spective, the Other of this total obfuscation would have to be the Other of discursive rationality, and therefore the Other of history: only from a messianic point of view can the analysis of *actual* reason still be understood as a critique of *false* reason.][26]

For Wellmer, a productive reappraisal of Critical Theory would include the earlier phases of the Frankfurt School and possibly a greater distance toward negative dialectics, as it appears in the theory of Jürgen Habermas. Yet, this is precisely the open question in the present German debate. Is Habermasian theory the only legitimate response to the unresolved problems of Adorno's late work? Or, to put it differently, how dialectical is Critical Theory allowed to be? Wellmer himself pleaded for the importance of Adorno's "mikrologisches Verfahren" (micrological method), that is, the immanent textual analysis that informed Adorno's philosophy.[27] It is significant for the present debate that Wellmer suggests a separation between Adorno's philosophical system (with its unmistakable links to the category of identity) and his method (of reading cultural artifacts)—clearly with an antisystematic intention: what Wellmer wants to rescue is the *implicit* theory of language and epistemology, especially those moments that Adorno did not fully articulate. In this formulation of the task, Wellmer goes beyond the project of a fragmentary philosophy that he defines as Adorno's legacy. Its radical nature lies in its break with Adorno's own intention. Clearly, however, this Adornian procedure is not compatible with the communication model of Habermasian theory. Hence one cannot refer to *the* discourse of Critical Theory today. In the context of the present West German debate, two models at least are competing with each

26. Albrecht Wellmer, "Die Bedeutung der Frankfurter Schule heute," in *Die Frankfurter Schule und die Folgen*, ed. Axel Honneth and Albrecht Wellmer (Berlin, 1986), 28. All translations, unless otherwise noted, are mine.
27. Ibid., 31.

other: namely, Habermas's communication model and the fragmentary aesthetic model of Adorno's late work with its stress on difference. Wellmer's suggestion that this model as a fundamental critique of traditional metaphysics is not too far removed from Heidegger's project shows how much this debate has moved away from Adorno's intentions, since Adorno himself did not admit any common ground between Heidegger and his own theory.

The present tensions within Critical Theory reflect, at least to some extent, also the heterogeneity of the Frankfurt School's past. In spite of Horkheimer's repeated attempts to define the project of the institute, it was always difficult, if not impossible, to find a common theoretical ground for its members. In making his strong claim to critical rationalism, Habermas invokes the early phase of Critical Theory—especially the early writings of Horkheimer and Marcuse—in order to distance himself from Adorno's fragmentism. In contrast, proponents of the aesthetic model would go back to Adorno's early music criticism, especially *Philosophy of Modern Music*, and to Benjamin's literary criticism with its links to the early romantics. Furthermore, the tensions mentioned above are related to significant shifts in the theoretical discourse during the 1970s. The emergence of sociological functionalism as well as systems theory, on the one hand, and poststructuralism, on the other, changed the configuration of the discourse to such an extent that Critical Theory, by responding to these new models, lost its old center and split into a variety of overlapping and competing paradigms. Only one of them, represented in the work of Oskar Negt, remains squarely in the tradition of Western Marxism. Neither the theory of communicative action nor the post-Adornian aesthetic model, although they occasionally relate to Marxian theory, are in terms of their epistemology and methodology exclusively based on Marxist premises.

I Neoromantic Anticapitalism: Georg Lukács's Search for Authentic Culture

In the more recent research on romanticism, Georg Lukács enjoys a reputation as a dogmatic and obstinate opponent of romantic literature. This view is certainly not without justification, for his essays of the 1930s and 1940s on authors such as Heinrich von Kleist and E. T. A. Hoffmann, as well as his *Skizze einer Geschichte der neueren deutschen Literatur* (Sketch of a history of modern German literature, 1953), reveal him to be an inexorable critic of German romanticism. Also, in his broadly conceived history of German ideology, *The Destruction of Reason* (1954), romantic philosophy (Schelling) stands at the beginning of a process of irrationalization of spirit that Lukács believed led the way into German fascism. Here we find one important explanation for Lukács's harsh critique of romantic thought: the affirmative reception of romantic themes and conceptualizations by the National Socialists determined the perspective of his criticism. For Lukács, romanticism moves in a cultural tradition that must be understood as an aberration of the German spirit. For the later Lukács, the history of German (and European) literature divides into two traditions struggling with each other: the Enlightenment stands on one side, leading by way of its liberal and democratic tendencies to a socialist literature; romanticism and its emerging irrationalism stand on the other side. Lukács believed that this irrationalism continued after 1848 in modernism and, in the twentieth century, in the avant-garde (expressionism). This conceptualization not only influenced the study of literature in East Germany up into the 1970s, it also affected in a lasting way the scholarly treatment of the Enlightenment in the Federal Republic: West Germany's rediscovery of the Enlightenment in the 1960s often contained a bias against romanticism.[1]

Lukács's attempt to deal with fascism was not the only important factor in his rejection of romanticism; another important motif for Lukács was orthodox Marxism's negative stance toward romantic anticapitalism. Orthodox Marxism's claim to an objective and scientific critique of bourgeois society seemed irreconcilable with an approach that derived its strength from a utopian alternative—even more so when this alternative project contrasted modern society and its division of labor with earlier idealized historical periods (whether antiquity or the Middle Ages). During the Second International, the romantic-utopian intellectual motifs of the Marxist tradition were forced increasingly into the background. The German social democracy supported by Engels separated itself more and more from this "utopianism" and appropriated the economic theory developed in *Capital* together with a conception of history that trusted in gradual evolution.[2] The German and Austrian socialists were justified in invoking Marx, for their theories emphasized genuine elements of his theory. At the same time, however, they repressed under the influence of this positivism other aspects of Marx's thought, more particularly those that stood nearer to the romantic conception of social critique. The crucial achievement of the early Lukács lies in his rediscovery of this dimension of Marxism even before Marx's Paris manuscripts (which illustrate this connection clearly) were published.

The materialism of *History and Class Consciousness* (1923)

1. See Klaus Peter's introduction to *Romantikforschung seit 1945*, ed. Klaus Peter (Königstein, 1980); see esp. 22–29.
2. On the question of "scientific" Marxism, see Alvin W. Gouldner, *For Sociology: Renewal and Critique in Sociology Today* (New York, 1973).

does not oppose itself to the romantic social critique as it is first formulated, for example, in the work of Friedrich Schlegel and Novalis. Instead, Lukács expands, criticizes, and renders these romantic beginnings more precise by bringing them into contact with the theories of Marx and Max Weber. Lukács thereby reexposed in 1923 genuine motifs of the Marxist tradition that had been extensively suppressed by the Second International. He was predestined for this task, as his intellectual development placed him on intimate terms with romanticism and his position toward romanticism developed against the backdrop of turn-of-the-century neoromantic tendencies. As Ferenc Fcher has shown, especially important for the development of Lukács's thought was his friendship with Paul Ernst, a radical naturalist who later became an extreme nationalist.[3] Other significant influences included Lukács's acquaintance with life philosophy (Wilhelm Dilthey, Georg Simmel) and his engagement with contemporary literature (Thomas Mann). Lukács's sudden decision to join the Hungarian Communist party in 1918 and to devote his life to the revolution did not extinguish neoromantic tendencies in his thought, rather, it pushed him to integrate these tendencies into the Marxist theory of the 1920s. Lukács thus achieved an enormous transformation of Marxist theory, which, as "Western Marxism," has traveled a path separate from that of the Third International since the 1930s.

We ought not to see Lukács's turn toward Marxism, however profound its biographical significance, solely as a rupture; the moment of continuity is equally strong. It reveals Lukács's continuing reflection on problems that he had been considering since his *Entwicklungsgeschichte des modernen Dramas* (The history and development of modern drama, 1912)—a contin-

3. See Ferenc Feher, "Am Scheideweg des romantischen Antikapitalismus. Typologie und Beitrag zur deutschen Ideologiegeschichte gelegentlich des Briefwechsels zwischen Paul Ernst und Georg Lukács," in *Die Seele und das Leben: Studien zum frühen Lukács*, ed. Agnes Heller (Frankfurt, 1977), 241–327.

uing reflection that certainly involved self-critique and changes in his own position. The question posed in *Soul and Form* (1911), "How is authentic culture possible?" was answered by the revolutionary theory of Marxism (Rosa Luxemburg, Lenin). The following solution emerged, then, in the early 1920s: authentic (aesthetic) culture can be built only on the basis of a far-reaching social revolution that extends beyond the establishment of a new political order.

As soon as one turns to the early Lukács, his existential proximity to romanticism becomes clear, while the Enlightenment that he later regarded so highly remains in the background or, when it appears, is viewed critically as part of the alienated world. This thesis leads us to the following question: Why did Lukács turn away from his romantic tradition in the 1930s? What led him to believe that the social protest of the romantics was at best a failed attempt to deal with the modern world, a failure that must be overcome by means of the liberal-democratic tradition? Only a step-by-step analysis can possibly answer these questions. My first step consists of reconstructing, at least sketchily, the position of the middle and late Lukács. In the second step, I will indicate the tradition in which Lukács placed himself after 1930 in his discussion of romanticism. In the third step I will treat the early Lukács's reception of romantic literature (first condensed in *Soul and Form* in 1911 and *The Theory of the Novel* in 1916 and 1920), in order finally to move into his elaboration of a new revolutionary theory in *History and Class Consciousness.*

Lukács formulated his later critique of romanticism most powerfully in the essay "Die Romantik als Wendung in der deutschen Literatur" (Romanticism as a turning-point in German literature), which first appeared in the volume *Fortschritt und Reaktion* (Progress and reaction) and later in *Skizze einer Geschichte der neueren deutschen Literatur* (Sketch of a history of modern German literature, 1953). While this essay attracted little attention in the West—or at least exercised no lasting influence on its literary research—it galvanized literary criticism in East Germany. The essay's impact is easy to recognize in the early work of Hans Mayer, Hans Dietrich Dahnke, and Claus Träger.[4] Lukács criticizes romanticism so strongly because he believes that romantic literature marked that point in German intellectual history where the German tradition separated from Western Europe, embarking on a special path that would eventually end in the National Socialists' seizure of power.

In order to understand the essay fully, one must place it in the broader context of the *Sonderweg* debate (the controversy over Germany's "special destiny"), which was taken up again after the Second World War by German historians and social scientists. In the historical and social sciences since the end of the nineteenth century, as well as in literary criticism, the prevailing voices had attributed to Germany a special destiny that, beginning in the late eighteenth century, distinguished it politically, philosophically, and literarily from the general European lot.[5] The theory of Germany's *Sonderweg* was generally presented by conservative historians in an emphatic manner: the importance of this thesis did not lie in its description of a demonstrable difference but, rather, in its legitimation of a desired special position that rejected the democratic civilization of the West in the name of German culture. The fall of the Third Reich rendered this particular tradition of thought and research highly questionable. From this point forward, the affirmative *Sonderweg* thesis was associated (not only by Lukács) with pre-fascist and fascist ideologies.[6] The philosophical and literary traditions that historical and literary studies in-

4. See Hans Mayer, "Die Wirklichkeit E. T. A. Hoffmann," in his *Von Lessing bis Thomas Mann* (Pfullingen, 1959), 198–246; Claus Träger, "Novalis und die ideologische Restauration," in *Sinn und Form* 13 (1961): 618–30; reprinted in Träger's book *Erläuterungen zur deutschen Literatur: Romantik* (East Berlin, 1967).

5. Bernd Faulenbach, *Ideologie des deutschen Weges* (Munich, 1980).

6. See Jürgen Kocka, "Der 'deutsche Sonderweg' in der Diskussion," in *German Studies Review* 5 (1982): 362–79.

voked in order to ground Germany's particularity also appeared spurious. Romanticism—already read by Wilhelm Dilthey (in terms of life philosophy) as part of a specifically German movement, and assessed in the literary history of Adolf Bartels (1901/1902) as the true German literature—belonged to that suspect tradition.[7]

For this reason, Lukács believed in 1945 that romanticism constituted that part of the German tradition that must be eliminated in order to make possible Germany's return into the community of democratic peoples. It is remarkable that Lukács adopted this *Sonderweg* thesis while repudiating its inherent valuation. In 1945, Lukács saw only one solution: romanticism must be canceled. Thus, according to Lukács, the correct evolution of German literature led from the Enlightenment to Weimar classicism, and from there to Heine and the Left-Hegelian opposition. Bourgeois realism (only weakly developed in Germany), which appeared to Lukács as the predecessor of socialist realism, was connected to these traditions. Significantly, this construction leaves no place for modernism or the avant-garde. Lukács's version of the *Sonderweg* thesis presupposes a schematic division of good and bad traditions. Lukács does not contest the modernity of romanticism; he understands romanticism as a movement involving bourgeois men of letters who, for the first time in Germany, had to deal with a modern society in the beginning stages of capitalism. But he rejects romanticism's worldview, which appears reactionary; protesting against modern society, romanticism reaches for premodern models. It is no coincidence that Novalis's essay "Die Christenheit oder Europa" (Christianity or Europe, 1799), in which Novalis seems to recommend the Middle Ages as an answer to the fragmentation and alienation of his own time, appears as the central proof of the reactionary spirit

---

7. On this topic, see Peter Uwe Hohendahl, "Bürgerliche Literaturgeschichte und nationale Identität," in *Bürgertum im 19. Jahrhundert*, ed. Jürgen Kocka (Munich, 1988).

of romanticism. Corresponding to Lukács's protest against modernism and the avant-garde, which he considered phenomena of decay, was his assessment of early romanticism—in particular, his assessment of Friedrich Schlegel—as decadent. Schlegel's theory of romantic irony appeared dangerous to Lukács because of its disengaged worldview. Only those writers (like Ludwig Uhland) who could be proven to stand in the tradition of political liberalism or those authors (like E. T. A. Hoffmann) who neared realism in their prose (even if in fantastical terms) were exempted from this judgment.

It need hardly be mentioned that for the late Lukács, Marx and Engels are separated from German romanticism by a wide chasm—such that both appear above all as critics of the romantic worldview. In other words, from Lukács's viewpoint the classics of Marxist theory speak for a particular tradition. This tradition can be traced from a Marxist literary critic like Franz Mehring and the Left-Hegelians Arnold Ruge and Robert Prutz to Heinrich Heine and G. W. F. Hegel. The mature Lukács incorporated this tradition's critique of romanticism into his own. In 1945, his own polemic reproduced many of its motifs and conceptualizations. Hence a brief summary of this tradition is in order.

In his *Romantic School* (1835), Heinrich Heine established the Left's assessment of German romanticism as a reactionary political movement—against the more favorable judgment of Madame de Staël, who was unable from her French position to conceive of the equation of romanticism and conservatism. This distancing from romanticism continued with Arnold Ruge and Ernst Theodor Echtermeyer's manifesto against romanticism in the *Hallischen Jahrbüchern* (1839).[8] In the tradition of Hegel, both critics accused romanticism of substanceless subjectivity, of an internality that failed before reality. Ruge and

---

8. See Peter Uwe Hohendahl, "Literary Criticism in the Epoch of Liberalism," in *The History of German Literary Criticism*, ed. Peter Uwe Hohendahl (Lincoln, Neb., 1988), 179–276.

Echtermeyer suggested even more explicitly than Heine that the romantics repudiated the progressive tradition of rationalism. In philosophy, they attributed this turn primarily to Friedrich Schelling.

At the same time, we find in the *Hallischen Jahrbüchern* an opposition of classicism and romanticism to which Georg Lukács would return a hundred years later. This opposition interprets Weimar classicism as the continuation and realization of the Enlightenment; classicism appears, therefore, as a secure literary basis for the cultural evolution of the nineteenth century. This assessment largely corresponds to Gervinus's judgment, in which Goethe and Schiller represent the zenith of German literature, and romanticism (and Junges Deutschland [Young Germany]) already manifests its decline.[9] Even Rudolf Haym, who presented in 1870 the first extensive scholarly discussion of early romanticism, obviously distances himself from the romantic worldview.[10]

Conversely, renewed interest in romanticism, appearing in the 1860s in the work of Wilhelm Dilthey and increasing in the last decades of the nineteenth century, should be understood as a critique of liberalism—a critique of an interpretation of history as well as a theory of society. After 1866, interest in articulating a specific German tradition was not limited to Dilthey. One also finds the desire to integrate romantic literature into the national canon in the criticism of Wilhelm Scherer, especially after the founding of the empire. This nationalism, which understood Bismarck's unification of Germany as the fulfillment of the old liberal demands, pushed the reception of romanticism toward the right, as Klaus Peter correctly notes.[11] The positive assessment of romanticism served

9. Georg Gottfried Gervinus, *Geschichte der Deutschen Dichtung*, 4th revised ed., 5 vols. (Leipzig, 1953).

10. Rudolf Haym, *Die romantische Schule: Ein Beitrag zur Geschichte des deutschen Geistes* (Berlin, 1870).

11. Peter, *Romantikforschung*, 5–7; see in addition, Peter Uwe Hohen-

a specific ideological-political function, although it was not always explicitly expressed: insofar as one understood romanticism as a parallel to the struggle against Napoleon (Scherer), as the emancipation from cultural domination by foreign powers, it belonged to the movements that prepared the way for the new empire.

This opposition between liberal animosity toward and nationalistic enthusiasm about romanticism clarifies Lukács's position at the end of the Second World War. By returning to the liberal-democratic tradition, Lukács believed he would be able to fight the dangerous German nationalism. With this strategy, Lukács also sacrificed the neoromantic cultural criticism of his earlier work. Cultural criticism of the late nineteenth century sympathetic to romanticism served to strengthen a Right-radical nationalism, which in turn fueled, among other things, the ideology of National Socialism In order to evoke this tendency, it is sufficient to mention the names of Paul de Lagard, Julius Langbehn, Friedrich Lienhard, and Möller van den Bruck.[12] Finally, the early work of Thomas Mann also belongs in this tradition. In his *Reflections of a Nonpolitical Man*, Mann protests in the name of romanticism against Western civilization. Common to these authors is a repudiation of modern capitalist society. They therefore followed with skepticism the modernization of Germany after 1870. One could invoke the older romanticism, which was the first to criticize the symptoms of modern society, precisely for this reason. The search for an authentic life led the neoromantic trends into a double opposition—against both the official empire nationalism and the technologically oriented ideology of

dahl, *Literarische Kultur im Zeitalter des Liberalismus 1830–1870* (Munich, 1985), 194–210 and 240–65.

12. See Fritz Stern, *The Politics of Cultural Despair: A Study in the Rise of the Germanic Ideology* (Berkeley, 1961), and George L. Mosse, *The Crises of German Ideology: Intellectual Origins of the Third Reich* (New York, 1964).

progress that was characteristic of positivism and the later stages of liberalism.

Paul Breines suggests with justification that this neoromantic opposition to capitalism is politically ambivalent.[13] Its critique of society can settle on either the right or the left side of the political spectrum. It can articulate itself in nationalistic or egalitarian terms. The work of the young Lukács arose within this constellation of tensions. His early treatment of German romanticism—more specifically, his discussion of Novalis, Friedrich Schlegel, Solger, and Schelling—stands as a fundamental protest against a modern world that denies any authenticity. This criticism contains, to be sure, no nationalism—an element not to be overlooked in the work of Thomas Mann. The test case was the outbreak of the First World War, when the German intelligentsia was suddenly forced to show its political colors. The majority, including Thomas Mann and Max Weber, placed themselves on the side of the Germans; a liberal minority, including Heinrich Mann, supported the Western powers. Lukács refused his fealty to both sides.[14] The reconstruction of Lukács's argument in the preface of the 1962 German edition of *The Theory of the Novel* is revealing in this regard. It reads: "the Central Powers would probably defeat Russia; this might lead to the downfall of Tsarism; I had no objection to that. There was also some probability that the West would defeat Germany; if this led to the downfall of the Hohenzollerns and the Hapsburgs, I was once again in favour. But then the question arose: who was to save us from Western civilization?"[15]

13. Paul Breines, "Marxism, Romanticism, and the Case of Georg Lukács," in *Studies in Romanticism* 16 (1977): 473–90.
14. See Andrew Arato and Paul Breines, *The Young Lukács and the Origins of Western Marxism* (New York, 1979), esp. 61–74; also Ernst Keller, *Der junge Lukács: Antibürger und wesentliches Leben* (Frankfurt, 1984), esp. 155–66.
15. Georg Lukács, *The Theory of the Novel: A Historico-Philosophical Essay on the Forms of Great Epic Literature* (Cambridge, Mass., 1971), 11;

The last sentence is above all worthy of note. The Western civilization that Heinrich Mann prescribed for the Germans held no charm for Lukács. The victory of the Western powers could not, therefore, represent the final word. At this time, the solution for Lukács lay much more in Russia, and *The Theory of the Novel* indicates the direction of this solution. When, in the last chapter of *The Theory of the Novel*, Lukács believes he has found in Dostoevsky the overcoming of the novel, he acknowledges the possible beginning of a new aesthetic culture. This obviously presented a religious-metaphysical solution that Lukács would no longer recognize a few years later. At the same time, however, this discussion was a preparation for the answer that Lukács would present in *History and Class Consciousness*.

In order to understand Lukács's conceptual position within the neoromantic trends, it is instructive to examine his relationship with Paul Ernst—a relationship that facilitated Lukács's interrogation and clarification of his own position in the period from 1910 until the writing of *The Theory of the Novel*. Lukács shared with Ernst a critical opinion of naturalism, which Lukács had already formulated in his history of modern drama. In that work, he described naturalism as a poetics of the purposelessness of bourgeois ideals, which hovered between socialism and an individualism strained to the point of sickness, between Stirner and Marx.[16] The naturalistic poet presents longing for a new life (Hauptmann), but his desire goes unrealized because the naturalist drama already contains the message that hope for change must remain unfulfilled. For Lukács, therefore, naturalism does not overcome the problems left behind by classical drama, but instead appears as an indecisive and consequently "powerless innovator."[17] Lukács and Ernst agreed that the positivistic notion of science, which the

---

in further references in the text, this work will be cited as *TN*, followed by page number.

16. On this topic see Feher, "Am Scheideweg," 246.

17. Translated from ibid., 247.

German social democracy largely appropriated, could not achieve a transition to a new way of life. Both shared—and therein lies their literary-critical alliance—an uncompromising anticapitalist position that does not rely on Marxist theory (from which Ernst much more decisively distanced himself). Of course, even from the very beginning, there lay in Ernst's and Lukács's alliance the seed of their later estrangement. Ernst, in search of a populist conception of life, moved in the direction of a nationalist worldview—and consequently approved of the war in 1914. Lukács, on the other hand, decisively rejected the possibility of a populist nationalism and saw the necessity of thoroughly rethinking the problem of authentic culture.

In his essay "Metaphysik der Tragödie: Paul Ernst," published in 1911, Lukács first articulated a program for a postnaturalist dramatic art. He called for a return to the classic form of tragedy, as it was presented in Paul Ernst's play *Brunhild* (1909). At this point in Lukács's development, Ernst's plays represented a possible solution to the problem of a new aesthetic culture—a solution that impressionism, according to Lukács, was precisely unable to achieve. For the theoretician Lukács, it was most important to carry the real life, which he emphatically separated from the empiricism of facts and data, over into the dramatic form. The irreality of the "real life," of that which leads beyond the banality of the everyday, should meet with the dramatic form. According to Lukács, this can happen only when empirical life is distanced from drama or, more accurately, when it is filtered such that it loses its historical-concrete temporality and spatiality. "Such existence knows no space or time; all its events are outside the scope of logical explanation, just as the souls of its men are outside the scope of psychology."[18] This position consistently opposes re-

18. Georg Lukács, *Soul and Form* (Cambridge, Mass., 1974), 156; henceforth cited in the text as *SaF*, followed by page number.

alism and naturalism. "Realism," argues Lukács, "is bound to destroy all the form-creating and life-maintaining values of tragic drama" (*SaF*, 159). Lukács believed in 1911 that Ernst's classical plays satisfied his demands, surpassing the banal empiricism of naturalism in order to condense "the pure soul-content of pure form" (*SaF*, 164), as Lukács formulated it in his discussion of *Brunhild*.

This championing of the classical tragedy by no means excluded treatment of romanticism. Exactly the opposite: Lukács's interest in tragedy is grounded, as his essay "On the Romantic Philosophy of Life: Novalis" illustrates, in a problem lying near to his detailed treatment of early romanticism. The early romantics, in their debate with the preceding generation (Goethe and Schiller), were the first to consider a question central to Lukács: in a world that has splintered into heterogeneous parts, how does the soul guard itself against falling prey to the mundane and philistine? How is poetics possible in the modern society? In his Novalis essay, Lukács takes up the culturally critical motifs of early romanticism and opens them up to debate, without deciding if the complete poetization of reality constitutes a sound solution. One can discern a note of sympathy, but also of distance, which is articulated through a quote from Heinrich Steffen's letter to Ludwig Tieck: "There was something unhealthy about the whole thing" (*SaF*, 42, 46, 51)—a sentence that will be repeated as a leitmotiv. There is thus in this early essay no lack of explicit reservations, many of which foreshadow Lukács's later objections to the romantics: the individualism of the romantics was always in danger of sinking into pettiness; the romantics, following Kant's critique of dogmatic reason, prided themselves on overcoming rationalism, but this attitude also undermined the program of Enlightenment; finally, Lukács's essay already invokes the comparison with Goethe, whose cult of self-formation he acclaims. The stereotypical liberal reproach, that romanticism was in essence no more than a literary clique, also appears in

Lukács's essay: "Of course the whole thing was really no more than a big literary salon, even if scattered over the whole of Germany" (*SaF*, 44).

It would nevertheless be overly hasty to evaluate Lukács's relationship to the romantic tradition solely on the basis of this confining and critical observation. It must instead be understood as a self-critical note—as an indication of the unsolved questions of his own life. The early Lukács took romanticism seriously—especially its search for a new mythology, which contained for Lukács the program of a new aesthetic culture. "Friedrich Schlegel believed that in the all-penetrating force of idealism... there lay concealed a myth-engendering force which only needed to be awakened into life in order to provide a ground which would be as strong and as collective as that of the Greeks for poetry, art and every life-expression" (*SaF*, 45). This allusion to the unity of Greek culture, which can be compared with the transcendental shelter of medieval culture, is extremely important to Lukács.

A few years later in *The Theory of the Novel* (in the tradition of early romanticism), Lukács would fashion a philosophy of history in which the desire to overcome the fragmented, heterogeneous modern world determined his perspective. Lukács's claim in his Novalis essay that the romantics used ancient Greece and the Middle Ages as "makeshift symbols for this new longing" (*SaF*, 46) is also true of his own understanding: *The Theory of the Novel*'s outline of Homeric culture as a closed and organic totality is a preliminary symbol for aesthetic culture not yet achieved. It does not occur to the young Lukács to understand the romantic interest in the Middle Ages, for example, Novalis's famous essay "Die Christenheit oder Europa," as a literal glorification of that period. The Novalis essay is in this regard remarkably free from the interpretive clichés that slipped into the writing of liberal literary history. Lukács similarly avoids the aestheticized interpretation of early romanticism easily accessible about 1900, which saw in the poetic theory of Schlegel above all an anticipation of symbolism.

Indeed, he explicitly rejects this position: "It is not art for art's sake, it is pan-poetism" (*SaF*, 47). Poetry is the "the One and the All." This "pan-poetism" brings life into poetry, such that the culture of romanticism includes "the whole of life" (*SaF*, 48). Lukács obviously uses the term "life" here in an emphatic sense, rather than as a referent for the everyday and its depressing facticity.

Lukács refers in a central passage of his Novalis essay to the dream of a golden age. This reference must be understood as a cipher for the utopian claims of romanticism: romanticism as the program for a utopian culture, in which the soul and life are in accordance. This is the viewpoint through which the young Lukács approached the early romantics, through which he imagined himself in their position, without entirely identifying himself with them. This process of approximation holds at the same time an element of critical resistance. The ambivalence reveals itself in Lukács assessment of romantic subjectivity—of the internality so rebuked by the liberal camp. Lukács makes clear that he accepts this internality as a legitimate expression of the romantic program: "Yet this path was the only possibility open to their longing for the great synthesis of unity and universality. They looked for order, but for an order that comprised everything, an order for the sake of which no renunciation was needed; they tried to embrace the whole world in such a way that out of the unison of all dissonances might come a symphony" (*SaF*, 48). On the other hand, Lukács is not willing to entrust himself completely to this dream. The romantics identified the longed-for organic world with the real one. "This gave their world the quality of something angelic, suspended between heaven and earth, incorporeally luminous; but the tremendous tension that exists between poetry and life and gives both their real, value-creating powers was lost as a result" (*SaF*, 50). To be sure, this objection hits the romantic synthesis squarely on the head; the synthesis reveals itself to be a mere semblance that exists at the expense of the resistance with which life opposes poetry—and here we should

35

probably understand the expression "life" as the empirical everyday. But it is not fully clear at this point if it is only the romantic synthesis that proves problematic, or if it is the assumption of a poetic synthesis per se; for when Lukács objects that the romantics failed to realize the border between poetry and action (such that it became necessary for them to awake as from a dream), the question arises whether the assumption of such a border, the insistence on the limited character of all life-praxis, must not in the end position itself against utopia altogether.

As is commonly known, the mature Lukács broke with the utopian approach of his early years and focused the question of life-praxis on the problem of proper collective action. In the course of his expressionism debate with Ernst Bloch, Lukács decisively formulated this realist position.[19] Lukács rejected the subjectivized notion of reality that guided Bloch's defense of the expressionist avant-garde and that was traceable to a (romantic) utopianism. Whether *History and Class Consciousness* already contains such a critique of the panpoetic utopia needs to be investigated. It undoubtedly does not appear in *The Theory of the Novel*, however, which, it must be remembered, was originally planned as the first chapter in a study of Dostoevsky. In the theory of the novel that Lukács wrote after the outbreak of the war, he cogently develops a utopian conception of history—which was only hinted at in the essays of *Soul and Form*—such that the depiction of Dostoevsky approached that of a conqueror of the modern world abandoned by God.

Lukács completes the step from life philosophy to philosophy of history in *The Theory of the Novel* without rejecting the life-philosophical or aesthetic-theoretical motifs of his earlier writing. His position regarding romanticism also changes with this transition. If the final objection to romanticism in the

19. See Georg Lukács, " 'Grösse und Verfall' des Expressionismus," in *Probleme des Realismus* (Berlin, 1955).

Novalis essay focuses on the biography of Novalis himself, who managed as an individual thoroughly to poeticize his life and death, then the historical process offers the starting point for a critique of romanticism in *The Theory of the Novel*. This critique realizes itself no longer in the form of an opposition between achievement and failure but, rather, as a critique of the history of spirit. The beginnings of this view are already evident in Lukács's essay "The Bourgeois Way of Life and Art for Art's Sake: Theodor Storm," which describes the poet Storm as an outmoded romantic in a bourgeois world. Under the conditions of a developed bourgeois society, as Lukács emphasizes, the work of art arises no longer through poetization but rather in connection with the capitalist ethic of work performance. With such an approach, the poet consciously abandons the synthesis of poetry and life. Memory replaces hope in the work of Storm; his is a "poetry of decay" (*SaF*, 63), exposed to the danger of sentimentality, which accompanies the attitude of retrospection. This viewpoint becomes central in *The Theory of the Novel*. This historical-philosophic construction stresses the loss of totality and thereby positions itself differently vis-à-vis the romantic epoch. First and foremost, it is important to note that Lukács introduces in his theory of the novel a notion of romanticism that is more extensive spatially as well as temporally. By expanding his view of European literature and at the same time including the later phases of romanticism, romantic literature appears in a different light. At this point, the contours of romanticism in Lukács's interpretation stand much nearer to Nietzsche's conception than they did in 1911.[20] In *The Theory of the Novel* the emphasis shifts from the moment of utopia to the modern character of romantic literature— that is, to the tension between abandonment by God and resistance to the prosaic.

20. For Nietzsche's conception of romanticism, see Ernst Behler, "Nietzsche und die frühromantische Schule," *Nietzsche Studien* 7 (1978): 59–87.

This transition was prepared for in Lukács's never-completed project, "Die Romantik des 19. Jahrhunderts" (Nineteenth-century romanticism), the plans for which have resurfaced in his posthumous works. This project was not only supposed to begin—in typical German fashion—with the philosophy of Fichte and Schelling, moving from there to a discussion of the Schlegels; it included also Baudelaire, Kierkegaard, Flaubert, and Storm.[21] Furthermore, Lukács evidently wanted to extend the project to deal with postromantic authors such as Ibsen, Holz, Tolstoy, and Dostoevsky. This plan clearly illustrates that Lukács wanted to articulate the connection between romanticism and his own epoch. In other words, romanticism is placed here explicitly in relationship to modern literature; it is understood as the beginning of that literature—as the first attempt to express poetically the postclassical situation. Remarkable in Lukács's organization of this project is not so much the inclusion of late romanticism, which appears simultaneously in the work of Ricarda Huch, and which even literary historians like Wilhelm Korsch and Gustav Roethe desired (out of nationalistic-populist motivations).[22] Far worthier of note is Lukács's explicit mention of Flaubert and Baudelaire. Such a conception embraces the modern, distancing itself decisively from the picture sketched by Dilthey in *Das Erlebnis und die Dichtung* (1905) and Oskar Walzel in his concise treatment of the subject (1908).[23]

Dilthey, whose efforts in this regard decisively influenced succeeding German interpretations of romanticism, was primarily concerned with integrating the romantic authors into the canon of the great German tradition. To this end, in his inaugural lecture at Basel (1867) Dilthey had already advocated a continuity between classicism and romanticism. Romanticism appeared as a part of a larger cultural movement that

21. See Keller, *Der junge Lukács*, 134–36.
22. Ibid., 136.
23. Wilhelm Dilthey, *Das Erlebnis und die Dichtung*, 14th ed. (Göttingen, 1965); Oskar Walzel, *Deutsche Romantik* (Leipzig, 1908).

extended from 1770 to 1830. From this perspective, romanticism and idealism proved to be the fulfillment of the German spirit—precisely in their difference from the West European Enlightenment. For this reason Dilthey explicitly declares his interest in "find[ing] in him [Novalis] several of the most important motifs of a world view that emerges in the generation following Goethe, Kant, and Fichte."[24]

The young Lukács had no intention of describing early German romanticism as the culmination of the German spirit. Instead, the sketches he left behind of his romanticism project anticipate *The Theory of the Novel*, in which the motif of disillusionment—of an irreconcilable discrepancy between the hopes and expectations of the subject, and the indifference of an external world which the individual can no longer infuse with meaning—moves to the forefront. Romantic theory of art, especially the romantic theory of irony, plays an important role in this context. By appropriating the romantic notion of irony—presumably on the basis of his extensive preliminary research for the book on romanticism—Lukács creates an odd situation in which he achieves his critique of historical romanticism with the help of an idea placed at his disposal by that same romanticism. But matters don't stop there: the critique of historical romanticism, which appears in *The Theory of the Novel* as a discrete stage of spirit to be overcome, salvages at the same time the utopian impulse that Lukács, in his Novalis essay, identified as the essence of the romantic program. The utopia of the good life and authentic culture were displaced by Lukács into the future: instead of the plans and programs of romanticism, it is the novels of Dostoevsky that act as ciphers for the golden age that must be rewon.

In order to illustrate this shift, we must first investigate the historical construction that lies at the basis of *The Theory of*

24. Translated from Dilthey, *Das Erlebnis und die Dichtung*, 188, my interpolations.

the Novel. In the preface to the second edition (written in 1962), Lukács emphasized that *The Theory of the Novel* represented the transition in his development from life philosophy to Hegel's philosophy of history (*TN,* 16). While motifs of Hegelian thought, such as the historicization of categories, should not be overlooked, it would nevertheless be a mistake to understand *Phenomenology of Spirit* as the basis of Lukács's theory. Lukács's theory emphasizes the loss of organic totality and the longing for a new age without alienation to an extent irreconcilable with such a claim. Lukács appears to stand nearer at this point to a romantic conception of history, similar to the one Novalis designed in "Die Christenheit oder Europa," than to the Hegelian logic of history. In order to legitimize the form of the novel, Lukács invokes the difference between antiquity and the modern world. The world of Homer, out of which the Greek epic emerged, represents a closed, organic totality in which "the essential difference between the self and the world, the incongruence of soul and deed" (*TN,* 29) do not yet exist. "It is a homogeneous world, and even the separation between man and world, between 'I' and 'you,' cannot disturb its homogeneity. Like every other component of this rhythm, the soul stands in the midst of the world; the frontier that makes up its contours is not different in essence from the contours of things" (*TN,* 32–33). This closed world is for Lukács the exclusive historical-philosophical locus of the epic. As soon as the organic totality of the antique world dissolves—and this begins already in Greek history—the epic loses its grounding and transforms into an abstract form that, although capable of being imitated, has nevertheless lost its authenticity. Thus the period of Greek tragedy, and even more the period of Greek philosophy (Plato), mark both the loss of "Homer's absolute immanence of life" (*TN,* 35) and the development of a transcendence that divides phenomena and ideas.

Lukács describes the novel as the suitable genre for a world in which unity has disintegrated, in which, consequently, there is no more "spontaneous totality" (*TN,* 38). This point is reached in the history of the genres with Cervantes. The jump from antiquity to the modern age appears to leave the question of how Lukács would classify the verse novel of the Middle Ages unanswered. The predominance of Christian metaphysics, with its strict division between the present world and the world to come, makes the assumption of an immanent totality of existence difficult. For the early Lukács, however, the decisive loss obviously first occurs when a metaphysical construction of reality becomes impossible. In this sense, the medieval world of a Dante or a Wolfram is indeed clearly differentiated from Homer's immanence of life. This difference, however, is smaller than that between Dante and Cervantes or Goethe. Lukács argues that the theology of the Catholic church, even though it strongly insists upon the transcendence of God, creates anew a complete world in which sensuality is preserved. "In Giotto and Dante, Wolfram von Eschenbach and Pisano, St. Thomas and St. Francis, the world became round once more, a totality capable of being taken in at a glance; the chasm lost the threat inherent in its actual depth; its whole darkness, without forfeiting any of its somberly gleaming power, became pure surface and could thus be fitted easily into a closed unity of colours" (*TN*, 37). The Middle Ages thus drew closer to antiquity under the aspect of totality and completeness; the break first enters with the dissolution of the Catholic world. This break, though, is final; every attempt to regain the Greek world (humanism) remains at the level of a "hypostasy of aesthetics into metaphysics—a violence done to the essence of everything that lies outside the sphere of art and a desire to destroy it" (*TN*, 38).

One popular notion of romanticism stresses the poets' turning back to the Middle Ages; one can refer in this regard to Wilhelm Heinrich Wackenroder and Tieck as well as to Novalis's "Die Christenheit oder Europa"—in which the modern age is compared with the closed world of the Middle Ages. According to conventional classification, classicism, in opposition to romanticism, refers to Greek culture. If we follow this classification, the early Lukács appears as a classicist—his championing of Paul Ernst's tragedies affirms this judgment. Upon closer examination, however, this association proves to be only superficially accurate. Lukács's construction of history draws upon the difference between the immanence of existence and the loss of that immanence; it stresses the opposition of a world in which the individual has his secure place to a world (the modern) in which the ego knows no pre-given coordinates.

The transcendental homelessness of the individual is the existential situation that Lukács assumes for the beginning and development of the novel. The novel is, according to Lukács's powerful formulation, "the epic of an age in which the extensive totality of life is no longer directly given, in which the immanence of meaning in life has become a problem, yet which still thinks in terms of totality" (*TN*, 56). The novel is for Lukács the form in which the internal and external worlds have separated, in which the ego can no longer recognize the external world as its own. With this formulation, the preeminence of the subject in the form of the novel is decided for Lukács. While the Homeric epic knew heroes but no individuality, the novel is distinguished by an individuality that corresponds only formally to the idea of the hero—and then often with ironic intent (Goethe).

Lukács succeeds romantic theory in more than one aspect here, probably most clearly with regard to his historical conception.[25] Still, Lukács's theory of the novel establishes a connection with ideas of early German romanticism. Liberal historians, reading the romantic interpretation of history as a conservative turn to the past, often misunderstood early romantic conceptualizations. It has become clear, most recently in the work of Hans-Joachim Mähl and Wilfried Malsch, to what extent the nineteenth-century liberal critique misperceived the romantic conception of history and its political im-

25. See also Michael Löwry, *Marxisme et romanticisme revolutionnaire* (Paris, 1979).

plications.[26] Malsch proves in detail that Novalis's Europa speech—still considered by Träger in 1961 to be the decisive anti-Enlightenment turning point—must be understood as a typological figure of thought.[27] Novalis perceives "in the old-new 'dialectical' perversion of history the effects of an opaque poetics, which wins its freedom through self-recognition as self-design. For this reason, he could begin the 'new' history of the self-recognizing poetics with the French Revolution, and he could take the 'old' path of history toward freedom from the revolution out of its 'conscious' transition into the 'old' realm of self-knowledge or of 'belief and insight.' "[28] In this typological interpretation of history by Novalis, the seemingly lost past is rediscovered as the future. Malsch rightly draws attention to the fact that the typological form of thinking found its continuation in the twentieth century in the philosophy of Ernst Bloch. Malsch could have just as accurately cited Lukács's early work, had it not been hidden by Lukács's later opposition to romanticism.

Continuing Richard Samuels's research, Mähl brings to the forefront even more thoroughly the crossing of past and future in the historical thought of Novalis. Mähl powerfully underscores the difference between this vision of history and the linear-progressive Enlightenment conception (Lessing, Kant): "For Novalis, by contrast, the process of history lies between that primitive state of humanity, which is characterized by

26. Wilfried Malsch, *"Europa" Poetische Rede des Novalis: Deutung der Französischen Revolution und Reflexion auf die Poesie in der Geschichte* (Stuttgart, 1965); Hans-Joachim Mähl, *Die Idee des goldenen Zeitalters im Werk des Novalis: Studien zur Wesensbestimmung der frühromantischen Utopie und zu ihren ideengeschichtlichen Voraussetzungen* (Heidelberg, 1965).

27. Claus Träger, "Novalis und die ideologische Restauration," reprinted in *Erläuterungen zur deutschen Literatur: Romantik*.

28. Translated from Malsch, *"Europa,"* 119. With this statement, Malsch moves Novalis nearer to Hegel and consciously removes him from the sphere of romanticism. He wants to distinguish a critical-orphic classicism (Goethe, Schiller, Novalis, Schlegel, Hegel) from romanticism (Brentano, Tieck, Hoffmann). On this point, see esp. 121.

childlike innocence and a fantastical harmony of the natural
and spiritual world, and that desired end condition of humanity, which re-produces this innocence and harmony on a higher
plane and cancels the limitations of time and eternity."[29] Novalis's triadic understanding of history incorporates mystical elements while nevertheless denying the possibility of a mystic
unification outside of history; this conception sees in the present signs of loss, but also of hope—and indeed, hope in the
sense of an openness toward the future. Therefore, the golden
age lies not only in the past but also in the future. "Memory"
and "anticipation" are interwined. "Nothing is more poetic
than memory and anticipation or representation of the future.
The representations of previous times draw us toward death,
toward disappearance. The representations of the future drive
us toward animation, toward abbreviation, toward an assimi-
lating efficacy." Thus wrote Novalis in Blüthenstaub-Fragment
of 1798.[30] Between the poles of the past and future lies the
present, whose critical negation Novalis demands. "Annihi-
lation of the present—apotheosis of the future, this truly better
world."[31] Malsch and Mähl both stress the prophetic, future-
oriented character of the romantic critique of the present. "Poetics preserves in the midst of a decayed present, dulled by
understanding, the memory of the 'previous time,' so that out
of it, as out of the death, out of the mystic, the idea of a true
future, the common golden age, may arise."[32]

The idea of conquering the world crisis through poetry—a
central idea of early romanticism—is preserved in Lukács's
Theory of the Novel, although Lukács had treated the project
of the Jena school with skepticism in his Novalis essay a few

29. Translated from Mähl, *Die Idee des goldenen Zeitalters,* 305.
30. Translated from Novalis, *Schriften,* ed. Paul Kluckhohn and Richard
Samuel, 2d expanded ed. (Stuttgart, 1965), 2:461.
31. Cited (and translated by Karen Kenkel) from Mähl, *Die Idee des
goldenen Zeitalters,* 318. All translations of quotations in this essay by
Karen Kenkel.
32. Translated from ibid., 319.

years earlier.[33] Possibly, Lukács can maintain this idea because from this point forward he places it at a distance from historical romanticism and associates it with the novels of Dostoevsky. Between the publishing of *Soul and Form* (in 1911) and *The Theory of the Novel* (in 1916), Lukács shifted his interest in romanticism. Already in his unrealized attempt at thoroughly representing European romanticism, the emphasis had shifted from German early romanticism to European late and postromanticism. The inclusion of Baudelaire and Flaubert in the arrangement of the work is characteristic. *The Theory of the Novel* continues in the same vein when it presents the disillusionment novel as the representative novel type of the nineteenth century, for the disillusionment novel, demonstrated by Lukács above all with the example of Flaubert's *Education sentimentale*, thematizes a postromantic situation, a situation in which the dream of a correspondence between the ego and the world is lost, but the desire for such a correspondence is not. If the form of the novel is first constituted through the separation of the ego and the world, which occurs in the *Neuzeit*, then the disillusionment novel is an extreme manifestation of this separation. "The elevation of interiority to the status of a completely independent world is not only a psychological fact but also a decisive value judgment on reality; this self-sufficiency of the subjective self is its most desperate self-defense; it is the abandonment of any struggle to realise the soul in the outside world, a struggle which is seen *a priori* as hopeless and merely humiliating" (*TN*, 114). The content of the disillusionment novel maintains the desire for the fusion of the ego and the world, the desire for a life filled with meaning. This is nevertheless a utopia that is "based from the start on

33. See also Friedrich Schlegel in his *Ideen* from 1800: "Humanity becomes an individual through the artists, for it is they who combine past worlds and coming worlds in the present. They are the higher organ of the soul, where the life-spirits of all of external humanity meet, and in which inner humanity has its first effects" (translated from *Kritische Friedrich-Schlegel-Ausgabe*, ed. Ernst Behler [Munich, 1967] 2:262).

an uneasy conscience and the certainty of defeat" (*TN*, 116). The coherence of Lukács's position with romanticism is preserved, however. For example, the poetization of life, an essential aspect of Friedrich Schlegel's and Novalis's theories of the novel, appears renewed in the disillusionment novel, of course only to be disappointed. "Life becomes a work of literature; but, as a result, man becomes the author of his own life and at the same time the observer of that life as a created work of art" (*TN*, 118). The "fulfilling itself" (*TN*, 118) of the ego is no longer possible. It therefore amasses and confines its energy in the internal, enriching internality at the cost of the external world, which has disintegrated into heterogeneous fragments. "The novel remains a beautiful yet unreal mixture of voluptuousness and bitterness, sorrow and scorn, but not a unity; a series of images and aspects, but not a life totality" (*TN*, 120).

For all that, the lost totality of life remains the unshakable focus of Lukács's theory; it is precisely with this focus that he maintains the project of early romanticism. According to the logic of *The Theory of the Novel*, however, totality can be attained only after the present, which is distant from God, is overcome. Between the years 1914 and 1916, Lukács conceived of this victory in terms of a new faith.[34] We need to remember that *The Theory of the Novel* contains not only a structural analysis of the novel but also a criticism of Lukács's own era. In 1914, this assessment of the present took a position against the civilization of the West, anticipating salvation from the East—especially from Russia's literature. At the end of his essay "Aesthetische Kultur," Lukács speaks of the "sanctified

34. See Ernst Keller, *Der Junge Lukács*, 172–75. Keller protests against the assumption that Lukács stood primarily under the influence of Hegel when he composed *The Theory of the Novel*, as Lukács himself later claimed; Keller emphasizes instead Lukács's agreement with the Neoplatonic understanding of history and connections with the thought of early romanticism.

names of our epic poets."[35] He is referring to Dostoevsky. Lukács joined his vision of an authentic life, in which Western individualism is overcome by community, with the work of this novelist. The focus of this program is the "greater closeness of nineteenth-century Russian literature to certain organic natural conditions, which were the given substratum of its underlying attitude and creative intention" (TN, 145). According to Lukács, it is this nearness that permits the Russian writers—first Tolstoy, but primarily Dostoevsky—to return to the form of the epic. Lukács remarks in this regard: "It is in the words of Dostoevsky that this new world, remote from any struggle against what actually exists, is drawn for the first time simply as a seen reality. That is why he, and the form he created, lie outside the scope of this book. Dostoevsky did not write novels, and the creative vision revealed in his works has nothing to do, either as affirmation or as rejection, with European nineteenth-century Romanticism or with the many, likewise Romantic, reactions against it" (TN, 152).

That Lukács settles the Russian novelist on the other shore, beyond the "perfected iniquity" of his own age, emphasizes once again how much he adheres to the utopia of the golden age while repudiating European romanticism. In the "Ethische Fragmente" (Ethical fragments, 1914–17), utopia does not concretize the idea of a just society but a conception of human solidarity. "Each one of us is guilty for everyone else and everything in the world—not only because of the common sins of the world, but also, each solitary individual is responsible for all of humanity and each member of it on this earth. Recognition of this is the climax of life."[36]

After entering the Communist party, Lukács rejected *The Theory of the Novel*. Accordingly, he describes this early work,

---

35. Cited and translated from ibid., 203.
36. Cited and translated from ibid., 214.

in the preface to the new edition of 1962, as abstract-utopian, searching for a resolution to the historical crisis of the First World War without being able to develop it theoretically or conceptually (*TN*, 12, 17). It is certainly correct that Lukács would soon radically alter his substantiation of the change, of the entrance of a new world condition. Still, this certainly does not mean that Lukács's utopian patterns of thought lost their power. Paul Breines rightly stresses that the decisive turn of Marxist theory, expressed in *History and Class Consciousness*, originates in the romantic impulse.[37] Lukács's success in breaking through the positivistic Marxism of the Second International is more easily explained by the fact that his thought did not originate in economic theory—theory that proved to be primarily antirevolutionary in the hands of the German Social Democrats. Instead, Lukács's thought derived from a romantically influenced theory of culture, in which the category of reification, though not developed out of social history, was nevertheless already contained in idealistic form. The central chapter on reification and proletariat consciousness in *History and Class Consciousness* was miles distant in its political objective from the vague hopes of *The Theory of the Novel*; conceptually, however, Lukács could follow closely his early theory of culture. The notion of totality (in its historical expression), as well as the concept of reification, which Lukács from this point on explicitly attributed to Marx's *Capital*, bear witness to the continuity of the (neo)romantic impulse.[38] Lukács became with this work the founder of Western neo-Marxism without ever belonging to it.

As soon as one has rendered visible the connection be-

---

37. On the question of this continuity, see Arato and Breines, *The Young Lukács*, 75–96; Ursula Apitzsch, *Gesellschaftstheorie und Aesthetik bei Georg Lukács bis 1933* (Stuttgart, 1977), esp. 83–85; and Michael Grauer, *Die entzauberte Welt: Tragik und Dialektik der Moderne im frühen Werk von Georg Lukács* (Königstein, 1985), esp. 67–69.

38. Breines, "Marxism, Romanticism, and the Case of Georg Lukács," 428–30.

tween a neoromantic theory of culture and a Marxist theory of revolution, a further question confronts us: How does Lukács's avowed hostility toward romanticism come about? After 1930, sympathy for romanticism is hardly detectable. Prior to Lukács's essay "Die Romantik als Wendung in der deutschen Literatur" (1945) and his studies of Kleist and E. T. A. Hoffmann, his antiromantic position is indirectly articulated in the expressionism debate of the 1930s. The attack on Ernst Bloch (and his defense of expressionism) constituted an attack on a position that Lukács himself had held between 1910 and 1920 but from this point forward repudiated as abstract utopianism.[39] In his critique of expressionism, Lukács draws attention to the political dangers of this position: that is, its potential proximity to fascism. His engagement with National Socialist literary scholarship—for instance, its Büchner and Kleist studies—strengthened these reservations toward the romantic tradition. Fascism's appropriation of romantic and neoromantic ideas and terms legitimized the fundamental decision that Lukács had already made in the 1920s. Coming to terms with the Marxist orthodoxy of the Third International, Lukács retracted the romantic motifs in his theory of society and revolution (without giving them up entirely) in order to maintain his connection with the party.[40] Accordingly, in 1933 (in his autobiographical portrayal "Mein Weg zu Marx" [My path to Marx]), Lukács had already identified and abandoned as error his own proximity to romanticism and his participation in neoromantic cultural criticism (Simmel, Bergson).[41]

Nevertheless, Lukács's essay "Heinrich Heine als nationaler

39. On this topic see Sandor Radnoti, "Bloch und Lukács: Zwei radikale Kritiker in der 'gottverlassenen Welt,' " in Heller, ed., Die Seele und das Leben, 177–91.

40. On the debate about Lukács, see Arato and Breines, The Young Lukács, 163–89; on Lukács's development, see Apitzsch, Gesellschaftstheorie, 112ff. and 139ff.

41. Georg Lukács, Schriften zur Ideologie, ed. Peter Ludz (Neuwied, 1967), 323–29.

Dichter" of 1935 illustrates that he preserved a continuity with his early work. It was not difficult for Lukács to rescue Heine politically: Heine was one of the Jewish authors banned by the National Socialists, and Heine himself had harshly criticized German romanticism in his *Romantic School* in a way that corresponded in part to Lukács's critique. Still, Lukács could not overlook the fact that within a European perspective, Heine had to be placed in the romantic canon. Therefore, Lukács argues—in a fashion similar to that of *The Theory of the Novel*—that Heine (as a member of the second generation of romanticism) had to destroy the illusion of the romantic utopia in light of a social situation in which emerging capitalism also increasingly determined literary relationships. Heine develops as an answer a poetic process of radical subjectivity that itself criticizes romantic subjectivity. According to Lukács, Heine does not simply continue to write romantic irony but instead critically overcomes it with an irony that always again rends the hope for a harmony of ego and world. The result is an ideological pessimism that Lukács nevertheless justifies as the last self-critical bourgeois position before the appearance of socialism. In other words, Lukács is able thoroughly to appreciate Heine's romantic, though self-critical, impulses. According to Lukács, Heine reaches his limit only when he comes into contact with Marxist socialism: "Heine had no idea of the socialist revolution as a concrete-historical process. In this regard he remained throughout his life at the methodological standpoint of utopianism: Socialism is for him a condition, an impending condition of the world."[42]

It is remarkable, however, that in his Heine essay Lukács assesses the postromantic—that is, modern—situation so much more cautiously than in his other studies of the same period. In other works (the contributions to the *Linkskurve*,

---

42. Translated from Georg Lukács, *Deutschen Realisten des 19. Jahrhunderts* (Berlin, 1952), 107; henceforth cited in the text as *DR*, followed by page number.

for example), he positions himself directly against modern-ism and the avant-garde. Although Lukács registers his nega-tive assessment of romanticism ("reactionary character of German romanticism," *DR*, 126), he alters his evaluation of the historical context. Lukács attributes to Heine a deeper understanding of the connection between romanticism and modern literature. "But secondly, Heine sees the inner con-nection of romanticism with the modern movement of liter-ature. . . . For example he belongs to those few who have grasped the ideological and methodological significance of the German philosophy of nature. He also understands that the return of romanticism to the popular (*Volkstümliche*), despite any re-actionary tendencies it contained, was an indispensable move-ment for the development of modern literature and culture in Germany" (*DR*, 127). Although it is questionable whether Heine believed that romanticism could be saved by a notion of the popular, he undoubtedly viewed himself as the progeny, critic, and executor of the last testament of romantic literature. The equally important question, to what extent Heine can be understood as an architect of modernism, is touched upon by Lukács, but significantly, he does not fully explore it.[43] Instead, he stresses the parallel to Balzac in order to describe Heine's place "in the development of West European bourgeois liter-ature of the 19th century" (*DR*, 131). According to Lukács, both authors distinguish themselves as still standing before the threshold of modernism. In short, in its overall judgment, the Heine essay corresponds to Lukács's basic antiromantic posi-tion of the 1930s and 1940s. The opportunity to deviate from predetermined tracks, however, lay above all in the person and the work of Heine. Heine's critique of romanticism allowed Lukács to return his consideration, at least indirectly and par-tially, to the romantic sources of his early work.

43. See Peter Uwe Hohendahl, "The Emblematic Reader: Heine and French Painting," in *Paintings on the Move*, ed. Susanne Zantop (Lincoln, Neb., 1989), 9–29.

In the case of Georg Lukács it is appropriate, if not almost necessary, to distinguish between his opposition to romanticism and his (objective) relation to it. While his position vis-à-vis romantic philosophy and literature changed many times during his life, his objective relation to the romantic tradition remained to a large extent constant. It exists even when Lukács expresses his antiromanticism, for instance, in his enmeshment in and duty to the philosophical tradition that enabled him radically to reformulate Marxist theory in the early 1920s. From the viewpoint of structural Marxism, which places renewed emphasis upon the scientific character of Marxist theory, Lukács's entire oeuvre appears to be romantic. From this perspective it makes no difference whether one speaks of the early or late Lukács. That Lukács begins in the 1930s to stress the line from the Enlightenment via Hegel to Marx does not alter the basic assessment of his thought, in that Marx, read through the philosophy of Hegel, appears idealistic and "romantic."

There are three ways in which Lukács, even in his antiromantic phase, remained bound to the romantic tradition (in the broadest sense): his adherence to the notion of totality as an indispensable tool for the materialistic interpretation of history; his insistence upon the Marxist notion of alienation (objectification) as a central concept in the Marxist critique of society; and finally his emphasis on a theory of consciousness in which both literature and art could play an important role in the historical process—not only as reflections of objective relationships, but also as factors that intervene and effect change. The distance toward Hegelian neo-Marxism brought about by the structuralist Marxism of the 1970s allows the romantic components of Lukács's work to appear more clearly than they did in the 1950s, when the debate between Western Marxism (Sartre, the Frankfurt School) and Lukács almost entirely obscured Lukács's affiliation with the romantic Marxist tradition.

2   *Art Work and Modernity:*
The Legacy of Georg Lukács

The debate between Georg Lukács and the Frankfurt School after the Second World War did not occur in a climate of mutual understanding. Even before they left Germany in 1933—Lukács emigrating to the Soviet Union and most of the members of the Frankfurt School to the United States—there were theoretical differences and disagreements on major political issues; after 1945, especially after the political division of Germany, there was even less of a basis for fruitful discussion. While Lukács became the most influential spokesman of orthodox Marxism in Hungary and East Germany (whether this role was an appropriate one is another matter), the members of the Frankfurt School, particularly Horkheimer and Adorno, moved far away from the Marxist premises of their early work, no longer sharing many assumptions with the Hungarian critic. At least this is what each side felt about the other when they looked at the work of their respective opponents. We remember Lukács's remark about the "Hotel Abyss" into which the members of the Frankfurt School had settled all too comfortably;[1] we also remember, of course, Adorno's essay "Reconciliation under Duress," written in 1958 as a response to Lukács's book *Realism in Our Time.*

---

1. Georg Lukács, *The Theory of the Novel* (Cambridge, Mass., 1971), 22; henceforth cited in the text as *TN*, followed by page number.

This highly polemical essay certainly helped to discredit Lukács as a philosopher and critic among young West German intellectuals of the 1950s and early 1960s. Offering a rigorous and vicious critique of Lukács's theory of realism, this text is in one way clearly a product of the cold war. Adorno, for instance, refers to the socialist countries behind the Iron Curtain only as the *Ostbereich* (Eastern sphere). Yet the essay goes beyond a mere rhetorical dismissal of the orthodox Marxist theory of art, containing at least elements of a more positive appreciation of Lukács, a reading which tries to situate the difference between Adorno's approach and Lukács's method within a broader philosophical context. Adorno, for instance, excludes Lukács's early work, especially *The Theory of the Novel*, from this negative verdict and acknowledges its major impact on the leftist intelligentsia of the 1920s and 1930s. As we shall see, the link between the early Lukács and the Frankfurt School was never entirely severed. Just as the project of Western Marxism can hardly be defined without reference to *History and Class Consciousness*, Adorno's theoretical endeavors can be understood only against the background of Lukács's early work—those texts their author transcended when he became a Marxist. While Lukács viewed his early literary essays as part of a phase that would ultimately lead him to the fundamental insights of orthodox Marxism, Adorno came to the opposite conclusion in "Reconciliation under Duress."[2] The real Lukács is not the mature Lukács, the proponent of the theory of realism and the advocate of the *Volksfront* (popular front) during the 1930s and 1940s, but the early Lukács, whose collection of essays, *Soul and Form*, established him as a major literary critic in Germany and whose *History and Class Consciousness* fundamentally changed the European understanding of Marx.

---

2. Theodor W. Adorno, "Reconciliation under Duress," in *Aesthetics and Politics*, ed. Ronald Taylor and Fredric Jameson (London, 1980); henceforth cited in the text as "RD," followed by page number.

If we were to focus exclusively on Lukács's literary theory or his philosophy of art, we might possibly disregard Adorno's polemic. Since it is our task to explore the relationship between Lukács and the Frankfurt School, however, we cannot overlook Adorno's critique. His essay provides a forceful, although certainly not neutral, statement about the two opposing positions. While Adorno occasionally, particularly at the end of the essay, attempts an intrinsic understanding of Lukács's theory, his attack for the most part measures Lukács's work against his own concepts and presuppositions. Hence he vehemently disagrees with Lukács's central thesis that modernism and the avant-garde must be seen as a phase of artistic decline when compared with nineteenth-century realism and twentieth-century socialist realism in the Soviet Union. Where Lukács sees a basic tendency toward literary and cultural deterioration after the failure of the 1848 revolutions, a loss of vigor he does not hesitate to call "decadence," Adorno emphatically insists that nineteenth-century modernism and the avant-garde movements of this century—Adorno does not systematically distinguish between these concepts—provide (precisely through their nonrealistic method) the moment of aesthetic truth that Lukács wrongly finds in realism. Modernist works of art unveil, without imitating, empirical reality. It is not progressive works of art— for example, the compositions of Arnold Schönberg—that fail to grasp and explore the social reality of their time, but rather, as Adorno emphasizes, the belated attempts to capture this reality through the method of bourgeois realism.

Adorno's opposition to Lukács centers on the latter's concept of the work of art, especially his insistence on defining the interconnection between art and social reality in terms of representation. Adorno argues against this. We have to understand the relationship between art and reality first and foremost as an opposition. Only by conceiving art as an antithesis to social reality can one unfold the inner connection between them. Adorno notes: "Art exists in the real world and has a function in it, and the two are connected by a large number of mediating links. Nevertheless, as art it remains the antithesis of that which is the case" ("RD," 159). Consequently, one cannot treat the content (*Gehalt*) of art works as a simile of historical reality, as if aesthetic presentation were no more than a vehicle that critical analysis quickly transcends in order to reach the essential core of the art work.

This criticism—we shall have to come back to it later—leads to two important points. First, Adorno argues that in his later work Lukács underestimates the significance of *artistic technique*. In reducing its importance, Lukács necessarily misunderstands the nonmimetic tendencies of modern art. In order to fend off this reduction, Adorno underscores the logic of aesthetic form. Progress in the realm of art does not result from proper imitation; rather, it stems from the intrinsic unfolding of technique. As Adorno remarks: "But can he really close his eyes to the fact that the techniques of art also develop in accordance with their own logic? Can he rest content with the abstract assertion that when society changes, completely different aesthetic criteria automatically come into force?" ("RD," 162).

Adorno's theory of the aesthetic forces of production developing their own historical logic through artistic techniques then necessarily turns—and this is the second point—against Lukács's normative concept of realism. Undercutting the opposition of formalism and realism, Adorno argues that the formal construction of the work of art, the relationship of its elements to each other, precedes the representation of empirical reality. The concept of realism, which is indeed crucial for the later Lukács, appears in Adorno's writings only as a dominant literary convention of the nineteenth century. Thus, for Adorno, the realism of Balzac, as it was praised by Lukács, turns out to be much less realistic than generally assumed—an argument that Adorno, however, does not use to belittle the literary importance of Balzac. For Adorno, Balzac's significance lies in his radical use of themes and formal elements, rather than in the reflection of contemporary French society.[3]

Obviously, the fundamental disagreement between Lukács and Adorno concerns the mediation of art and society in their respective theories. This confrontation can be traced on two levels. First, they disagree about the correlation between art and social reality. Whereas Lukács conceptualizes this correlation on the level of content, Adorno insists on the priority of form; and while Lukács introduces the concept of *reflection* at this juncture, Adorno refers in his aesthetic theory to the notion of a *monad*. As he reminds us, the Leibniz monad is without windows, yet the inside contains the outside.[4]

On a second level, Lukács and Adorno also cannot agree on the evaluation of social reality. As far as the perils of late capitalism are concerned, they come to more or less the same conclusions (reification and alienation). They part ways, however, in their understanding and evaluation of the future. Adorno no longer accepts Lukács's conviction that the reification of advanced capitalism can be overcome through the proletarian revolution. Adorno's critique of Lukács's aesthetic theory has its exact parallel in his critique of Lukács's social theory, especially of the socialism of the Soviet Union and its Eastern allies. Therefore, in Adorno's eyes, Lukács's concept of socialist realism is no more than the expression of Stalinist terror. It effaces, among other things, the essential category of aesthetic autonomy.

Still, as a reader of *Realism in Our Time*, Adorno is also careful to accentuate those elements of Lukács's theory that do not support the official literary theory of Hungary or the GDR. At the end of his essay, he tries to rescue some of Lukács's concepts, but this does not get very far, since Adorno basically judges the work of the mature Lukács by the standards of the

3. Theodor W. Adorno, "Balzac-Lektüre," *Noten zur Literatur II* (Frankfurt, 1961), 10–41.
4. Theodor W. Adorno, *Aesthetic Theory* (London, 1984), 257–60; henceforth cited in the text as *AT*, followed by page number.

early Lukács. The last sentence of his essay makes this very clear: "The magic spell which holds Lukács in thrall and which prevents his return to the utopia of his youth that he longs for, is a re-enactment of that reconciliation under duress he had himself discerned at the heart of the absolute idealism" ("RD," 176). At least Adorno is willing to admit that Lukács's aesthetic theory cannot be dismissed as a simplistic concept of thematic reflexion. Structural and formal questions are important for Lukács as well. As Adorno concedes, Lukács's critique of certain forms of socialist realism contain elements of critical resistance that, if elaborated rigorously, could be used to defend the avant-garde. When Adorno makes this point, incidentally, he does not fail to refer again to Lukács's early work, with its emphasis on the crucial difference between intensive and extensive totality.

This, then, is precisely the common ground between Lukács and Adorno. When Adorno develops the difference between theoretical and aesthetic knowledge, he introduces the concept of totality. "A work of art only becomes knowledge when taken as a totality, i.e. through all its mediations, not through its individual intentions" ("RD," 168). As much as Adorno distances himself from Lukács's preference for the cognitive aspect of the art work, they share the category of totality, although not its construction and application in the realm of aesthetic theory. Obviously this category refers to their common heritage in Hegel's philosophy as it was reformulated by Marx and the Marxist tradition. We might, as Peter Bürger does, conclude from this intertextual relationship that both Lukács's and Adorno's theories are variations of the same basic Hegelian model.[5] This approach, however, obscures the historical difference between Lukács and Adorno; it represses the historical causes that discouraged Adorno from simply explicating Lu-

5. Peter Bürger, *Theory of the Avant-Garde* (Minneapolis, 1984), 83–94.

kács's theory. Both Lukács and Adorno are indebted to the Hegelian tradition, but their debt must be understood in terms of transformation and modification. Adorno's transformation of Lukács results in a position to which the latter is fundamentally antagonistic. To put it differently: Adorno's critique of Lukács makes use of concepts and categories that were partly taken from Lukács's early work and in which Lukács had to recognize himself. In the prefaces to the second edition of *The Theory of the Novel* (1962) and the reprinted edition of *History and Class Consciousness* (1967), Lukács makes it very clear that he fully understands this intertextual connection.

The Theory of the Novel is key to the debate between Lukács and the Frankfurt School; both sides refer to it explicitly or implicitly. Only with this text in mind can we fully understand both the Frankfurt School's compatibility and its conflict with Lukács. This claim, however, must be specified. The members of the Frankfurt School did not simply read *The Theory of the Novel* as a continuation of Lukács's earlier work; rather, they read it backward, so to speak. Their interpretation included the social theory of *History and Class Consciousness*, especially the concept of reification. In the late 1920s, Benjamin and Adorno gave *The Theory of the Novel* a revisionist Marxist reading, but in doing so they repressed certain parts of Lukács's theory. This is particularly true of Adorno's aesthetic theory, which fails to pick up Lukács's attempt to return to the totality of the epic in the closing discussion of Tolstoy and Dostoevsky. Instead, Adorno uses Lukács's concept of the novel—the form that articulates the condition of the modern world—as the basis for his own theory. When Lukács developed the idea that the novel is historically grounded in an age marked by alienation, he provided Adorno's theory with two significant elements. First, he insisted on the historicity of aesthetic forms—an important step toward a sociology of forms; second, he underscored the legitimacy of the structure of the novel, that is, the legitimacy of its fragmentary, nonorganic character. Adorno's thesis that technique is more important than content was already anticipated in Lukács's emphasis on the nonorganic structure of the novel.

It is important to unpack this aspect of *The Theory of the Novel*. Lukács delineates the concept of the novel by differentiating the homogeneous world of the Greek epic from the modern world. While the early Greek age is characterized by a life-world filled with immediate meaning, this extensive totality has become problematic in the postmedieval modern world. The individual faces an alienated reality; the meaning of life is no longer guaranteed by traditional social practices. Still, the demand for totality does not vanish. It is precisely this historical configuration that generates and determines the novel form. "In a novel, totality can be systematized only in abstract terms, which is why any system that could be established in the novel—a system being, after the final disappearance of the organic, the only possible form of a rounded totality—had to be one of abstract concepts and therefore not directly suitable for aesthetic form-giving" (*TN*, 70). The early Lukács, precisely because he emphasizes the concrete, rounded totality of the world of the Greek epic, insists on the modern world's lack of rounded totality. Organic form therefore has been replaced by abstract structure, an abstract form that can only allude to the rounded totality of the epic, since the "immanence of being" (*TN*, 71) no longer coincides with empirical reality. To put it differently, there is an unbridgeable hiatus between the immanent meaning of life and outer reality, between the subject and the objective world. The novel responds to this configuration by articulating this hiatus through its formal structure. As Lukács remarks: "The composition of the novel is the paradoxical fusion of heterogeneous and discrete components into an organic whole which then is abolished over and over again" (*TN*, 84).

Two aspects of this formulation must be underlined. On the one hand, Lukács points out that the form of the novel differs significantly from the epic form yet is not illegitimate. In fact,

Lukács insists on the historico-philosophical necessity of its abstract, nonorganic composition. On the other hand, Lukács suggests that there is a longing for an organic whole that can only be suggested and must be repeatedly canceled in the context of the modern world. In *The Theory of the Novel*, Lukács is primarily concerned with the legitimation of the novel, yet we also find an attempt to stipulate organic composition as the ultimate goal of history. Lukács articulates this idea in a more pronounced fashion especially when confronting the question of whether and how the novel form can be overcome in the final chapters.

Let us look at this problem more closely. If the structure of the novel cannot reach the authentic organic form of the epic, then the question becomes how abstract elements can form a whole at all—and here we do not speak of a conceptual but of an aesthetic unity. The early Lukács clearly separates these two aspects. While he grants the feasibility of systematically constructing an extensive totality through concepts, he assumes that the attempt to grasp this extensive totality through aesthetic means would be problematic. It can be realized, however, at least approximately. Lukács solves this dilemma by introducing the concept of *irony*, although his concept must not be confused with the rhetorical figure where the true meaning is simply the opposite of what is said. In *The Theory of the Novel*, irony describes the attitude of the creative subject (the writer) toward reality after he has realized his own problematic status in this world. This self-consciousness—the insight into the discrepancy between his own desire for a meaningful life and the alienated reality—articulates itself in the novel as the reflexivity of the narrator. The form of the novel, the patterns of its composition, grows out of the tension between the reflexivity of the narrator and the world as it appears in the narrative (the given material). The never-completed but always-anticipated synthesis of abstract elements is brought about through the narrator's self-awareness, which thematizes the gap between the interior and the outer world, between the longing for meaning and a trivialized empirical reality. As Lukács notes, irony "extends not only to the profound hopelessness of the struggle, but also to the still more profound hopelessness of its abandonment—the pitiful failure of the intention to adapt to a world which is a stranger to ideals, to abandon the unreal ideality of the soul for the sake of achieving mastery over reality" (*TN*, 85–86). Hence the plot, narrating the development of the hero, is not the final word. Through the reflexivity of the narrator, the narrative transcends itself. The form of the novel, therefore, is not only abstract but also self-critical. The aesthetic appearance, as it materializes in the characters and the plot, is not the ultimate level of meaning. "Irony, the self-surmounting of a subjectivity that has gone as far as it was possible to go, is the highest freedom that can be achieved in a world without God. That is why it is not only the sole possible *a priori* condition for a true, totality-creating objectivity but also why it makes that totality—the novel— the representative art-form of our age: because the structural categories of the novel constitutively coincide with the world as it is today" (*TN*, 93).

Again, I want to underscore that the form of the novel does not cancel the longing for rounded totality. Lukács, as we remember, insists on the longing for totality; yet this totality is not a given essence. Rather, it is an attempt that is regularly undermined through irony. The appearance of organic wholeness is no more than a suggestion to be problematized by the narrator. At the same time, we have to keep in mind that for Lukács the novel is only a transitional genre. It is the form that corresponds to the age of alienation. As soon as this age has been overcome and the rupture between the subject and reality has been healed, the novel form loses its raison d'être. Thus, at the end of *The Theory of the Novel* Lukács is faced with the question: What will be the adequate genre after the demise of the novel? In certain ways, Lukács argues, the novels of Tolstoy already transcend the structure of the novel and return to the epic mode, although in Tolstoy it is more a matter of intent and *gestus* than a question of historical necessity. Lukács further suggests that Dostoevsky's narratives are no longer novels, without, however, explaining what the basis of this transformation might be. Still, the underlying argument becomes quite apparent: under certain historical conditions, the problematic totality of the novel will be replaced by a renewed organic totality of the epic.

It is evident that Lukács's later Marxist position deviates significantly from this theory. As he points out in the preface to the 1962 edition of *The Theory of the Novel,* his early theory looks like a utopian construct without historical and social foundations. The hope for a restoration of epic totality and organic form is not firmly grounded in social history. Nonetheless, I would argue, this motif does not entirely disappear from Lukács's work. He brings it into his later criticism by redefining the task of the novel. Adorno and Benjamin, on the other hand, who in many ways stay much closer to the impetus of *The Theory of the Novel,* do not follow Lukács when he later emphasizes the need for organic form in the novel. Adorno asserts the abstract character of modern art; and in his criticism, the nonorganic composition of the novel becomes the model for the advanced work of art in general.

This strategy can be studied by looking at Adorno's music criticism of the 1930s and 1940s. The prime example is the essay "Schönberg und der Fortschritt" later incorporated into *The Philosophy of Modern Music.* In a different way, the same argument prevails in the famous chapter on the culture industry in *Dialectic of Enlightenment,* where Adorno works out the difference between administered art and authentic autonomous works of art. First, Adorno continues the move toward historical understanding of forms and genres, as it was introduced by the early Lukács (who, of course, already inherited this idea from Hegel's aesthetics); second, Adorno sharpens the focus and transforms the philosophical interpretation of form into a sociological one. This revision is closely connected to Lukács's own development. The changes in Lukács's position when he wrote *History and Class Consciousness* clearly left their traces in the work of the Frankfurt School. In particular, Lukács's theory of reification, as synthesized from the writings of Marx and Weber, had a major impact on the work of Benjamin and Adorno. Whereas the concept of commodity fetishism in Marx's *Capital* refers primarily to the material practices of human beings, Lukács extends the concept by fusing it with Weber's notion of rationalization in modern societies and applies it to cultural configurations as well. The philosophy of German idealism, for instance, the epistemological theory of Kant, comes as much under the spell of reification, Lukács argues, as the social relations between human beings.

This is the early Adorno's point of departure in the 1930s. His essays on music—for example, his famous essay on the regression of listening in advanced capitalist societies—concentrate their effort on the social context of musical production and reception under late capitalism.[6] Adorno means to demonstrate that neither the production nor the reception of music can be treated as natural and transhistorical phenomena. Listening is determined by the fact that modern society is almost totally reified. The process of reification extends to culture as well. Works of art are transformed into cultural goods that have only exchange value and no use value. I do not wish to pursue the later development of this argument in *Dialectic of Enlightenment;* instead, I want to have a closer look at its other side, the fate of the autonomous work of art under advanced capitalism.

Adorno's analysis of Schönberg's music combines the historical definition of modernity set forth in *The Theory of the Novel* with the theory of reification unfolded in *History and Class Consciousness.* While the early Lukács was concerned with the legitimation of the aesthetic form of the novel,

6. Theodor W. Adorno, "On the Fetish Character in Music and the Regression of Listening," in *The Essential Frankfurt School Reader,* ed. Andrew Arato and Eike Gebhardt (New York, 1978), 270–99.

Adorno, using Schönberg's music as an example, wanted to legitimize the experiments of the avant-garde vis-à-vis traditional romantic music. Adorno argues that the decline of romantic music, that is, the transition from tonal to atonal methods of composition, is a logical process justified by the material itself. This material, which confronts the artist in previous works of art, calls for the destruction of tonal conventions as soon as the artist defines his or her task vis-à-vis a postliberal capitalist society. For Adorno, exterior and interior motives (social context and intrinsic structure) are of equal importance.

In *The Philosophy of Modern Music*, Adorno insists on the impossibility of an organic work of art in the modern age, much as Lukács did in *The Theory of the Novel*. Schönberg only followed the internal logic of evolution in music when he diverged from the late romantics and refused to compose rounded and closed works of art. Adorno notes: "Under the coercion of its own objective consequences, music has critically invalidated the idea of the polished work and disrupted the collective continuity of its effect."[7] Hence, the only legitimate works of art are those compositions that are no longer works of art in the traditional sense. Adorno uses this insight when he criticizes Alban Berg's opera *Wozzeck*: its final form returns to a more traditional notion of an opera, especially in comparison with the first draft.

Lukács's idea of the fragmentary and artificial character of the modern novel becomes even more radical in the writings of Adorno. Adorno favors the idea of a thoroughly fragmented, open work of art, a text emphatically distanced from a cultural tradition that has been integrated into the culture industry. Where Lukács emphasized the heterogeneous nature of the aesthetic elements that have to be fused by the novelist's creative subjectivity, Adorno uses the concept of the material following

7. Theodor W. Adorno, *Philosophy of Modern Music* (New York, 1973), 29; henceforth cited in the text as *PhMM*, followed by page number.

its own logic. The composer's sensibility has to differentiate between those forms that have become obsolete and those that are adequate responses to the social context. Thus Adorno remarks on the historical logic of musical harmony: "The isolated appearance of chords does not in itself decide their correctness or incorrectness. These are to be judged only from the perspective of the level of technique adhered to at a given time" (*PhMM*, 84). Consequently, the technique applied in a work of art—and this is the other side of the coin—would also elucidate its social meaning and function. In other words, for Adorno the social meaning of the work of art is expressed through technique rather than through specific themes and motifs.

In music, the concept of representation or imitation as a way of correlating art and reality is not particularly fruitful. Yet Adorno's preference for formal, technical analysis is by no means limited to the field of music. In his literary essays, Adorno later uses the same concept of technique in reading novels and poems. The idea of mimesis plays only a very minor role in Adorno's literary criticism. Instead, Adorno's theory is centered on the concept of aesthetic autonomy. Modernism and the avant-garde are particularly determined by their radical separation of the aesthetic realm from social and political reality. The more modern society is defined by reification—a situation that has become reality under monopoly capitalism—the more the work of art has to distance itself from its social as well as its political context. Its critical power derives from its refusal to participate in a largely commercialized tradition. Therefore, Adorno already radicalizes the concept of aesthetic autonomy in his 1940 Schönberg essay to such an extent that it ultimately undercuts the traditional notion of aesthetic appearance. Art, as Adorno later notes in *Aesthetic Theory*, "challenges its own essence, thereby heightening the sense of uncertainty that dwells in the artist" (*AT*, 2). This element of heightened uncertainty does not, however, encourage Adorno to retract the claim that truth is expressed in art. In *Aesthetic*

Theory, Adorno emphatically opposes the Kantian approach to art, which views the act of aesthetic judgment purely as a matter of taste. Adorno, following the early Lukács, insists on the objective truth content of art works, although this truth value cannot be reduced to the level of cognitive knowledge.

Although Adorno's authentic work of art, particularly that of the avant-garde, may be isolated and far removed from the cultural tradition, it is nevertheless closely connected with reality through its *Gehalt* (Adorno's concept of the synthesis of form and content). Hence the concept of totality, which is central to Lukács's criticism, is crucial to Adorno's as well. In *Aesthetic Theory*, this emphasis must not be understood as a plea for affirmation. Rather, Adorno needs this category to situate the fate of the modern work of art. Especially when Adorno moves from an intrinsic analysis to a contextual interpretation that brings the historical configuration to bear on the reading of the art work, the category of totality becomes essential. Without it, the relationship between the aesthetic sphere and empirical social reality (including its organizations and institutions) would be reduced to monocausal correlations. The relationship between art and reality, Adorno argues, cannot be reduced to a field of causal connections. Rather, art works are to be conceived as monads that contain and therefore mirror the totality of social reality. For this reason, Adorno is not interested in the communicative aspect of art. The notion of communication would result, as Adorno maintains against empirical sociology, in affirmation. For Adorno, the relationship of the art work to the whole of the social system can be understood only as concrete negation (*bestimmte Negation*).[8]

In emphasizing the importance of the concept of totality in Adorno's work, we have to underscore at the same time the particular nature of this category in his writings. In his study *Marxism and Totality*, Martin Jay correctly points out that the

8. For an explication of this concept, see Theodor W. Adorno, *Negative Dialectics* (New York, 1973).

Frankfurt School moved away from the concept of totality developed in *History and Class Consciousness*.[9] This category loses its dogmatic character, especially in Adorno's work. Hegel's dialectical struggle for synthesis is replaced by a negative dialectic that refuses the completion of synthesis and thereby continually calls the notion of stable truth into question. Truth and totality are mutually exclusive. The whole, according to Adorno, is the false. Still, the concept of totality has a place and a function in *Aesthetic Theory*. It serves as a reference point for the mediation between art and reality, the aesthetic and the social realm. But the totality of the social system absolutely cannot serve as a goal. For the modern artist, reconciliation is strictly prohibited. The concept of totality must be restricted to the sphere of art. As Adorno remarks in *Aesthetic Theory*: "The road to the integration and autonomy of the art work leads to the death of its moments in the totality. As art works transcend their own particularity, they flirt with death, the epitome of which is the totality of the work" (*AT*, 78). Even this use of the category distances itself from Hegel's affirmative dialectic. For Adorno, Lukács's Hegelian concept of totality in *History and Class Consciousness* is only the negative foil against which he defines his own approach.

With this point we return to where we began. Adorno's "Reconciliation under Duress" made it very clear that the Frankfurt School was unable to identify with the critical writings of the later Lukács. Yet this rigid opposition calls for scrutiny, because the hostility between Lukács and Adorno is grounded in a shared tradition of concepts and categories. There are three ways to understand and evaluate this common ground. If one maintains the unity of Lukács's oeuvre, if one stresses the continuity of his writings from the early essays to his late aesthetic theory, the position of the Frankfurt School appears to be an unfortunate deviation from the path of Western Marx-

9. Martin Jay, *Marxism and Totality* (Berkeley and Los Angeles, 1984), 241–75.

ism. Fredric Jameson at least comes close to this point of view. For him, Lukács's writings can be understood as the continuous unfolding of a basically identical theory.[10] The contrary position is more prominent among Adorno's disciples in Frankfurt. They accept Adorno's critique of Lukács as a premise of their own work and therefore eliminate Lukács's writings after 1930 from any further consideration. Consequently, Lukács's heritage is limited to his early work, especially to *The Theory of the Novel* and *History and Class Consciousness*. In *Marxism and Totality*, Martin Jay takes a similar position when he stresses the fact that the Frankfurt School criticized and transformed Lukács's concept of totality.[11]

In his *Theory of the Avant-Garde*, Peter Bürger challenges this point of view, maintaining that it stays too close to the subject matter and therefore takes the differences between Lukács and Adorno as absolutes. According to Bürger, it is not difficult to show that both critics share basic presuppositions— exactly those elements that remain outside the controversy. Hence Bürger insists that the theories of both Lukács and Adorno, though they seem contradictory, are actually cut from the same cloth. They share certain limitations that must be articulated and overcome. In order to transcend these limitations, we have to historicize not only Lukács's writings, but Adorno's as well. Thus Bürger argues: "the intention of the theory sketched here is to demonstrate that the debate itself is historical. To do so, it must be shown that the premises of the two authors are already historical today and that it is therefore impossible to simply adopt them."[12]

According to Bürger, both Lukács and Adorno basically developed theories of the art work without attending to the institutional context. "The dispute between Lukács and Adorno concerning the legitimacy of avant-gardiste art as outlined

---

10. Fredric Jameson, *Marxism and Form* (Princeton, 1971), 160–63.
11. See Jay, *Marxism*, 196–219 and 241–75.
12. Bürger, *Theory of the Avant-Garde*, 86.

above is confined to the sphere of artistic means and the change in the kind of work this involves (organic versus avant-gardiste)."[13] Since both theories are grounded in the concept of aesthetic autonomy, their authors underestimate the avant-garde's challenge to the principle of autonomy. Arguing about the specific character of the modern art work, both overlook the fact that the avant-garde movements fundamentally problematized the status of art. These movements aimed, as Bürger holds, at the cancellation of the institution of art in general. They meant to destroy the very institution that served as the foundation for the ongoing debate about modern art.

This is not the place for an extensive discussion of Peter Bürger's theory. His thesis that both Lukács and Adorno have become historical has lost much of its shock effect. It would be difficult today to find many orthodox students of Lukács's literary theory, nor are there dogmatic practitioners of Adorno's philosophy of art. Our problem is not so much to achieve distance but to come to terms with this heritage, the tradition of Western Marxism. Is it superfluous baggage to be thrown overboard in order to get the boat floating again? Or would it be better to rescue parts of Lukács's and Adorno's theories? Bürger's solution to this problem, the move toward historical distance, is not sufficient, since it is basically negative, a warning against the dogmatic use of Lukács's and Adorno's theories. Bürger does not discuss the usefulness of revisions, and his solution is schematic. Lukács's and Adorno's theories do not occupy the same historical space (as it may have appeared in West Germany during the 1960s). Rather, we must note the historical filiation: the aesthetic theory of the early Lukács, together with the social theory of *History and Class Consciousness*, is the basis for the Frankfurt School and Adorno. As we have seen, Adorno appropriates and develops a position that Lukács sketched in *The Theory of the Novel* (the nonorganic work of art), while Lukács himself later favored different

13. Ibid.

aspects of his early theory, for instance, the notion that the crisis of bourgeois society has to be overcome—in both the social and the aesthetic sphere. Since the proletarian revolution in Russia has transformed the structure of a bourgeois society, Lukács suggests, we may also expect a new organic art form. Socialist realism is this new organic art that differs so significantly from the formal experiments of bourgeois modernism. We must not overlook the correlation between the political and the aesthetic development in Lukács's theory. Similarly, Adorno's resistance to Lukács's normative theory of realism is grounded in a different assessment of the class conflict and its outcome in the twentieth century. Adorno is convinced that the emancipatory potential of the proletarian revolution failed. In Germany, the fascists seduced the proletariat; in Russia, the revolution resulted in Stalinism. Thus Adorno's aesthetic theory is confronted either with late capitalism or with pseudo-socialism. According to Adorno, neither system allows change.

This assessment of the condition of modern society has a major impact on Adorno's aesthetic theory. Adorno wants to constitute a realm of critical resistance against the overwhelming power of the reified social system. Therefore he emphatically embraces the concepts of aesthetic autonomy and aesthetic appearance. For the same reason he is less interested in those tendencies of the avant-garde movements that would undermine and ultimately destroy the institution of art, for this thrust could only weaken the resistance against the pressure of the system.

As I have tried to demonstrate for both Adorno and Lukács, the problem of cultural tradition cannot be separated from political theory and the evaluation of the concrete political situation. Yet recent history has not exactly supported either theorist. In this respect, Peter Bürger has rightly emphasized that their theories are no longer immediately applicable to the present situation. The political and literary practices of the socialist countries could legitimize socialist realism only for a limited time. The most advanced authors of these countries have moved closer to the formal structures of modernism and the avant-garde, particularly since the 1970s. These tendencies must be understood as signals that the social reality of these countries cannot be grasped through the concept of epic totality. On the other hand, the literary practices of Western countries after the Second World War do not easily conform to the concept of the avant-garde. Adorno was aware of these changes when he discussed the evolution of modern music. He defined these changes as a process of aging without, however, adjusting his aesthetic theory in major ways. In this case, the correlation between aesthetic and social theory functions as a block. Since Adorno stresses the reified character of the social system—that is, the lack of dynamic change—he is unable to anticipate new forces that would break with the status quo. Hence the work of art is locked into place, and aesthetic autonomy must be the final answer to the pressure of the system of late capitalism.

Our historical distance from Lukács and Adorno is hard to deny. It restricts dogmatic readings of their theories and unmediated application of their theses. Since the institutional structure of art has changed, and with it the function of art, we can no longer share some of Lukács's and Adorno's implicit presuppositions. For instance, our view of the relationship between authentic art and mass culture has changed. Both Lukács and Adorno—in this they are heirs of romantic theory—have a defensive attitude toward mass culture. They exclude that which cannot be subsumed under the category of autonomy from the concept of art. This aggressive stance, especially in Adorno's case, always risks becoming a defense of an affirmative elite culture. This danger should not, however, blind us to Lukács's and Adorno's theories. Adorno's critical procedure, negative dialectic, is still a powerful and decisive instrument for critical analysis of our present social and cultural reality. And, although Adorno would find this difficult to admit, it has incorporated a good deal of Lukács's theory.

Adorno's model of negative dialectic reflects Lukács's concept of totality—totality not as reconciled reality (as in the age of the Greek *epos*) but as a hypothetical concept that refers to a notion of wholeness. This hypothesis then allows the critic to understand and criticize the individual and concrete moment. In other words, the element of deconstruction in Adorno's theory, his insistence that the individual moment is not identical with its concept, cannot forgo the category of totality, because without it the critical approach would be reduced to the collection and ordering of facts or the phenomenological description of individual elements. This emerges, for instance, in Adorno's strong criticism of empirical sociology of art. In his essay "Theses on the Sociology of Art," he states: "Sociology of art, in the strict sense of the word, contains all aspects of the relationship between art and society. It is impossible to reduce this discipline to one aspect, for example the social impact of art works. This impact is only one moment in the totality of this relationship."[14] Lukács would have agreed with this, as much as he differs from Adorno when it comes to working out the mediation between an art work and society.

Adorno's concept of totality does not, however, imply the notion of an organic construct. Organic totality is only a hypothetical model, and in his historical analyses of modern art, Adorno clearly does not use such a concept. It could be argued that Adorno's category of immanence makes the presupposition of totality superfluous. This would lead to a defense of Adorno's intrinsic method of reading against Lukács's historical reading, which apparently transcends the text. This dichotomy cannot do justice to the problem at hand, however, since Adorno's emphasis on an intrinsic procedure is a matter of methodological priority rather than an attempt to restrict the interpretation to the text and exclude historical reality. Adorno does not mean to dissolve history. His concept of the monad makes this very clear. When we understand the art work as a monad, we assume that the totality of the social system

14. Theodor W. Adorno, "Thesen zur Kunstsoziologie," in *Ohne Leitbild* (Frankfurt, 1967), 94.

(against which we read the text) is not simply outside but inside as well. At the same time, this model retains a notion of objective meaning—it retains the concept of the truth content (*Wahrheitsgehalt*) of the work of art, which, since it is "begriffslos" (conceptless), challenges decoding.

3   Autonomy of Art:
      Looking Back at Adorno's
      Aesthetische Theorie

Theodor W. Adorno's major contribution to the philosophy of
art, his *Aesthetische Theorie*, appeared in 1970.[1] The work was
almost completed when the author died in 1969. Adorno meant
to rewrite the introduction, but otherwise the text needed only
stylistic revisions, which were carried out by Rolf Tiedemann,
Adorno's faithful disciple and editor. Tiedemann rightly felt
that *Aesthetische Theorie* deserved immediate publication,
since it was the legacy of Critical Theory. Yet it was precisely
this aspect that marred the reception of the book. Except for a
few voices in the liberal and conservative camp, the response
was surprisingly negative. One might have expected that the
East German critics would denounce Adorno's theory as a typical example of Western ideology—which they did; more alarm
ing was the unfriendly or at least cool reception among the
West German Left. If the members of the Frankfurt School
considered *Aesthetische Theorie* Adorno's legacy, it turned out
to be a legacy that was clearly unwelcome. The charges varied,

1. For a full account of the genesis of *Aesthetische Theorie*, see Rolf
Tiedemann's "Editorisches Nachwort" (editorial afterword), in Theodor
W. Adorno, *Gesammelte Schriften: Aesthetische Theorie* (Frankfurt,
1970), 7:537–44. The quotations and page numbers cited in the text will
be translations from this edition, which will be abbreviated as *AT*, followed by page number. An English translation has been published as *Aesthetic Theory* (London, 1984).

but there was almost a consensus among the critics of the Left that Adorno's last book did not offer the materialist theory of art that everybody was looking for. It was particularly Adorno's insistence on the autonomy of the art work and his well-known indictment of *Tendenz* (tendentiousness) and political art that angered the Left. Adorno evidently had not changed his position. In his last work he reiterated his critique of unmediated engagement and once more presented modernism and the avant-garde as the only viable responses to the increasing brutality of advanced capitalism. His renewed claim that, in the final analysis, only the authentic work of art overcomes the stultifying atmosphere of the culture industry met with disbelief and outspoken disapproval. The hostility was so strong that the German Left dismissed the book out of hand and left the appropriation to the conservatives, who at this point were inclined to use some of Adorno's arguments for the defense of their aesthetic and moral beliefs.

What were the reasons for this bizarre development? After all, the leftist movement in Germany owed most of its theoretical insights to the Frankfurt School and especially to Theodor W. Adorno, who taught the younger generation the critical approach to literature and music. When *Aesthetische Theorie* came out, the West German student movement had reached the climax of its public influence. At the same time, it faced its first major crisis. The remarkable public recognition did not translate into a lasting, serious impact on the social system they critiqued and attacked. Unlike the American students, the West German students tried to solve this problem by forming more structured political organizations or moving closer to established political parties. In 1970 the student movement, entering its second phase, turned against its initial belief in spontaneous political expression and rallied around more orthodox leader figures like Lenin, Trotsky, or Mao Tse-tung. As much as these various groups fought among themselves and disagreed about strategy, they had one thing in common: their dislike of the Frankfurt School and its interpretation of Marxism.[2] They redefined their goals in terms of immediate political action and tried to establish a closer connection with the working class. Critical Theory became the victim of this reorientation. Since the New Left had been under the influence of the Frankfurt School at least until 1969, this critique was more than anything else a self-critique and therefore carried out with uncommon harshness. The members of the Frankfurt School were openly condemned as bourgeois, and their theory was denounced as liberal middle-class ideology. The liberal element in Adorno's writing—not only his concept of genuine culture, which clearly owed much to the eighteenth and nineteenth centuries and showed the *Bildungsbürger* in Adorno, but also his defense of individual freedom against the demands of the state and political parties—made him definitely unpopular with a movement that struggled to transform the social structure of West Germany.

Using the yardstick of orthodox Marxism, Adorno's leftist critics found it easy to dismiss his late work, especially *Aesthetische Theorie*, as irrelevant for the Marxist project. It was either Lukács or Brecht and Benjamin who became the new cultural heroes, and their theoretical work was appropriated to develop an alternative position. Ever since the famous Benjamin issue of *alternative* in 1967 (no. 56/57), the extremely complicated personal relationship between Walter Benjamin and the younger Adorno, who became Benjamin's disciple, critic, and editor, was presented as a clear-cut opposition: on the one hand, the smug Adorno who tried to suppress certain parts of Benjamin's oeuvre because they did not agree with his understanding of Benjamin's essential philosophy (an accusation that cannot be denied); on the other hand, Walter Benjamin, who moved closer to Brecht, transcended idealism and developed a truly materialist theory of art. We have to under-

2. For the development of the West German student movement and its impact on literature, see *Literatur und Studentenbewegung*, ed. W. Martin Lüdke (Opladen, 1977); also see *Nach dem Protest: Literatur in Umbruch*, ed. W. Martin Lüdke (Frankfurt, 1979).

stand this emotionally charged debate as a political rather than philological discourse. The heart of the matter for the New Left was a defense of Benjamin's oeuvre against the authority of Adorno and its integration into the dogma of the Frankfurt School.[3]

The interest in Benjamin, particularly in his essays of the thirties, which support the Communist party, reflects the yearning of the New Left to grasp and revive the element of political praxis in aesthetic theory. Since the Left placed the emphasis primarily on those elements in Benjamin's work that agreed with Brecht and overlooked other traditions, Adorno's critique of these essays, which he advanced already in letters during the 1930s, could only fuel the aversion toward the devious influence of Adorno's aesthetic elitism.

Although this debate has not yet come to an end—the question of Benjamin's Marxism seems to be as undecided as ever—there is a growing consensus among the Left and its various factions that the initial approach and the way it shaped the discourse has lost its usefulness and its critical edge. While Benjamin scholars have realized that we have to get out of the old mold if we want to appropriate Benjamin's writings for the present time, the discussion about Adorno's theory seems to linger without any direction.[4] It is time to take another look at *Aesthetische Theorie* and Adorno's essays on literature. This is not to make Adorno less controversial and thereby more acceptable to the established forces of the academy. The per-

3. See Jürgen Habermas, "Bewusstmachende oder rettende Kritik: Die Aktualität Walter Benjamins," in *Zur Aktualität Walter Benjamins* (Frankfurt, 1972), 175–223; also see Philip Brewster and Carl Howard Buchner, "Language and Critique: Jürgen Habermas on Walter Benjamin," *New German Critique* 17 (1979): 3–14.

4. Among the contributions to Adorno research, see especially Richard Wolin, "The De-Aestheticization of Art: On Adorno's *Aesthetische Theorie*," *Telos* 41 (Fall 1979): 105–27; and Anson Rabinbach, "Critique and Commentary/Alchemy and Chemistry: Some Remarks on Walter Benjamin and This Special Issue," *New German Critique* 17 (1979): 3–14.

spective that guided the interpretation and critique of Adorno in the early 1970s was rooted, as I have tried to show, in a singular historical situation—the struggle between the student movement and the West German establishment. The historical distance from these events, which only the nostalgic observer can overlook, calls for a reappreciation. In this rereading we cannot simply dismiss the arguments of the early 1970s and pretend to face the text for the first time, but we must be conscious of the limitations imposed on the interpretation at that time.

According to the Left, Adorno refused to apply his own theory to the political realm. He indulged in pessimism. Indeed the social theory of the Frankfurt School, which started out in the thirties as a Marxist project, became increasingly pessimistic with respect to Marx's prognosis that capitalism would ultimately self-destruct and give way to a socialist society. Faced with fascism in Germany and Italy and monopoly capitalism in the United States, Horkheimer and Adorno concluded in the 1940s that the Enlightenment, which was supposed to bring freedom and emancipation, had resulted in barbarism and slavery, not as an accidental relapse—as the liberal mind preferred to see this development—but rather as the logical outcome of the historical process. In their *Dialectic of Enlightenment* Horkheimer and Adorno argued that the political unfolding of *ratio* would lead to the increasing domination of nature by man, who then would become the victim of his own structure of domination. Since Horkheimer and Adorno, unlike Lukács, had given up the belief that the proletariat would revolutionize the given social structure, their analysis of advanced capitalism did not include the revolutionary perspective of traditional Marxism.

The Frankfurt School reached the position that man can analyze the logic of history but not organize political opposition. As late as 1969, shortly before his death, Adorno defended this stance against the demands of the students. The unity of theory

79

and praxis, he argued, tends to privilege action.[5] And this emphasis becomes irrational when imposed on philosophy. Adorno denounced the call for praxis as dogmatic and insisted that the uncompromising rigor of theory that defends its realm against the onslaught of positivism offers the truly critical opposition. This last effort to preserve the priority of theory came close to the very position that the Frankfurt School castigated as traditional in the 1930s. Adorno's use of the category of negation became abstract and thereby lost its critical edge.

Although Adorno refused to view his attitude as pessimistic, we cannot overlook the widening of the gap between theory and praxis in his later writings. His late work tends to dwell on the importance of art. It is not accidental that Adorno's last book deals with aesthetic rather than social problems. His concern with social questions leads to aesthetic rather than political theory. Adorno's philosophy of art is his final answer to the dilemma of social praxis. Adorno offers the authentic work of art as that emphatic opposition that can no longer materialize in political organizations. This perspective might look more attractive today than twenty years ago when there appeared to be hope that the age of capitalism might come to an end. But is this kind of relevance a good reason for us to return to Adorno's criticism? Is Adorno perhaps becoming fashionable again because his aestheticism and pessimism appeal to the readers of the troubled 1990s? By asking these questions I do not want to discredit the legitimacy of our present interests and simply restore the authority of Adorno and the Frankfurt School. Still, the question of what *Aesthetische Theorie* offers us today should be coupled with the complementary question of what we offer to Adorno's theory and from where we look at it.

Let me begin with a broad description of Adorno's philosophy. His oeuvre is clearly grounded in the tradition of German

5. Theodor W. Adorno, "Resignation," in his *Kritik: Kleine Schriften zur Gesellschaft* (Frankfurt, 1971), 145–50.

idealism, particularly in Hegel. The same can be said about Georg Lukács, but the results are strikingly different. When Lukács moved from an idealist to a Marxist position and attempted to work out a materialist basis for his criticism, he adopted Lenin's reflection theory, which is supposed to support Lukács's concept of the organic work of art as the only authentic form of art. Adorno rejects this more traditional part of Hegel's aesthetics and insists that the rigorous historical approach should be extended to basic aesthetic norms and rules. Lukács also historicizes art and literature. Coming from reflection theory and a general concept of realism, however, he favors those forms of literature that express the interest and concerns of the proletariat—in other words, social realism. Adorno, who admired the early Lukács, refused to accept this argument. In his essay "Erpresste Versöhnung," he distances himself from Lukács's theory of realism and at the same time harshly critiques Lukács's concept of the organic work of art.[6] Adorno denounces Lukács's struggle against modernism—writers like Kafka and Joyce—as the regressive part of Hegel's influence—a reduction of the work of art to considerations of content. Adorno on the other hand defends modernism precisely because he shares the historical approach with the Hegelian tradition. To put it more concretely: he rejects the attack on modernism because it is rooted in an ontological, ahistorical understanding of the organic work of art. Modern writers are not decadent and therefore unable to synthesize content and form; rather, they try to work out the dialectic of social change and aesthetic innovation. What we call the history of literature, changes of style and genres, is not just a sequence of facts and events; it consists of a dialectical process in which the individual work is seen against the background of conventions and norms. Authenticity is reached only through the negation of

6. In Theodor W. Adorno, *Gesammelte Schriften* (Frankfurt, 1974), 11:251–80; an English translation has appeared as "Reconciliation under Duress," in *Aesthetics and Politics*, ed. Ronald Taylor and Fredric Jameson (London, 1980).

thc affirmative tradition. This stress on novelty should not be mistaken for an apology of the fashionable, it rather indicates that the aesthetic material itself is drawn into the historical process.

Adorno follows the idealist tradition of Kant, Schiller, and Hegel and emphasizes the autonomy of the art work. Unlike the aesthetic theory of the later nineteenth century in Germany, which tends to view aesthetic principles as metahistorical, Adorno is much closer to Hegel's intention when he applies the historical critique also to the basic aesthetic categories—including the concept of autonomy. The legitimacy of this category is limited to the period between the eighteenth and twentieth centuries, although Adorno is never quite clear whether this period has come to an end. In his famous lecture in 1957 on poetry and society, Adorno refers to the collective *Grundstrom* (deep undercurrent) in the poems of Brecht and Lorca, without indicating whether this grounding in a collective spirit marks the beginning of a new progressive era or the decline of poetry as a medium of philosophical truth.[7] I shall come back to this ambiguity later. First I would like to develop another important aspect of Adorno's theory: the correlation between the aesthetic and the social sphere.

When literary theory in the late eighteenth century developed the notion that art is autonomous, the intention was to free the art work from the demand of social praxis. The result is an abstract opposition between the social and aesthetic sphere. By historicizing the major categories of aesthetic theory Adorno brings these realms closer together again. Ultimately art and society belong to the same stream of history. This insight is certainly not new. The Left-Hegelians, beginning with Hcine, used Hegel's model of history to understand the evolution of literature as representative for the development

---

7. Theodor W. Adorno, "Rede über Lyrik und Gesellschaft," in *Ge-sammelte Schriften* (Frankfurt, 1974), 11:48–68; translated as "Lyric Poetry and Society," in *Telos* 20 (Summer 1974): 56–71.

of social and political history. Adorno's approach stands in this tradition, but he is very much aware of its dangers. While he insists on the dialectic of art and society (the art work is also a social fact), he does not, like Lukács, conceive of it in terms of reflection. Adorno's *Aesthetische Theorie* is his final effort to grasp and theoretically refine the dialectic of the social and the aesthetic spheres.

Adorno's theory not only defends and legitimizes modernism and the avant-garde, it may well be called a theory of the avant-garde. Its author is clearly on the side of those historical forces that undermine the rule of European classicism. Adorno is a distant and skeptical observer of the ideas of Johann Winckelmann. Looking back at Greek classicism Adorno points out the material conditions of Greek history, which were anything but ideal: brutal warfare, slavery, and oppression are the reality that have to be suppressed before we can enjoy the notion of perennial beauty and harmony in Greek art.

Neoclassicism presented a unity of the general and the particular which already in the Attic period could not be attained, much less later. It is why the classic statues gaze at us with those empty eyes which, instead of radiating noble simplicity and silent greatness attributed to them by the neoromantic period, give us an archaic scare. What is forced upon us as classicism has nothing to do with corresponding European classicism in the era of the French Revolution and of the Napoleons, not to speak of the time of Baudelaire. (*AT*, 241)

The object of this critique is the neohumanism of Weimar and its glorification of Greek art. This seemingly historical polemic has a methodological aspect that I want to bring to the foreground: Adorno, at least implicitly, speaks here against the model that was used by the early Lukács to situate the novel form. Adorno undercuts the fundamental assumption of Lukács's *Theory of the Novel* that early Greek literature was grounded in social conditions that were free of alienation.

This critique of classicism becomes important because it is

at the same time a critique of a model that was further developed by Lucien Goldmann. For Goldmann the task of the critic and sociologist of literature is to establish a homology between the social and the literary structure.[8] Adorno's theory looks similar, yet this similarity is deceptive. While Adorno shares with Goldmann the interest in formal structure and rejects any kind of *Inhaltssoziologie* (sociology of content) as vulgar materialism, he is careful not to press the correlation into the homology model. The difference becomes apparent when Adorno defines his approach as *immanent*. The critic is starting out from the text rather than beginning with an analysis of the social structure. It is the explication of the work of art that offers insight into the social conditions that defined the production of the work of art. In his essay "Rede über Lyrik und Gesellschaft" (Lyric poetry and society) he unfolds the notion that the social meaning of the poem is expressed through its language. The poem relates to social history only indirectly. Adorno calls the poem a philosophical and historical sundial; by deciphering the structure of the poem the critic decodes the meaning of social history. Again, this sounds like Goldmann's theory, but we have to note the distinction: the interpretation of the poem refers to the meaning of history, not to the facts or objective structures. The two realms are mediated by philosophy—more specifically the philosophy of the early Marx. Unlike Goldmann, Adorno would never identify the work of art with an individual social group or class. This procedure, which is typical of Goldmann's criticism, is unacceptable to Adorno on principle. The correspondence between art and society, the aesthetic and the social meaning, transcends the particular group or class. Authentic are only those works representative of the whole. The choice of the sundial as the key metaphor signals that for Adorno the important element in the text is its expressive force and not so much the author and his

8. Lucien Goldmann, *Pour une sociologie du roman* (Paris, 1964); see also his *Recherches dialectiques* (Paris, 1959).

or her intentions to build up a coherent vision of the world. The individual author enters the sphere of criticism only as the human voice, the historical subjectivity that objectifies the expression through the work. Thus the emphasis is placed on the objective side: the authentic work of art is given the status of a permanent testament of human history—it embodies the hopes and sufferings, the expectations and contradictions, of the human race.

In *Aesthetische Theorie* Adorno tries to unfold this argument: "If [the authentic work of art] stands in opposition to empirical reality by means of its formal moment—and mediation between form and content cannot be comprehended without this differentiation—then a certain degree of mediation is to be found in the fact that aesthetic form is but a sediment of content" (*AT*, 15). Or another definition: "Only by separating itself from empirical reality—a separation possible, based on the need of art to manipulate the relationship between the whole and its parts—can a work of art become a being of second power" (*AT*, 14). Here Adorno, following Walter Benjamin, introduces the concept of the monad. By comparing art works with monads, Adorno tries to explore the dialectic of art and reality. Monads are closed—they have, so to speak, no windows and therefore offer no immediate access to reality. This, as it turns out, is quite necessary, since the outside world is already contained in a monad. Adorno then applies this idea to the understanding of aesthetic forms: "The unresolved antagonisms of reality recur in the works of art as immanent problems of its form. This and not the introduction of concrete moments define the relationship of art and society" (*AT*, 16). These unanswered questions provide literary and art history with their dynamic force. The increasing contradictions of reality show up as dissonances of form, they propel the evolution of art to the point where the avant-garde artist negates the very principle of the art work itself. Thus only those works deserve to be called authentic that question their own formal structure.

By stressing the formal aspect of literary history Adorno arrives at a position close to that of Russian formalism. He also argues that aesthetic criticism should be primarily concerned with questions of technique. The detailed analysis of seemingly technical points, in other words close readings, throws light on the social meaning. The comparison with Russian formalism is fruitful with respect to considerations of form. There are also important differences. Adorno would have rejected the formalist notion that literary history can be fully understood in terms of its intrinsic evolution. As we shall see, Adorno insists on the totality of history no less than Hegel or Lukács. Therefore the approach of Tynjanov—that the critic has to look first at the literary sequence, then at the political or economic evolution, and finally try to relate these sequences—would be shunned as undialectical and positivistic.[9] While Adorno shares the concern of the Russian formalists with technique, his interpretation of history follows a model that is quite different.

In spite of his outspoken critique of the traditional dialectic, which moves from thesis to antithesis and finally ends with a synthesis, Adorno's philosophy is still grounded in Hegel's philosophy of history. The concept of history proposed by the formalists, although analytically sound, is unacceptable to Adorno because it deprives the work of art of its emphatic truth value (*Wahrheitsgehalt*). Adorno's interest in literary evolution is not that of the historians who are satisfied when they have demonstrated how a genre changes or a motif is expressed in different ways. Adorno's theory puts a high premium on aesthetic innovation. Patterns, forms, genres, are not fixed entities but historical categories. The notion of change and innovation, however, must not be fetishized. Its meaning can be understood only as a part of a larger historical context. Close reading is for Adorno, strange as this may sound, a contextual reading. When Adorno postulates that the sociologist of art must begin with

9. Jurij Tynjanov, "Ueber die literarische Evolution," in *Texte der russischen Formalisten*, ed. Jurij Streidter (Munich, 1969), 1:393–431.

the text, he presupposes a model of history in which the various spheres—social, political, philosophical, aesthetic—are part of a unified process. Thus Adorno's claim to *Immanenz* should not be interpreted as a German version of New Criticism, the equivalent of Emil Staiger, for instance. Stressing the intrinsic approach means the opposite: it is the attempt to overcome the reification of traditional interpretation. Formalized professional scholarship insists on the rigorous definition of its object, the separation of the researcher and his or her material, without paying attention to their dialectical relationship in which the subject is very much part of the object and the seemingly objective material is the result of the subject's activities. When we talk about Adorno's approach we have to realize that he refuses to offer an objectified scientific method that can be abstracted from the individual act of understanding and then applied to various works.

Among the three approaches to the work of art, the interest in the origin and production of art, the interest in its structure, and the interest in its impact and reception, Adorno favors, as we have seen, the structural procedure. He is less sympathetic to studies that try to understand art in terms of communication. Adorno argues:

> The objectification of art [from a social standpoint, its fetishism] is in itself a social product of the division of labor. Thus, an examination of the relationship between art and society should not zero in on the sphere of reception as it precedes reception: it is to be found in the sphere of production. The interest in the social de-coding of art should turn to production and not be satisfied with analysis and classification; for societal reasons, they often are completely divergent from the works of art and their objective social content. (*AT*, 338)

This hostile remark against reception studies is primarily directed against positivism in musicology, which tried to develop a quantitative method to demonstrate the success and significancc of music.[10] Adorno himself was clearly interested in reception and wrote a number of important essays on the sociology of listening.[11]

Adorno's emphasis on production as the key to the understanding of the art work deserves closer scrutiny. What does he mean? Certainly not the kind of studies popular in the late nineteenth century, when the critic explained the work of art by documenting its sources and demonstrated the roots in the biography of the author. In Adorno's criticism the individual author and his or her intentions rarely receive more than fleeting attention. Biography is in most cases treated on the anecdotal level. Adorno would agree with Lukács's argument that Balzac's intentions and the meaning of his novels were not identical. He carefully refrains from praising the genius, knowing well that this category is part of the liberal ideology: the self-promotion of the artist who has to deal with the marketplace. Adorno defines production of art in terms of the general economic and social conditions under which the artist has to work—feudal patronage, the competition of the capitalist market, or the situation of the culture industry in advanced capitalist societies. Second, Adorno wants to emphasize artistic labor: the concrete struggle of artists with the techniques available at a certain time. By focusing attention on the process of production the critic at the same time reveals its meaning and truth value.

An example from *Aesthetische Theorie* will serve to demonstrate what Adorno has in mind. There is no doubt that Adalbert Stifter was a conservative author. Both his critical prose and his works of fiction express a moderate and cautious stance. It is not accidental therefore that Stifter's reading public consisted to a large extent of educated conservative German

10. Theodor W. Adorno, "Thesen zur Kunstsoziologie," in *Ohne Leitbild* (Frankfurt, 1970), 94–103.

11. See Theodor W. Adorno, *Einleitung in die Musiksoziologie* (Frankfurt, 1962); translated as *Introduction to the Sociology of Music* (New York, 1976).

Bürger (bourgeois citizens), while the leftist camp remained indifferent or hostile. Typically enough, Lukács denied Stifter the status of a major German writer. Adorno agrees with neither side. His interpretation wants to rescue Stifter's work from his conservative admirers, who find their own ideology confirmed in the message of the novels. Adorno is fully aware that this effort is problematical when he notes: "The strata which granted him his somewhat esoteric popularity has since disappeared. This is not the last word about him, however. Especially in his late period, there is too much of reconciliation and reconcilability. Objectivity becomes a mere mask and the conjured life a ritual of resignation. But throughout his middle period, we perceive the suppressed and renounced suffering of the alienated subject and an unreconciled situation" (*AT*, 346). This statement, however, is followed by another one that demonstrates Adorno's understanding of the authentic value within the conservative ideology: "The ideological overtension present lends [Stifter's] work its mediated nonideological truth content and guarantees its superiority over literature that can offer only solace and the overrated privacy of the countryside. It gives him the authentic quality Nietzsche so admired" (*AT*, 346). Adorno clearly differentiates between the meaning Stifter wanted to express in his writings and the *Gehalt* (Adorno's adaptation of the Hegelian idea of a synthesis of form and content) hidden in the structure of the work. In the case of Stifter, Adorno sets the utopian element apart from the conservative ideology of the author. This is a significant move. The sociologist who concentrates on the plot and the characters of, say, *Nachsommer*, can read this novel as a typical example of the conservative mood of the 1850s. The overriding themes offer plenty of evidence for this thesis. Adorno, to be sure, does not deny the validity of this aspect, yet ultimately the thematic conservatism of Stifter's novels is seen as part of a larger context. Adorno's reading links the conservative component to the industrial revolution of the 1850s. The legitimacy of *Nachsommer* is its negation of the new industrial society.

The category of negativity is crucial for Adorno's philosophy. Through its negativity the work of art secures its authenticity and sets itself apart from the conventions of its time and genre. Indeed, Adorno de-emphasizes conventions because, as socially accepted models of artistic expression, they indirectly also affirm the social status quo. This is the reason why Adorno never feels quite comfortable with older literature or music. The works of the sixteenth and seventeenth centuries rely heavily on conventional devices and moreover fulfill immediate social functions. They are still embedded in social and cultural traditions of individual social groups and classes. For Adorno they are less valuable because they belong to a specific social setting and are not fully autonomous. Their truth value appears to be more limited.

This bias shows that Adorno's criticism is not just another form of criticism of ideology. In this respect Goldmann's theory is certainly closer to Marxist orthodoxy. Goldmann focuses on a specific social and historical situation—for instance, the situation of the *noblesse de robe* in France—and then relates his findings to the structure of individual works of literature, Racine's tragedies, for example. In the final analysis he maintains a base-superstructure model. Adorno, on the other hand, makes use of the critique of ideology to undermine ossified structures and reified thought patterns. He firmly holds that those works of art that deserve to be called *gelungen* (that is, genuine and excellent) cannot be reduced to the status of documents that reflect the ideas of a particular class. Although the authentic work of art is grounded in its historical moment, its truth value (*Wahrheitsgehalt*) transcends the historical moment. This truth value, on which their rank ultimately rests, Adorno argues in a key passage of *Aesthetische Theorie*, is historical through and through: "Truth value is not related to history in a way that it, together with the status of works of art, changes with the passing of the period. To be sure, some variations are possible; works of art of high quality, for example, may unfold throughout history. This does not mean, however, that truth value and quality devolve on historicism" (*AT*, 285). Against any relativistic notion, Adorno maintains that there is an objectively correct historical consciousness: "Ever since the potential for freedom disappeared, correct consciousness... will be advanced consciousness about contradictions, with their possible reconciliation on the far horizon" (*AT*, 285). The aesthetic analogies of this advanced consciousness are the forces of production within the art world, the craftsmanship of the artist, mastering the material, struggling against the general trend toward conformity. Artistic innovation, in other words, is the equivalence of the advanced historical consciousness.

It should be obvious by now that Adorno's theory summarizes the development of the last century. Its examples are the composition of Schönberg and his disciples and the evolution of modern poetry since Baudelaire. Whether this philosophy can be applied to medieval art seems doubtful, since the category of autonomy is central to the basic argument. This brings us back to my initial question. After outlining what Adorno "has to offer," we must ask ourselves where we stand and how we relate to this theory today. If we mean to take Adorno's philosophy of art seriously, we cannot evade this question, because theory itself is no less historical than literature and music. And Adorno was quite aware of this problem. In the introduction to *Aesthetische Theorie* he states, "Just as the concept of system or moral, the notion of a philosophical aesthetics today seems antiquated" (*AT*, 493). Then the question arises: How can we develop a systematic aesthetic theory when most of the traditional categories on which this theory was built have become obsolete? The fact that recent history has liquidated basic concepts like the beautiful makes any attempt to systematize aesthetics highly problematical.

Thomas Baumeister and Jens Kulenkampff have argued that Adorno could no longer follow Hegel's philosophy of art, which places the emphasis on content rather than form, because it privileges rational discourse and therefore imposes its concepts on art in such a way that art loses its status as an independent mode of expression.[12] Those elements of the work of art that cannot be grasped by theoretical concepts are indeed most meaningful ones for Adorno, who is distrustful of rational discourse. By the same token Adorno cannot hark back to a more traditional genre theory that rests on metahistorical norms. Nor can he turn to Kant's aesthetic theory, which is concerned with aesthetic experience. Still, Adorno is convinced that modern art and literature are in need of aesthetic theory. Appreciation as a mode of criticism is not enough. Since philosophical criticism aims at the truth value of art, the critics must not confine themselves to subjective experience. The task is to decipher objective meaning and this can be accomplished only with the help of a theoretical framework. Especially the complexity of modern art calls for a theoretical approach. Adorno notes: "Precisely those moments of art which cannot be reduced to subjective experience and cannot be comprehended in their plain immediacy need consciousness, that is, philosophy. It is part of every aesthetic experience as long as it is not barbaric, alien to art. Art expects its own explication" (*AT*, 524). So Adorno, in spite of his skepticism against rational discourse, clearly relates back to the tradition of philosophical aesthetics and turns explicitly against the concept of experience offered by positivism and pragmatism. He defines the goal of aesthetic theory as follows: "Aesthetics today should be above the controversy between Kant and Hegel without trying to form it into a synthesis" (*AT*, 528).

This reference to Kant and Hegel—Adorno's shorthand for two types of aesthetic theory—locates the realm in which Adorno tries to work out the tension between theory and history. He suggests that the categories of idealism still help us capture the emphatic meaning of modern art and literature, although modernism and the avant-garde are no longer

---

12. Thomas Baumeister and Jens Kulenkampff, "Geschichtsphilosophie und philosophische Aesthetik: Zu Adornos Aesthetischer Theorie," *Neue Hefte für Philosophie* 5 (1973): 74–104.

grounded in idealism. Adorno is fully aware of the dilemma. The philosophical concepts of criticism are at the same time indispensable and inadequate. Because of this ambiguity the late work of Adorno tends to identify philosophy and art, since the process of deciphering and preserving—in other words, criticism—is the only way in which truth in an emphatic sense can be revealed. Genuine art, for Adorno the last bastion that has not yet capitulated, is the sphere where the deception of instrumental reason is without consequence. This vision owes its force to Hegel, although it does not share Hegel's negative attitude toward postclassical art. For Adorno, art and philosophy are inseparable but not identical. This position allows him to cling to the concepts of the work of art and truth value as his categories. When philosophy in the phase of late capitalism has lost most of its emancipatory functions, as Adorno claims, it becomes the task of the authentic art work to stand in and defend the tower of truth.

I started this essay with some remarks about the hostile reception of *Aesthetische Theorie* in the early 1970s. This animosity was partly caused by the frustration of the student movement. The students were looking for a leader in their political struggle and had to realize that Adorno was unwilling and also unprepared to step into this role. This explanation, however, is insufficient. The lack of appreciation the younger generation showed in 1970 must be related to a broader phenomenon. Between 1967 and 1970 West Germany witnessed an almost unparalleled breakdown of the literary system. The radicals called for the end of literature and criticism, since the capitalist system had turned them into meaningless toys of the establishment. This crisis undermined the belief in the autonomy of art, which Adorno defended against *Tendenz*. This debate is only the foreground for a deeper problem that had been lingering since the Second World War. I mean the fate of the avant-garde. Adorno's philosophy of art is closely related to the avant-garde of the early twentieth century. He takes most of his examples from works written or composed between

1890 and 1930. Seldom does he refer to later works. His literary criticism favors authors of the nineteenth and early twentieth centuries, such as Heine, Balzac, Joseph Eichendorff, Stefan George, Frank Wedekind, Karl Kraus, and Benjamin. The notable exception is his interpretation of Beckett's *Endgame* (1957)—a play that speaks very much to the mood of Adorno's late years.[13] Occasionally Adorno would play with the idea that the concept of autonomy of art might not be fully appropriate for the period that followed the Second World War. Here and there he cautiously alludes to the end of the avant-garde, yet he fails to pursue this perspective with any rigor.

Today it would be futile to suppress this question: Did the neo-avant-garde still have the same critical edge Adorno saw in the works of the previous generation? The New Left answered in the negative. They appropriated the arguments of Horkheimer and Adorno's *Dialectic of Enlightenment* that there is no room for genuine culture in advanced industrial societies and therefore rejected the notion of aesthetic opposition. As I mentioned earlier, they discovered Benjamin's writings and followed his thesis that the autonomy of art, which was grounded in its ritual function, faded away with the advent of mechanical mass reproduction. Benjamin had argued: "But the instant the criterion of authenticity ceases to be applicable to artistic production, the total function of art is reversed. Instead of being based on ritual, it begins to be based on another practice—politics."[14] This thesis guided the theoretical efforts of the student movement. They wanted to tear down the walls of the aesthetic ghetto and apply the arts to the political realm. By 1975 it was clear that this movement had failed to reach its goal. The literary system slowly but surely returned to its earlier status quo. I cannot go into the political and philosoph-

13. Theodor W. Adorno, "Versuch das Endspiel zu verstehen," in *Gesammelte Schriften*, 11:281–331; translated as "Trying to Understand Endgame," *New German Critique* 26 (1982): 119–50.

14. Walter Benjamin, *Illuminations*, ed. Hannah Arendt, trans. Harry Zohn (New York, 1969), 224.

ical reasons for this failure.[15] My argument is exclusively concerned with the critique of Adorno's *Aesthetische Theorie* as it emerged from the crisis of the literary system.

As soon as we focus on this question we begin to realize what separates our situation from that of Adorno in the 1960s. We notice that Adorno's philosophy of art has become historical. Adorno stresses the precarious state of modern art and emphasizes the negative impact of capitalism on culture, yet he maintains that the function of art has not changed since the advent of modernism. To put it differently: Adorno's theory takes the institution of art for granted. Peter Bürger advanced the argument in his *Theory of the Avant-Garde* (1974) that Adorno failed to provide a critique of the concept of autonomy.[16] It was the aim of the avant-garde movement, according to Bürger, to overcome the gap between the aesthetic and practical spheres and regain political impact by eliminating the traditional aesthetic autonomy. Bürger convincingly demonstrates that Adorno, in spite of his hostility toward Lukács, shares basic philosophical assumptions with him. Their disagreement about realism and modernism is based on a common notion of the autonomous work of art. While Lukács tilted toward a model of organic works of art, Adorno placed the emphasis on the raison d'être of tensions and contradictions. In Bürger's analysis the sharp edge of the historical dialectic finally turns against Adorno himself. Following Benjamin, Bürger describes the avant-garde movement in terms of a self-critique that denounces the complacency of modern aestheticism. Compared with this radical stance, where art moves toward its own destruction, Adorno's aesthetic theory reads

15. See Peter Uwe Hohendahl, "Politisierung der Kunsttheorie: Zur ästhetischen Diskussion nach 1967," in *Deutsche Literatur in der Bundesrepublik seit 1965: Untersuchungen und Berichte*, ed. Paul Michael Lützeler and Egon Schwarz (Königstein, 1980); Chapter 6 in this volume is a translation and reworking of this essay.

16. Peter Bürger, *Theorie der Avantgarde* (Frankfurt, 1974), 117–27; translated by Michael Shaw as *Theory of the Avant-Garde* (Minneapolis, 1984).

like a somewhat belated summary of modernism—a recapitulation that is not quite ready to accept the extreme conclusions of the twentieth-century avant-garde.

Not all critics and theorists have agreed with Bürger's thesis. W. Martin Lüdke for instance, in a response to Bürger, questioned whether *Theory of the Avant-Garde* does justice to Adorno's category of modernism (*Moderne*).[17] He takes issue with Bürger's presentation of Adorno's theory of aesthetic innovation, and finally tries to show that Bürger's critique is not really intrinsic but, rather, inspired by the social theory of Jürgen Habermas. Lüdke's rejoinder is persuasive as an interpretation of *Aesthetische Theorie*, but it is ultimately beside the point. Adopting a Habermasian position, that is, looking at the Frankfurt School from a stance that has modified some of the basic tenets, enables Bürger to situate Adorno's aesthetic theory historically. Precisely because he stands outside of Adorno's theory he can point out that the logic of this theory is limited to a specific period of European art. Although it may not be obvious at first sight, this argument has far-reaching consequences. It undercuts Adorno's key metaphor: the art work is no longer the sundial of history. The period after 1945, according to Bürger, is marked by a legitimate coexistence of different styles and tendencies. There is no stringent correlation between social and art history.

Bürger's critique and its strategy are sound and convincing. Yet I would like to go one step further. To some extent Bürger himself still operates within the confines of Adorno's model. His major thesis—that the production and reception of literature between 1780 and 1910 were determined by the concept of autonomous art—is obviously derived from Adorno. Looking back at this period today and viewing it within the broader context of preceding and following literary history, we realize

17. W. Martin Lüdke, "Die Aporien der materialistischen Aesthetik—kein Ausweg? Zur kategorialen Begründung von P. Bürgers *Theorie der Avantgarde*," in *Antworten auf Peter Bürgers Bestimmung von Kunst und bürgerliche Gesellschaft*, ed. W. Martin Lüdke (Frankfurt, 1976), 27–71.

that Adorno's idea of autonomy, which was then historicized by Bürger, never covered more than a part of the actual literary production of the nineteenth century. Much of the Restoration period (1815–48), with Heinrich Heine as the prime example, would not fit. Aesthetic autonomy as an episode of history: this perspective looks more familiar to us than to Adorno. He was not prepared to accept this interpretation, because it would have deprived him of any meaningful approach to history. In his essay "Das Altern der Neuen Musik," Adorno is ready to concede that modern music was more radical in its beginnings than in its later phases.[18] Still, he refuses to unfold the implications of this argument. He laments this development as a loss. His remark about Béla Bartók's later work is typical of this attitude: "Partial responsibility for this is borne by the naiveté of the professional musician who goes about his business without partaking in the movement of the objective spirit."[19] This reference to the objective spirit indicates that Adorno, in the final analysis, relies on a Hegelian model of history in which all strands relate to one single center. The application of this model, however cautiously Adorno proceeded, seems to blind him with respect to the divergence of artistic trends and movements. While Adorno certainly rejected a reductive reading of history and was also skeptical of historical laws, his thinking is deeply rooted in the concept of a unified historical process. This idea, then, since the project of the Enlightenment has failed, leads him to the notion that the evolution of modern music is regressive because there is less personal freedom and an increasing amount of alienating bureaucracy in our society.[20] In a way, this argument puts the blame on history for not following the course that the philosopher has mapped out for it.

What is problematical in Adorno's philosophy of art, in other

18. This essay has been translated as "The Aging of the New Music," and has appeared in *Telos* 77 (Fall 1988): 95–116.
19. Theodor W. Adorno, *Dissonanzen* (Göttingen, 1972), 140.
20. Ibid., 157.

words, comes from the historical determinism he inherited from the Hegelian and Marxian tradition. The link between this tradition and the Frankfurt School is the work of Georg Lukács, especially *History and Class Consciousness*. Those orthodox Marxists who denounced Adorno's theory as liberal ideology failed to notice that they did not share his concept of the work of art and his approach to criticism but based their aesthetic theories on the same understanding of history: history as a dialectical process in which the concrete is by definition part of the whole. For Adorno there is no philosophy without *Universalgeschichte* (universal history). As Russell Berman puts it, "This historical scheme, an attempt to retain the universal history of Hegel and Marx, evidently precludes the possibility of perceiving the qualitatively new, for the new is only more of the old."[21] Although Berman underestimates the difference between Adorno and orthodox Marxism, he has a valid point.

What are we to learn from this critique? Does it mean that any project of defining aesthetic theory in historical-philosophical terms has become impossible, as Rüdiger Bubner claims?[22] Or are we to take the advice of Hans R. Jauss and turn to a system of aesthetic experience? Both Bubner and Jauss are prepared to eliminate history.[23] This way they hope to regain a less problematical theory of art. I would not be willing to pay this price, for the loss of history would imply a fragmentation of experience, decreasing its meaning.

21. Russell Berman, "Adorno, Marxism, and Art," *Telos* 34 (Winter 1977–78): 165.
22. Rüdiger Bubner, "Ueber einige Bedingungen gegenwärtiger Aesthetik," *Neue Hefte für Philosophie* 5 (1973): 38–73.
23. Hans R. Jauss, *Kleine Apologie der ästhetischen Erfahrung*, (Constance, 1972).

4   *Dialectic of Enlightenment* Revisited: Habermas's Critique of the Frankfurt School

A well-known newspaper caricature, printed some twenty years ago, pictures the Frankfurt School as a closely knit group with Max Horkheimer as a large father figure watching over the other members of the school, among them Theodor W. Adorno and Jürgen Habermas. This view of the relationship between the members of the Frankfurt School was quite common in Germany at that time: Habermas was seen not only as a member of the school but more specifically as a disciple of the older generation, someone who had started out from the position of Critical Theory, as it was developed in the 1940s and 1950s by Horkheimer, Marcuse, and Adorno. Although this interpretation cannot account for all of Habermas's early work, notably not for his *Strukturwandel der Oeffentlichkeit* (Structural transformation of the public sphere, 1962), it was plausible enough to find wide acceptance. Yet it was no accident that Habermas's first major study, which traces the evolution of the public sphere from the eighteenth to the twentieth century and stresses the need for an enlightened and rational reconsideration of the public sphere under advanced capitalism, never found Adorno's and Horkheimer's complete acceptance. Their own critique of the process of Enlightenment differed so markedly from the position Habermas outlined that there could be no full consensus. In a certain way, I would argue, the later differences, especially those between Adorno and Habermas, were already foreshadowed in *Strukturwandel,* although Habermas, when describing the decline of the liberal public sphere under organized capitalism, made use of the critique of mass culture formulated by the older generation and certainly did not indicate that he was in disagreement with the analysis offered in *Dialectic of Enlightenment.* On the whole, however, conventional wisdom, treating Habermas as a junior member of the Frankfurt School, was justified for the 1960s, when Habermas, for instance, defended the position of the Frankfurt School in the Positivism Dispute against Karl Popper and his allies of the Cologne school. While Adorno and Popper in their addresses to the German *Soziologentag* (sociology conference) of 1961 decided to suppress rather than highlight their theoretical and methodological differences, the younger generation, represented by Habermas and Hans Albert, did not hesitate to use a highly polemical rhetoric, in order to undermine the position of the enemy camp.[1] Habermas's insistence on the limitations of rational positivism and his emphasis on the need for a grounding of the humanities and the social sciences that is different from the methods of the natural sciences, clearly defended the position of Adorno. At least it was much closer to Adorno's understanding of the social sciences than that of Popper and the Cologne school.

The change of paradigm: Seen against the background of the rivalry between the Frankfurt and the Cologne schools during the 1950s and 1960s in Germany, there can be no doubt that Habermas's early work from *Theory and Practice* (1963) to *Knowledge and Human Interests* (1969) is part of the Frankfurt School, since it makes use of and relies on the analyses of the older generation, especially those of Horkheimer and Herbert Marcuse. Not only does Habermas share with classical Critical Theory a goal—the search for an

---

1. Jürgen Habermas, *Zur Logik der Sozialwissenschaften* (Frankfurt, 1970), 9–38 and 39–70.

emancipated and free society—he also continues, although not without modifications, the discourse of his teachers. More openly than Adorno and Horkheimer, Habermas returns to the Marxist problematic of Critical Theory, attempting to clarify the validity and function of Marxian theory vis-à-vis advanced capitalism. It is precisely this critical reexamination of Marxian theory, I would argue, that propels Habermas during the 1970s on a trajectory that distances him more and more from the position of Horkheimer and Adorno. By the end of the decade, friendly gestures notwithstanding, this process reaches a point from which, given the systematic development of Habermas's own theory, a return to the discourse of the old Frankfurt School is no longer possible. It seems that at this juncture Habermas wants to stress the break rather than the continuity. While the chapter devoted to Horkheimer and Adorno in *The Theory of Communicative Action* is still characterized by critical sympathy, his reassessment of *Dialectic of Enlightenment*, published under the title "The Entwinement of Myth and Enlightenment" in 1982, not only sharpens the critique of Horkheimer and Adorno but also displays a certain amount of acrimony absent from Habermas's earlier essays.[2] Habermas states in no uncertain terms that something went wrong in the evolution of Critical Theory during the 1940s. This harsh verdict is directed against Horkheimer's and Adorno's work from *Dialectic of Enlightenment* on. In particular, it is directed against Adorno's *Negative Dialectics* and *Aesthetic Theory*.

This turn in Habermas's appreciation of the older generation definitely calls for an explanation. I believe that there is more involved than just an increasing theoretical estrangement be-

2. Jürgen Habermas, "The Entwinement of Myth and Enlightenment: Re-reading *Dialectic of Enlightenment*," *New German Critique* 26 (Spring/Summer 1982): 13–30; reprinted in *The Philosophical Discourse of Modernity*, trans. Frederick Lawrence (Cambridge, Mass., 1987), 106–30.

tween the older and the younger generation. Habermas's earlier attempt to reformulate Marxian theory, by discarding a number of orthodox dogmas on the one hand and differentiating between labor and interaction on the other, did not result in a break because the open revision of Marxian theory in many ways simply spelled out what Horkheimer, Marcuse, and Adorno had already tacitly changed in their own theories since the early 1940s. Equally, the turn toward a theory of communicative action, the so-called linguistic turn in Habermas's work after *Legitimation Crisis* (1973), did not in itself necessitate the noticeable distress. There is an additional element that, taken together with Habermas's attempt to work out a communicative grounding of his theory, intensified the disagreement. What is ultimately at stake for Habermas is no less than the idea of rationality and the notion of a legitimate rational society. Rereading *Dialectic of Enlightenment*, Habermas discovers that Horkheimer's and Adorno's critique of reason owes as much if not more to Nietzsche than to Marx and the Marxist tradition. It is the Nietzsche connection that is, I think, responsible for the somewhat hostile tone, especially in the second essay. Again, I will argue, it is not Nietzsche's work in itself that creates the distress—Habermas had offered a critique of Nietzsche as early as *Knowledge and Human Interests*—but the intellectual atmosphere of the late 1970s and early 1980s in West Germany, where the revival of interest in Nietzsche was largely caused by the emergence of poststructuralism. As we shall see, it is Foucault's interpretation of Nietzsche that fuels Habermas's critical rereading of *Dialectic of Enlightenment* and of the later work of Horkheimer and Adorno.

Using explicit statements and implicit arguments from Habermas's systematic writings, I first want to document the growing rift between Habermas and the orthodoxy of the Frankfurt School. In a second step I want to look more specifically at the above-mentioned chapter in *The Theory of Communicative Action* and the essay on *Dialectic of Enlightenment*.

This should finally lead us to a reexamination of the fundamental problems involved in the grounding of Habermas's own theory. My interest in Habermas's reassessment and critique of Horkheimer and Adorno, to state it explicitly, is not primarily historical. The question whether Habermas's interpretation is historically correct or not is, in the context of my argument, secondary at best. The evidence, for instance, that Habermas misunderstands the intention of Horkheimer and Adorno in *Dialectic of Enlightenment*—a case that could possibly be made—will not be used as an argument against the critique of a specific position attributed to Horkheimer and Adorno.

Habermas's critique of the Frankfurt School: Axel Honneth has given a persuasive account of the changes of paradigm within Critical Theory.[3] "Habermas implicitly takes the first step toward a reorientation of social criticism to re-establish critical theory's tenuous claims within the present historical context."[4] Honneth rightly states that Habermas's own essays dealing with Marcuse, Adorno, and Benjamin do not systematically address the reasons why Habermas turned away from the position of the Frankfurt School in a late phase and challenged its historical and theoretical presuppositions. There are, however, clear indications that I want to bring into the foreground. While Habermas admires the aphoristic and stylistic qualities of Adorno's writings in his short essay "Theodor W. Adorno: Ein philosophierender Intellektueller" (A philosophizing intellectual, 1963)—which was, incidentally, not included in the later English edition of *Philosophical-Political Profiles*—the second essay on Adorno, published in 1969, already focuses on the problem that was to become crucial for Habermas's later reading of Adorno (and Horkheimer): Haber-

3. Axel Honneth, "Communication and Reconciliation in Habermas' Critique of Adorno," *Telos* 39 (Spring 1979): 45–61.
4. Ibid., 46.

mas concentrates on the dialectic of reason and Adorno's pessimistic conclusions.

As Habermas points out, for Adorno, "mastery of nature is chained to the introjected violence of humans over humans, to the violence of the subject exercised upon its own nature."[5] Thus the Enlightenment, since it remains unreflected, cannot attain the level of rationality that it claims for itself; rather, this process stays on the level of self-affirmation gone wild (*verwilderte Selbstbehauptung*). Habermas then suggests that he has some doubts about this view and hints that he would not necessarily concur with the analysis of reason lying behind it, but in 1969 he does not fully develop these thoughts because he seeks to understand Adorno's position as the result of his biography and the historical experience of his generation. He traces Adorno's concept of negative dialectic, concentrating on its challenge to both formal logic and orthodox Hegelian dialectic, which favors synthesis, but he does not emphasize the difference between his own project and Adorno's philosophy. In the final paragraphs Habermas merely touches on these differences when he problematizes his own psychological interpretation of Adorno and calls for a more systematic treatment of the fundamental epistemological questions raised by Adorno's concept of negative dialectic. He points out that Adorno cannot overcome the basic contradiction between his insistence on negativity (*bestimmte Negation*) and his use of the idea of reconciliation (*Versöhnung*), a state that would transcend the gesture of negation.

At this juncture the alternative project, as it was announced and partially developed in *Knowledge and Human Interests*, comes into the foreground. Habermas argues: "The idea of truth, already implicit in the first sentence spoken, can be shaped only on the model of the idealized agreement aimed for in communication free of domination. To this extent the truth

---

5. Jürgen Habermas, *Philosophical-Political Profiles* (London, 1983), 101.

of a proposition is bound up with the intention of leading a genuine life."[6] This statement, in which free communication becomes the basis for an authentic life, implicitly cancels the logic of reification on which Adorno's negative dialectic is modeled. Habermas is keenly aware that Adorno would not have accepted his premises and tries to explain why the older generation of the Frankfurt School would have resisted the idea of communication without domination as a real possibility for social organization. *Versöhnung*, the key term for Adorno's gesture toward an authentic social totality, must be grounded in a prerational understanding of nature, an understanding in which the dichotomy between subject and object does not exist. In Habermas's words, "Adorno (and also Benjamin, Horkheimer, Marcuse and Bloch) entertained doubts that the emancipation of humanity is possible without the resurrection of nature."[7] Habermas concluded in 1969 that the "dialectic of Enlightenment," that is, the historical logic of rationality, is profoundly ambivalent with respect to the chances of humanity's escaping the logic of domination.

So the question arises: Is universal reconciliation ultimately no more than an extravagant idea? Habermas's cautious statements seem to indicate that he differs from the older generation in two respects. First, he is unwilling to accept the logic of total reification that dominates *Dialectic of Enlightenment*, and second, he distances himself from a concept of reconciliation based on the notion of primal nature. In philosophical terms, Habermas at this point has moved away from the philosophical discourse of Hegel and the various schools that depend on the model of dialectical mediation.

By the late 1970s this critical stance becomes much more explicit in Habermas's work. This change, however, does not occur as a leap from one model to another, but rather as a critical reexamination that results in the development of a

6. Ibid., 107.
7. Ibid.

radically transformed discourse, using linguistic theories, theories of social action, and systems theory. The new model, which I cannot even sketch here, both replaces the Marxist Hegelian foundations of the Frankfurt School and calls for a systematic critique of these foundations. In *The Theory of Communicative Action* Habermas undertakes this reevaluation by tracing the concept of reification from Weber through Lukács to Horkheimer and Adorno. The charge is that Horkheimer and Adorno, by taking over and even broadening Lukács's concept of reification, maneuvered themselves into a position that did not allow them to conceptualize forces of resistance against the totally administered society.

In his reconstruction Habermas comes to the conclusion that Horkheimer's and Adorno's radical critique of reason (in its subjective and objective version) ultimately undermines the possibility of critical reflection itself. If critical thought, as Horkheimer and Adorno maintain in their later work, cannot formulate truth because it is already contaminated by the logic of instrumental reason, then the force of critical arguments is endangered. Critical reflection in its Adornian version can only hint at truth in the form of mimesis, but it cannot be developed as a theory with formal and methodological consequences. Habermas states this aporia in the following way: "The paradox in which the critique of instrumental reason is entangled, and which stubbornly resists even the most supple dialectic, consists then in this: Horkheimer and Adorno would have to put forward a theory of mimesis, which according to their own ideas, is impossible."[8] To put it differently, according to Habermas the critique of instrumental reason through the concept of reification makes it impossible to ground theory in communicative interaction. The business of philosophy would come to an end because discursive methods would lose their

8. Jürgen Habermas, *The Theory of Communicative Action*, vol. 1: *Reason and the Rationalization of Society*, trans. Thomas McCarthy (Boston, 1984), 382.

validity under the spell of identifying thought. By the same token—and this should be kept in mind—without discourse there is no space left for social praxis. It is precisely for this reason that Habermas does not follow Horkheimer's and Adorno's critiques. Instead, he wants to show how the Hegelian-Marxist tradition, relying heavily on the concept of reification, must end up in an aporetic situation.

Before I retrace the line of Habermas's argument, I want to call attention to its context. The critique of the Frankfurt School at the end of the first volume of *The Theory of Communicative Action* is part of a larger argument explaining the change of paradigm from a theory of teleological action to a theory of communicative action. The point of reference is the potential of rationality embedded in speech and linguistic communication, a rationality that remains, as Habermas claims, undeveloped in Max Weber's theory of action. Specifically, Habermas refers to the difference between rationality in the life-world and the rationality of systems and subsystems (economy, political system). By reconstructing the tradition of Western Marxism, Habermas wants to demonstrate that the heritage of Max Weber's theory of rationalization, as it can be found in Lukács well as in Horkheimer and Adorno, ultimately explodes the bounds of the philosophy of consciousness. The point of his argument is that the Frankfurt School, because of its dependence on the Weberian model of rationalization, fails to do justice to the problematic of the life-world—despite its own intentions.

Focusing on Horkheimer's *Eclipse of Reason*, Habermas underlines the similarity between Weber's and Horkheimer's interpretation of modern capitalist societies: their theories share an essentially identical model of rationalization. The history of modernity is seen as a process of disenchantment, with reason undermining the unquestioned validity of religion and ontology. Thus modern consciousness is characterized by a growing rift between knowledge and belief systems. This implies that morality and art are decoupled from the scientific pursuit of truth. Modern reason functions primarily as a tool for the promotion of self-interest and survival. Similarly, both Weber and Horkheimer stress the loss of individual freedom in modern society, Weber by calling attention to the impact of increasingly complex bureaucracies, Horkheimer, favoring psychological arguments, by pointing to the growing pressure of the social system on the individual. Habermas rightly acknowledges, however, that Horkheimer's conclusions differ significantly from Weber's reading of modern social organizations. He argues that these differences have to do with the impact of Lukács's theory of reification on the Frankfurt School.

Lukács, relying equally on Marx's theory of commodification and on Weber's theory of rationalization, fuses the concepts of reification and rationalization. As Habermas reminds us, this move in *History and Class Consciousness* allows Lukács to go beyond Weber and at the same time, I would add, to supplement Marxian theory. Habermas, however, is primarily interested in the theoretical limitations of this approach that are caused by Lukács's Hegelian reading of Marx. He sees two major deficiencies. First, Lukács's concept of reification relies exclusively on the concept of exchange value in *Capital* and therefore reduces all forms of rationalization in modern Western societies to a variation of reification caused by capitalism. As long as capitalism dominates social organization, reification is inevitable, not only in the sphere of social organization, but also in the realm of philosophy. Lukács argues, however, that this logic can be overcome because there are epistemological as well as social limits to the reification of reason. Also, this argument, in Habermas's opinion, depends on the use of Hegel's logic, a form of metaphysical thought that cannot be resurrected after its critique by post-Kantian philosophy.

Against Lukács's thesis of total reification under capitalism Habermas suggests that instrumental reason "establishes itself at the cost of practical rationality."[9] Then he concludes:

9. Ibid., 363.

"Thus it makes sense to ask whether the critique of the incomplete character of the rationalization that appears as reification does not suggest taking a complementary relation between cognitive-instrumental rationality, on the one hand, and moral-practical and aesthetic-practical rationality, on the other, as a standard that is inherent in the unabridged concept of practice, that is to say, in communicative action itself."[10] To put it differently, Hegel's logic of reconciliation, applied by Lukács to the problem of rationalization, remains a fiction, as long as it is carried out in the realm of theory only. This brings us to the second criticism: Habermas is equally opposed to the political solution of Lukács. He calls Lukács's notion of a proletarian revolution guided by Marxian philosophy a mistake, because the revolutionary avant-garde as the standard-bearer of theory would need a knowledge of the total structure of society that is empirically not available.

Habermas's critique of Lukács emphasizes two points: he challenges the reduction of rationalization to the level of reification caused by the capitalist economy, and he refuses to depend, as Lukács does, on a Hegelian reading of Marx that tries to solve the problem of practice in the sphere of philosophy. As we shall see, this critique reiterates many of the explicit or implicit arguments of the older Frankfurt School against Lukács—though I would like to add that a crucial part of Habermas's argument is not based on his reading of Horkheimer and Adorno but on his own theory of social practice. As much as he attempts to carry through an immanent critique, using the nexus of intellectual history, he reverts occasionally to the systematic framework of his own theory. This is equally true of his reading of *Dialectic of Enlightenment*.

The following steps of the argument unfold in a rather straightforward manner. Since the Frankfurt School, especially Horkheimer and Adorno, find it difficult to follow Lukács's Hegelian solution of the reification problematic, they have to

10. Ibid., 363–64.

reconsider the question of rationalization. They do this by decoupling the concept of reification from the historical development of capitalism. It seems that Habermas, who accuses Lukács of a reductive interpretation of rationalization and reification, approves of this criticism, yet at the same time he insists that this very move leads to the aporia I mentioned before. Habermas is distressed not so much by the way in which Horkheimer and Adorno de-historicize the concept of reification when they uncover the emergence of instrumental reason already in early Greek history, as by their tendency to blur the contours of the concept of reason itself. His criticism is carried out on two levels. He presents historical arguments in order to explain the strategy of the Frankfurt School, and he offers theoretical arguments to show why this strategy could not be successful.

The historical thesis, based on the work of Helmut Dubiel, can be summarized in the following way: (1) the Frankfurt School was faced with the peculiar development of Marxism in Russia, that is, Stalinism; (2) in Germany and Italy they encountered fascism, a political system that proved that capitalism could overcome its crisis by reorganizing the political order; and finally (3) they experienced in the United States the success of a capitalist system that integrated the underprivileged masses through organized mass culture (the culture industry).[11] As a result, so the argument goes, Horkheimer and Adorno could no longer rely on Lukács's theory of reification. While they still shared with Lukács the notion of a modern society largely determined by alienation, they could not share Lukács's view that this situation could be changed by the consciousness and the revolutionary action of the proletariat. To put it succinctly, their theory of fascism demonstrated why the consciousness of the masses would support advanced capitalism under the disguise of a new social order, and their theory

---

11. Helmut Dubiel, *Wissenschaftsorganisation und politische Erfahrung* (Frankfurt, 1978).

of the culture industry shows how the commodification of culture supplied the means for the integration of the masses into the existing social system.

The theoretical line of the argument is built on these historical considerations. In particular, Habermas wants to clarify why Horkheimer and Adorno, by radicalizing the theory of reification and/or rationalization, undermine the basis of their own critique. Habermas suggests that the rejection of Hegel's logic of mediation, to which Lukács could still resort in order to solve the problem of reification, leaves a vacuum that weakens the structure of the theory. Critical reflection in its attempt to grasp and break through the barriers of reified social relations is left only with the procedure of negative dialectic—a procedure that forgoes the attempt at reconciliation. The suspicion that even Lukács's critique of the reified mind is based on a philosophy grounded in the concept of identity (Hegel) leads to the eclipse of reason altogether. There are no weapons left to fight against the phenomena of reification, at least not within the sphere of rational discourse.

This is the center of Habermas's criticism, an argument I have to unfold. The question is, How can critical theory, fighting against positivism on the one hand and attacking ontology on the other, grasp and demonstrate its own validity? Habermas suggests two possibilities: either this critical reflection must be grounded in a general theory "that elucidates the foundations of the modern natural, social, and cultural sciences within the horizon of more encompassing concepts of truth and knowledge," or it has to be linked to a form of self-reflection "that reaches down into the lifeworld foundations, the structures of action and the contexts of discovery, underlying scientific theory-construction or objectivating thought in general."[12] The second alternative is clearly the one favored by Habermas. Yet this observation is of secondary importance in my context. More important, by

12. Habermas, *Theory of Communicative Action,* 375.

setting up this opposition, Habermas prejudges the following reading of Horkheimer and Adorno. He argues that Horkheimer's response to the theoretical dilemma does not fit into his classification of the possible solutions, for Horkheimer calls for a self-reflection that demystifies the social processes that determine the boundaries of systematic thought. Habermas takes this statement as a first step toward a self-reflection of scientific theory, as it was carried out by the next generation of social scientists and philosophers. Yet he rightly stresses that the Frankfurt School did not pursue this project. Rather, Horkheimer and Adorno insisted on a radical critique of reified subjective reason, of instrumental reason.

Habermas suggests that this critique was doomed because it destroyed the basis of critical reflection altogether. The first step of his argument reconstructs the strategy of Horkheimer and Adorno in *Dialectic of Enlightenment*. Habermas arrives at the following conclusion:

Horkheimer and Adorno detach the concept [of reification] not only from the special historical context of the rise of the capitalist economic system but from the dimension of interhuman relations altogether; and they generalize it temporally (over the entire history of the human species) and substantatively (the same logic of domination is imputed to both cognition in the service of self-preservation and the repression of instinctual nature). This double generalization of the concept of reification leads to a concept of instrumental reason that shifts the primordial history of subjectivity and the self-formative process of ego-identity into an encompassing historico-philosophical perspective.[13]

In his second step Habermas extrapolates the historico-philosophical horizon of Horkheimer's and Adorno's strategy. Through instrumental reason the human race attained

13. Ibid., 379–80.

the domination of nature, but the price it had to pay for this achievement was the repression of subjectivity. This dialectic works against the traditional notion of Enlightenment as a process of human emancipation. Instead, history turns into a self-imposed catastrophe from which there is no escape. Confronted with the failure of reason, Horkheimer and Adorno attempt to anchor their own critique of this process in an approach that is not trapped in the dialectic of instrumental reason. They mean to overcome the constraints of rational discourse by moving to a procedure that retraces a state without the separation between subject and object. In the words of Horkheimer and Adorno: "But the constellation under which likeness is established—the unmediated likeness of mimesis as well as the mediated likeness of synthesis, assimilation to the thing in the blind discharge of life as well as the finding of likenesses in what has been reified in the process of scientific concept formation—is still the sign of terror."[14]

Habermas rejects this move to philosophical hyperspace, since it does not provide the basis for rational discourse, for communicative interaction. In other words, Habermas claims that this radical critique of instrumental reason cannot be validated in theoretical terms. It has accepted the distinction of classical philosophical systems on the one hand and has disclosed the horrifying consequences of instrumental reason on the other. As a result, it finds itself in limbo. In order to criticize modern positivism, it must revert to the fundamental concepts of classical philosophy such as truth; in order to show the ideological nature of the older philosophical tradition, it uses the instruments of modern rationality. Habermas concludes that the Frankfurt School paid a very high price for its skeptical turn during the 1940s. In this context his own project can be understood as a return to the problematic of the early Frankfurt

14. Max Horkheimer and Theodor W. Adorno, *Dialectic of Enlightenment* (New York, 1972), 181.

School, though he definitely does not mean to rely on their position in any dogmatic sense.

The dangerous influence of Nietzsche: Before I turn to Habermas's answer to the dilemmas of Horkheimer's and Adorno's later work, I want to address his essay "The Entwinement of Myth and Enlightenment" of 1982, which not only radicalizes his critique but also develops more clearly the contemporary background of the debate. In *The Theory of Communicative Action* Habermas suggested in passing that the later writings of Adorno were not too far removed from the philosophy of Heidegger—in spite of their own intentions. This suspicion is intensified in Habermas's rereading of *Dialectic of Enlightenment* in 1982. Although the essay is just as much concerned with the problematic of the foundations of a critical theory, both the strategy and the rhetoric differ significantly. The emphasis is placed on the critique of ideology and its increasing radicalization in modern European history. Again Habermas means to demonstrate that the approach of Horkheimer and Adorno in *Dialectic of Enlightenment* leads to a paradoxical situation: it results in a critique denouncing reason, though it is based on reason itself. Thus Habermas insists that Horkheimer and Adorno cannot fend off the consequences of Nietzsche's critique of rationality, whatever their own intentions may have been. "Nietzsche's critique," as Habermas puts it, "consumes the critical impulse itself."[15]

To position Nietzsche and his significance for Horkheimer and Adorno, Habermas describes the history of modern consciousness as a three-phased process. Whereas the initial intention of the Enlightenment aimed at the explosion of traditional worldviews, the second and third phases used a different model, namely the critique of ideology. The older model of ideology critique (Marx) works with the assump-

15. Habermas, "Entwinement of Myth and Enlightenment," 23.

tion that the truth claims of theories can and must be questioned because these claims possibly rest on premises not derived from principles of reason but from presuppositions that reflect the self-interest of the theorist and his or her social group. This model maintains the ideas of the Enlightenment and uses them as the critical standard for the evaluation of existing social practices.

The following, more radical model of ideology critique extends the suspicion to the procedures of reason itself. "With this type of critique Enlightenment becomes reflexive for the first time; it now carries out the project on it own products, i.e. its theories. But the drama of Enlightenment reaches its peripeteia or turning point when the critique of ideology itself is suspected of no longer producing truth—it is only then that Enlightenment becomes reflexive for a second time."[16] This final phase is that of Nietzsche and of *Dialectic of Enlightenment*. In *Dialectic of Enlightenment* "this critique of ideology describes the self-destruction of the critical faculty."[17] More specifically, Habermas argues that *Dialectic of Enlightenment* owes its dangerous force to Nietzsche's philosophy; from Nietzsche, Horkheimer and Adorno take over the interpretation of reason as a mere instrument of self-preservation and power.

In this context I can develop neither Nietzsche's theory of truth nor Habermas's reading of it. It must suffice to summarize Habermas's arguments. Habermas emphasizes the aesthetic turn in Nietzsche's philosophical writings, a move that cancels established values of knowledge and morality. Nietzsche, Habermas suggests, "enthrones taste, 'the Yes and No of the palate' as the sole organ of knowledge beyond Truth and Falsity, beyond Good and Evil."[18] This move consistently undercuts the rationality of Yes/No positions. Thus both descriptive and

16. Ibid., 20.
17. Ibid., 22.
18. Ibid., 25.

normative statements are reduced to expressions of evaluation. (The sentence "x is true" should be read "I prefer x.") In Nietzsche these value judgments are no longer grounded in cognitive principles that can be demonstrated; rather, they express a claim to power. The core of this approach is an aesthetic sensibility and productivity, the excitement of the will by the beautiful. The theory of the will to power, however, is untenable, Habermas argues, because it is contradictory. It is unable to valorize its own claims. In Habermas's words: "If, however, all proper claims to validity are devalued and if the underlying value judgments are mere expressions of claims to power rather than to validity, according to what standards should critique then differentiate? It must at least be able to discriminate between a power which deserves to be esteemed and a power which deserves to be disparaged."[19]

The section on Nietzsche in Habermas's Adorno essay is of crucial importance in two respects: it serves to demonstrate the deficiencies of a totalizing critique of ideology, and it calls attention to the present poststructuralist debate. Habermas holds that Horkheimer and Adorno, under the impact of Nietzsche's theory of power, end up in an aporia similar to that of Nietzsche. Thus their own version of Critical Theory loses its critical edge because it follows a self-contradictory strategy. This conclusion concurs with the analysis presented in *The Theory of Communicative Action*. In the Adorno essay of 1982, however, Habermas stresses the impact of Nietzsche rather than the Marxist heritage because he wants to bring into the foreground an unresolved problematic embedded in *Dialectic of Enlightenment*. The procedure of unmasking the Enlightenment, showing that reason ultimately reverts to myth, leads to a theory of power deprived of possible strategies to overcome the impasse. Negative dialectic, always turning back to the abyss of yet another turn of suspicion, cannot address this problematic. It remains unresolved.

19. Ibid., 27.

Habermas and Foucault: Habermas comes to almost identical conclusions in *The Theory of Communicative Action* and his Adorno essay of 1982, although in the first case he puts the blame on the heritage of Western Marxism (reification), whereas in the second he makes the influence of Nietzsche responsible for the wrong turn of the Frankfurt School. This convergence is slightly puzzling: from the point of view of intellectual history, the two traditions that Habermas uncovers in *Dialectic of Enlightenment* are not easily reconcilable. In theoretical terms the two arguments do not necessarily belong together. The thesis that Horkheimer and Adorno, under the influence of Nietzsche, developed a totalizing critique of ideology is not identical with the thesis that Horkheimer and Adorno, by generalizing the concept of reification, arrived at a radical critique of instrumental reason. One could argue, however, that the two claims at least support each other. When we describe the history of modern consciousness as stages of an increasingly radical critique of its own presuppositions, we can also use this framework to position the transformation from Lukács's theory of reification to the critique of instrumental reason in the writings of Horkheimer and Adorno. We observe the same move toward a totalizing critique of reason undercutting the rationality that was used to carry out the project in the first place. Still, the logic of reification, as it was first fully developed in *History and Class Consciousness*, is significantly different from the theory of power in the writings of Nietzsche and Foucault. For Habermas, however, who is primarily looking at the strategical aspect, the two positions converge because they both aim at the destruction of rationalism.

Historically, I feel, Habermas is on safer ground when he develops the problematic of the late Frankfurt School out of the tradition of Western Marxism. For the strategy of his own project, on the other hand, the confrontation with the poststructuralist interpretation of Nietzsche, particularly that of Foucault, has become more crucial. The reason for this turn is as follows: since Habermas has consistently maintained that

Lukács's solution to the problem of reification is no longer viable, the defense of rationalism has become at the same time more difficult and more urgent. If Foucault's critique of reason is correct, Habermas's own theory of communicative action built on rational consensus through speech acts is in jeopardy. The skepticism of Foucault's geneaological history is a position that Habermas has to challenge in order to secure the viability of rational discourse. By the same token, incidentally, Habermas has to confront Luhmann's systems theory, which argues in favor of social systems without subjects and meaning (*Sinn*). The common denominator is "positivism," or the elimination of claims for meaning and validity.[20] Foucault's radical rereading of history results in relativism, since the genealogical historian cannot sustain his or her position when confronted with the question why a specific view of history should be preferable to another one (the same problem that Habermas found unresolved in Nietzsche).

Hence Habermas uses a similar strategy against Foucault: the inner logic of genealogical historiography becomes the target of his critique. Specifically, he wants to demonstrate that the seemingly objective approach of discourse analysis simply represses the fundamental hermeneutic configuration involved in the encounter between the historian and the material. The historian, whether it is explicitly stated or not, always takes a position. If we follow Foucault's position and assume that all knowledge is power and therefore critical only vis-á-vis other forms of knowledge/power, we undermine the basis of genealogical history. In this case the knowledge provided by critical historiography is as much part of the will to power as the practices under investigation. Habermas concludes: "Every counter-power moves within the horizons of the power which

20. See Jürgen Habermas, "Genealogische Geschichtsschreibung: Ueber einige Aporien im machttheoretischen Denken Foucaults," *Merkur* 38 (Oct. 1984): 745–53.

it opposes, and as soon as it is victorious transforms itself into a power complex which then provokes a new counter-power. The genealogy of knowledge cannot break out of this vicious circle."[21] As soon as critical knowledge has successfully challenged established knowledge/power, it becomes power, a vicious circle from which the genealogy of knowledge cannot escape. Hence, Habermas concludes that a critique that does not reflect on its own methods and theoretical premises is chained to this aporia.

While I think that Habermas's formal argument is persuasive, I am less certain whether it is strong enough to challenge Nietzsche's and Foucault's assumption that there is no ultimate meaning in history. To put it differently: the proof that Foucault's project is contradictory in terms of its own logic is not the same as proving that his pessimistic view of history is wrong. The rational critique can demonstrate the contradictions, but this strategy does not automatically secure the meaning of history. In particular, it does not prove that social practices are embedded in reason. The rationality of social practices, especially the validity of certain social practices in comparison with others, and the assumption that human history can be deciphered as a meaningful process toward a goal, have to be grounded in a different way. Foucault, who does not share Habermas's conviction that human practices are determined by rationality (in its emphatic sense), makes a different use of rational methods. His genealogical analysis seeks to undercut the presumed foundations of knowledge and the teleological constructs of history relying on unquestioned notions of continuity and logical sequence. "The search for descent," Foucault writes in his discussion of Nietzsche, "is not the erecting of foundations: on the contrary, it disturbs what was previously considered immobile, it fragments what was thought unified; it shows the heterogeneity of what was imagined consistent

21. Ibid., 749.

with itself."[22] In this context the concept of emergence takes on a meaning different from Habermas's usage. While Habermas seeks to understand genealogy in Nietzsche as the search for validity (the validity of the older forms), Foucault wants to stress the dangers of historical reconstructions along the lines of development or evolution. "As it is wrong to search for descent in an uninterrupted continuity, we should avoid thinking of emergence as the final term of an historical development. . . . These developments may appear as a culmination, but they are merely the current episodes in a series of subjugations."[23] Yet Foucault overstates his claim when he goes on to say that history is the "endlessly repeated play of dominations" and concludes: "The domination of certain men over others leads to the differentiation of values; class domination generates the idea of liberty; and forceful appropriation of things necessary to survival and the imposition of a duration not intrinsic to them account for the origin of logic."[24] This view of history totalizes the process of history as much as the liberal view stressing progress. While we can possibly agree that in all historical situations known to us human interaction has been determined by domination, it does not *eo ipso* follow that this insight can be generalized and extrapolated into the future. This, then, is the case that one can make for Habermas's position: granted that human practices have been shot through with violence, granted further that history has been propelled by the drama of power, we cannot logically exclude the possibility of change, unless we believe in eternal laws of history for which we would need more than empirical examples. The question then arises whether and how human beings can escape the fate of power, how they can become masters of their own history. This is obviously the central Marxian question.

Let me briefly state Habermas's answer. He infers from his

22. Michel Foucault, *Language, Counter-Memory, Practice* (Ithaca, 1977), 147.
23. Ibid., 148.
24. Ibid., 150.

analysis of Horkheimer's and Adorno's writings that the approach of the philosophy of consciousness to a subjectivity not contaminated by instrumental reason has failed and cannot be restored. Attempts by Dieter Henrich and others to rescue subjectivity by differentiating between subjective and instrumental reason result in the same aporia already diagnosed by Adorno. Hence, this approach has to be replaced with an intersubjective orientation undercutting from the very beginning the logic of reification inherent in instrumental reason. This project, Habermas believes, can be developed out of existing social theorics, especially those of George Mead and Emile Durkheim. So Habermas proposes a shift of focus rather than a new philosophy. "The focus of investigation thereby shifts from cognitive-instrumental rationality to communicative rationality. And what is paradigmatic for the latter is not the relation of a solitary subject to something in the objective world that can be presented and manipulated, but the intersubjective relations that speaking and acting subjects take up when they come to an understanding with one another about something."[25] Habermas understands this approach as the alternative to systems theory as well as the genealogy of knowledge, approaches where concepts like subject and object can be replaced by system and *Umwelt* (environment) and the problematic of subjectivity hence can be reformulated in terms of complexity aimed at self-preservation. Instead, Habermas offers a different reading of modernity. The process of disenchantment, the "decentration of our understanding of the world and the differentiation of various universal validity claims," seen by Luhmann as the historical background of systems theory, prepares the way for a reconsideration of intersubjective relations.[26] The very lack of fixed, overarching worldviews calls for an intersubjective interpretation of reality. Only a theory of communicative action, Habermas is con-

25. Habermas, *Theory of Communicative Action*, 392.
26. Ibid., 397.

vinced, can combat the reduction of subjectivity to the level of mere self-preservation (and power games). Obviously, this theory, unlike systems theory, cannot limit itself to the explanation of facts and structures; it is involved in claims for validity. Habermas emphasizes this element when he states: "The utopian perspective of reconciliation and freedom is ingrained in the conditions for the communicative sociation (Vergesellschaftung) of individuals; it is built into the linguistic mechanism of the reproduction of the species."[27]

Systems theory and the life-world: It is not my task in this book to analyze the foundations of this theory. Still, I want to discuss some of its aspects. In contrast to Parsons's systems theory, Habermas suggests a dual focus: he differentiates between system and life-world. The concept of the life-world, taken from phenomenological sociology (Schütz), refers to ordinary social situations where human beings interact. The life-world can be described in terms of narrative presentations of historical events and social situations. Among them are cultural events, for instance, aesthetic projects the function of which is to express the worldview of a social group and thereby help to integrate its members. The phenomenological analysis of the life-world primarily uses a hermeneutic approach; it reconstructs the life-world from the point of view of the participating actors. (The meaning of the events is seen through the eyes of the involved actors.) The actors, operating inside of their life-world, are involved in reaching a common understanding about the facts, the experiences, and the norms of their reality. Hence, it is also the transcendental horizon of their agreements and disagreements, their disputes and their claims. This pertains especially to language and culture. The actors cannot distance themselves from culture and language in the same way they can detach themselves from the objective

27. Ibid., 398.

reality of facts. Since communication is based on speech acts, the actors are always involved in the use of language.

Now, Habermas's thesis is this: a theory of communicative action must be grounded in the hermeneutic understanding of the life-world, but it cannot stay on this level because social relations cannot be reduced to social interaction. Therefore, the view from the inside has to be supplemented by the external perspective offered in systems theory. "I would like to suggest conceiving societies as simultaneously system and life-world."[28] Societies are conceived in terms both of systems and of life worlds. This dual approach would also apply to the cultural sphere. While hermeneutic theories (Gadamer) interpret the relationship between the subject and the work of art as a dialogue between two subjects (both raise questions and give answers), Habermas insists on the systematic and functional character of culture as well. By this I mean that culture has to be treated as a part of the social system in which it operates. When the analysis moves to this level, we step out of the commonly acknowledged cultural tradition of our life-world and shift to a functional reading of the events, norms, and objects in which we normally participate as actors. Yet, Habermas does not simply want to replace the first perspective by the second—which would be a structuralist notion. Rather, he wants to combine them. He calls attention to the short-comings of the phenomenological interpretation of the life-world (the bias for cultural aspects) and postulates a reorientation that would include the legitimate aspects of systems theory.

On the other hand, Habermas reminds us that the life-world cannot automatically be subsumed under the system. More specifically, he argues that the historical differentiation of the social system resulting in increased complexity leads at the same time to a situation where system and life-world are clearly

---

28. Jürgen Habermas, *Theorie des kommunikativen Handelns*, vol. 2 *Zur Kritik der funktionalistischen Vernunft* (Frankfurt, 1981), 180.

detached from each other. The process of differentiation implies a rift between system and life-world. "The social system definitively explodes the horizon of the life-world, removes itself from the pre-understanding of communicative everyday praxis, and remains accessible only to the counter-intuitive knowledge of the social sciences that have developed since the eighteenth century."[29] The result is the *Versachlichung* (reification) of the life-world; this would apply not only to the spheres of morality and law, but also to the cultural sphere. System differentiation, then, leads to the formation of new institutions dealing with specific problems in terms of their own logic.

Let us consider the implications for the realm of art more closely. As soon as the differentiation occurred in the sphere of art and literature in the eighteenth century, we observe the emergence of a new institution. This institution, the institution of art, performs specialized functions that cannot be duplicated by other social institutions. Thus validity claims in the sphere of art do not have the same meaning as claims made by moral or scientific theories. Specifically, Habermas, following Parsons, defines the claims of art to meaning as expressive values. Accordingly, the autonomous institution of art prescribes the reception of the individual work of art. That work is primarily received under the auspices of *Wahrhaftigkeit* (authenticity), as distinguished from *Wahrheit* (truth). The process of differentiation within the social system, in other words, assigns art a specialized function. This reorientation both sharpens and limits art's specific validity claims. To put it bluntly: as part of the cultural subsystem, art loses the central place it occupied in traditional societies, where it was bound to religion and morality.

Literary criticism and the life-world: We have to contemplate the consequences of this strategy. The grip of systems theory

29. Ibid., 258.

marginalizes art by insisting on its expressive function as the primary one. The aesthetic experience is detached from cognitive and moral truth. In Habermas's work, however, this analysis should not be understood as a plea for aestheticism. On the contrary, Habermas is well aware of the critical force of modern artistic movements. In his critique of Daniel Bell he argues—and this brings him close to Adorno again—that the avant-garde of the twentieth century fulfilled an important critical task. He writes: "These discontents [of modern societies] have not been called into life by modernist intellectuals. They are rooted in deep seated reactions against the process of *societal* modernization. Under the pressure of the dynamics of economic growth and the organizational accomplishments of the state, this social modernization penetrates deeper and deeper into previous forms of human existence."[30] In this context, Habermas stresses the critical function of modern art and vigorously defends it against the neoconservative praise of unquestioned tradition. He calls on communicative rationality in order to undercut the power of the economic and administrative logic that determined the historical process of modernization. Yet, on the level of systems analysis, he accepts the separation of art from science and morality. Hence, the standards for the appreciation and evaluation of art are different from those developed by ethical and scientific theories. In the realm of theoretical analysis (dealing with the system) we are left therefore with an unbridgeable gap between the specialized institution of art (as part of the cultural subsystem) and the life-world. (Like Peter Bürger, Habermas is convinced that the attempts of surrealism to destroy the institution of art and reconnect art and life-world have failed.)[31] Still, as we have seen, the task for Habermas is to relink system and life-world. In our example this would mean the specialized institution of

30. Jürgen Habermas, "Modernity versus Postmodernity," *New German Critique* 22 (Winter 1981): 7.
31. See Peter Bürger, *The Theory of the Avant-Garde*, trans. Michael Shaw (Minneapolis, 1984).

art and the use of art in everyday life have to be brought together again; the alienated analysis of the expert and the impoverished experience of the layperson have to be reintegrated. But how good are the chances for this project? Habermas is cautious enough to voice his doubts because the logic of the social system has been more powerful than the resisting forces within the life-world.

It seems that Habermas has maneuvered himself into a difficult position: on the one hand, using systems theory, he traces the process of social differentiation that leads to the institutional detachment of art from the life-world; on the other hand, he postulates the revival of the life-world and with it the revival of a common aesthetic experience that can be connected to other modes of experience, such as the moral sphere. Yet, this task of relinking is not an easy one because the differentiation of values, as it has been accepted by the institution of literary criticism, denies an immediate integration of the various modes of experience. This was one of the reasons why Adorno in his aesthetic theory heroically refused to support a strictly Kantian interpretation of art (through the category of taste) and insisted on the *Wahrheitsgehalt* of the work of art, on a moment of truth that is at least equivalent to, if not more valid than the truth claims of philosophical discourse. Thus Adorno does not acknowledge the dichotomy between the life-world and the institution of art. His analysis, which is clearly that of an expert critic, relies on hermeneutic procedures that must satisfy the institutional level as well as the experience of the life-world. The truth claims of the work of art cannot be restricted to one level. In fact, Adorno maintains that the redemption of the reified life-world can be conceived only through the understanding of the authentic work of art. This claim, of course, leaves him with the problem of explaining how the extreme complexity of the modern work of art can be related to our daily experience. The more Adorno emphasizes the validity of modern art by contrasting its aesthetic structure with the depraved language of everyday communication, the more he widens the gap between the work of art and the general public. Obviously Habermas does not want to pursue this approach, primarily, as we have seen, because he does not share Adorno's notion of a completely reified reality under advanced capitalism. He clearly means to redeem the life-world in its various modes. But how can this be done in the realm of art?

Two strategies are conceivable for the solution of this problem: either one has to find a mediating element between the system and the life-world, between the institution of art and everyday aesthetic experience, or one has to undercut the dichotomy by showing that it is a false one, by showing, in other words, that the use of language in ordinary communication and its use in fictional literature are not fundamentally different. In the second case the autonomy of art would be erased. Brecht's aesthetic would be a step in this direction. Habermas has not favored this approach, however. In his most recent essay on the distinction between philosophy and literary criticism, he has argued instead that the leveling of language in the project of deconstruction leaves us with no means to confront and solve the problems we encounter in our life-worlds. Most notably, he argues that Richard Rorty's notion of language as a permanently floating process would destroy the possibility of a meaningful practice because this concept of language cancels the yes and no of communication. "The yes and no of communicatively acting players are so prejudiced and rhetorically overwhelmed by linguistic contexts, that the anomolies that appear in phases of exhaustion are depicted only as symptoms of a diminishing vitality, as part of the aging process, as processes analogous to nature—and not as the result of failed solutions to problems and inadequate answers."[32] Against the"holistic" approach of Jacques Derrida and Richard Rorty, Habermas emphasizes the process of linguistic differentiation:

32. Jürgen Habermas, "Exkurs zur Einebnung der Gattungsunterschiede zwischen Philosophie und Literatur: Ueber Idealisierungen im Alltag" (1985, manuscript), 34–35.

thc discourses of science, law, and morality have become separate and therefore each has developed according to its own logic. Consequently, Habermas in his attempt to relink system and life-world must favor a model of mediation. Literary criticism, to give an example, has the task of mediating between the literary system, as it is articulated in the institution of art, and the ordinary language of communication. Since modern art beginning with romanticism is increasingly inaccessible to the general public, it becomes the mission of the critic to translate the *Erfahrungsgehalt* (experience content) of the art work into the language of ordinary communication. A similar function, incidentally, is assigned by Habermas to philosophy. It is supposed to mediate between the expert discourses of science, law, and the like, and ordinary communication.

My reservations about this model are twofold: first, I have some doubts about the chances for the success of this translation. Given the complexity of expert discourse, it is problematic to assume that ordinary language is adequate for the articulation of subtle aesthetic problems. This is, of course, one of the reasons why literary criticism has lost its mediating function between the advanced work of art and the general reading public. The rhetoric of modern criticism is no more accessible than the structure of advanced works of art. Second, Habermas's approach, much like that of the Young Hegelians, is a one-way street: it traces only the flow from the level of the system to the level of the life-world. Yet it would be crucial also to explore the possible impact of ordinary language on expert discourse. What can ordinary language contribute to the discourse of the experts?[33] In what way is the analysis of the critic also grounded in his or her daily experience? In certain ways Adorno's aesthetic theory can do justice to this dialectic by holding on to a notion of aesthetic truth that integrates the expert discourse and ordinary experience through the idea of

33. See Peter Uwe Hohendahl, *The Institution of Criticism* (Ithaca, 1982).

mimesis—an idea that Habermas wants to limit to the prerational phase of human development. In a different way Derrida's project of deconstruction undercuts the logocentric tradition of European philosophy. Habermas seems to underestimate its critical potential when he charges that Derrida reduces philosophical and literary writing and reading to the problem of rhetoric. Instead of assuming with Habermas that deconstruction aestheticizes all language (everything becomes literary criticism), one can also argue that deconstruction is an attempt to relink the formal discourse of the experts and ordinary language by problematizing both. In the realm of literary criticism this means, as Habermas notes critically, that the special status of poetic language is denied. But it is not quite evident why Habermas is not willing to use the critical force of deconstruction against the logic of differentiated systems. It seems that Habermas overstates his case when he describes deconstruction as a purely literary approach without concern for problem solving in the realm of the life-world. Thus my suggestion would be: if we want to free the life-world from the contraints of the overarching system and its institutions, there is room for the project of deconstructive criticism, precisely because it questions the logic of systems.[34]

One reason why premodern literary criticism—say that of the seventeenth century—could more easily connect literature and life in its discourse is that ordinary language and poetic language were not yet conceived of as fundamentally different. Both followed the same rules of rhetoric. Only with the emergence of the concept of aesthetic autonomy in the eighteenth century does the transition from poetic to ordinary language become problematic. Although it is not likely that we can return to the literary system of premodern classicism, its historical existence should remind us that the autonomy of art is

34. See, for instance, Michael Ryan, *Marxism and Deconstruction: A Critical Articulation* (Baltimore, 1982), and the critical remarks of John O'Kane, "Marxism, Deconstruction, and Ideology: Notes toward an Articulation," *New German Critique* 35 (Fall 1984): 219–47.

not a transhistorical category but rather a concept grounded in specific historical conditions. Looking back at the evolution of the institution of art from the eighteenth to the twentieth century we can understand the claim for the autonomy of poetic language as a critical response to the process of differentiation at the level of the social system. Yet this process had its own dialectic: as soon as the concept of autonomy was firmly installed in the institution of art, it became conventional. Today it hardly has the subversive force it had about 1800. Similarly, Habermas's attempt to rescue the autonomy of art as the sphere where language playfully creates new worlds and thereby offers counterfactual possibilities—as Habermas emphasizes against Mary L. Pratt—no longer has the same critical edge.[35] The whole issue of the life-world, I suggest, is still an open question in Habermas's recent work—a question that definitely deserves further attention and possibly has to be reformulated to reach the goal that Habermas has in mind.

35. Mary L. Pratt, *The Speech Act Theory of Literary Discourse* (Bloomington, Ind., 1977).

5 Habermas's *Philosophical Discourse of Modernity*

In September 1980, when he accepted the Adorno Prize from the city of Frankfurt, Jürgen Habermas provoked his audience by insisting that the discourse of modernity, which supposedly had collapsed, was by no means obsolete; moreover, he stressed that it was still waiting for its ultimate fulfillment. Habermas openly attacked the notion that we have reached the age of postmodernism, because this assumption would necessarily result in a flawed assessment of our future. Instead, Habermas insisted on the continuation of the Enlightenment project, even if this project, as he readily conceded, should not be pursued through the use of instrumental reason or in the mode of traditional subject philosophy. The reason for Habermas's polemic was his fear that the contemporary critique of rationalism would play into the hands of conservative forces—not only in West Germany but also in the United States. Habermas's provocation was answered in similar fashion: both in France and in the United States poststructuralist theorists angrily rejected the positing of a logical link between postmodernist theory and political neoconservatism. Jean-François Lyotard, for instance, responded by arguing that it was Habermas's logocentric theory that should be called conservative and hopelessly outdated.[1]

1. Jean-François Lyotard, *The Postmodern Condition: A Report on Knowledge* (Minneapolis, 1984).

It seems as if Habermas had entered a debate for which he was ill-prepared. Before 1980 he had not had many serious encounters with French theory. He had acknowledged neither Foucault nor Derrida and his deconstructionist disciples in this country. His own interest in the Anglo-American and French tradition had clearly favored theories that came out of the European Enlightenment, among them analytic philosophy and the pragmatism of John Dewey, Charles Peirce, and George Herbert Mead. In *The Theory of Communicative Action* (1980), French structuralism and poststructuralism are simply absent. There are biographical and historical reasons for this gap. For a German intellectual who grew up during the Third Reich, the most influential forerunners of contemporary French theory—Nietzsche and Heidegger—are politically dubious because of their impact on or their involvement with German fascism. This distrust of the Nietzsche-Heidegger connection continues in Habermas's latest book. His doubts concerning the validity and the political implications of poststructuralist theory are grounded in his hostility toward the German mastertexts on which French theory is based. Between 1980 and 1985, however, Habermas clearly moved away from the relatively simple opposition of Enlightenment versus postmodernism, or of progressive versus conservative traditions. The distance between Frankfurt and Paris decreased, although it would be misleading to call Habermas's position poststructuralist. It can be said, however, that Habermas's intensive readings of George Bataille, Foucault, and Derrida have resulted in a more precise and also more fruitful statement of the theoretical differences between Paris and Frankfurt. Whether his French colleagues would agree with his interpretations of their texts is another matter. The recent attempt to bring "German" and "French" theory together in Paris was, as Rainer Rochlitz has suggested in his instructive account of the meeting, unsuccessful.[2] Both

2. Rainer Rochlitz, "The Missed Meeting—A Conference Report of French and German Philosophy," *Telos* 66 (Winter 1985/86): 124–28.

sides were ultimately unwilling to make a leap and familiarize themselves with the opposing arguments. It seems doubtful that Habermas, who participated in the meeting only as an observer, could have prevented the disaster. Even his *Philosophical Discourse of Modernity* would in all likelihood have been rejected by Derrida and his disciples as a defense of a position that still relies on the unquestioned premises of European rationalism.[3] After all, Habermas did not change his position in the process of reading French theory. Still, there is one major agreement. It concerns the critique of the philosophy of consciousness, which Habermas fully shares with Foucault and Derrida. Thus, Habermas welcomes their attempts to move beyond the problematic concept of modern subjectivity, although his own critique of the subject differs significantly from the poststructuralist approach. Habermas shares with contemporary French theory the preference for a linguistic paradigm, yet he clearly does not support an understanding of language in which words function as a chain of signifiers for which a signified can never be established with certainty. This rhetorical interpretation of the function of language is unacceptable to Habermas because it makes intersubjective understanding and consensus impossible.

Some critics have argued that one cannot equate poststructuralism and postmodernism because poststructuralist discourse remains closer to modernism than to postmodernism. Poststructuralist theory is concerned with the texts of classical modernism. When Habermas refers to modernism (*Moderne*) he has a broader historical period in mind. He means the phase from roughly 1500 to the present, for which German historians have coined the term *Neuzeit* (as opposed to *Mittelalter*). More specifically, he refers to the philosophical discourse that began with the Enlightenment of the eighteenth century and reached

3. Jürgen Habermas, *The Philosophical Discourse of Modernity: Twelve Lectures*, trans. Frederick Lawrence (Cambridge, Mass., 1987); cited henceforth in the text as *PD*, followed by page number.

its maturity in the philosophy of Hegel. This is the moment when the theoretical awareness of historical modernity is fully developed. Hence, for Habermas the question of whether the present age is still part of modernity or whether it is already a phase of postmodernity can be answered only by addressing the accumulated philosophical problems of the last 150 years. This approach differs rather drastically from that of either Heidegger or Derrida, who argue that the problem of modern thought, that is, its logocentricity, goes back to ancient philosophy (Plato). Here, Habermas seems to be closer to Foucault, who assumes a fundamental epistemological break in the late eighteenth century. Even in this case, however, the differences are undeniable: while Foucault insists on the rupture between the classical episteme and modernism, Habermas views the German idealism of the early nineteenth century as a continuation of the Enlightenment, which began with Descartes.

Habermas defines modernity in the narrow sense (*Moderne* as opposed to *Neuzeit*) as the second stage of a philosophical discourse stretching from German idealism to the present. Modernity is understood as that historical moment when philosophy, by fully appropriating its own history, calls for its own cancellation (Marx) or at least radically questions the unproblematic continuation of its project (Left-Hegelians). Therefore, Habermas claims that the philosophical discourse following Hegel's system—both its more conservative and its more radical branches—is still relevant today. Although they hardly offered lasting solutions, the positions developed in Germany during the 1840s still have a (mostly unacknowledged) impact on present philosophical discussion.

For this reason, Habermas's debate with French theory begins with its German forerunners in the nineteenth century. At the center of this discussion we find Nietzsche, who clearly influenced Heidegger and also directly and indirectly had a major impact on contemporary French thought. It is not accidental that Habermas calls Nietzsche's work a *Drehscheibe* (turntable) of European philosophy. In the fourth chapter, which deals with Nietzsche's critique of the Enlightenment, Habermas underscores the radical nature of this polemic, which not only questions the content of previous philosophical discourse but attacks the episteme of rationalism itself—its method and its function. While Hegel saw reason as "reconciling self-knowledge" and the Left-Hegelians defined reason as "emancipatory appropriation" by and for human beings, Nietzsche decides to cancel the project of rational critique. "Nietzsche ... renounces a renewed revision of the concept of reason and *bids farewell* to the dialectic of enlightenment" (*PD*, 86). When Nietzsche undertakes a critique of the Enlightenment he does this with the "goal of exploding modernity's husk of reason as such" (*PD*, 86).

This formulation may remind us of Lukács, for whom Nietzsche was one of the most important precursors of German fascism. Still—and this makes a major difference—Habermas does recognize the importance and validity of the historically accumulated epistemological problems, and he also differentiates much more clearly between Nietzsche's utopian project and its reactionary appropriation by the German fascists. In order to demonstrate the problematic nature of Nietzsche's program, Habermas links Nietzsche's thought with German romanticism (with Richard Wagner as the connecting link). He tries to explain the difference between Nietzsche's position and the romantic approach to the problem of truth. As specifically romantic, Habermas defines the concept of a new mythology, a program to which Nietzsche remains indebted. "The idea of a new mythology is of Romantic provenance, and so also is the recourse to Dionysius as the god who is coming. Nietzsche likewise distances himself from the romantic use of these ideas and proclaims a manifestly more radical version pointing far beyond Wagner" (*PD*, 88). It is not the interest in Dionysius that is original in Nietzsche's writings but, as Habermas underscores, the displacement and revision of the Dionysius figure. In Nietzsche the god Dionysius is clearly separated from the Christ figure—a separation that does not occur in romantic thought. By cutting the link with Christian mythology—the presence of which he criticizes in Wagner's writings—Nietzsche redefines the utopian program in purely aesthetic terms. Thereby he undermines the liberal claim for an understanding of history that should culminate in the emancipation of humanity. "And as a counterauthority to reason, Nietzsche appeals to experiences that are displaced back into the archaic realm—experiences of the self-disclosure of a decentered subjectivity, liberated from all the constraints of cognition and purposeful activity, all imperatives of utility and morality" (*PD*, 94). To put it differently, Habermas views Nietzsche—and, of course, he is not the first critic to see Nietzsche in this light—as the proponent of a radical aestheticism that rejects all cognitive and moral norms.

Expectedly, Habermas is highly critical of this position. He is especially critical of Nietzsche's theory of power, which later resurfaces in Bataille and Foucault. This theory, Habermas maintains, is ultimately unable to legitimate itself because its major thesis (everything is grounded in power relations) makes it impossible to ground theory rationally. As Habermas points out, this type of radical critique of rationality necessarily ends in an aporetic situation: the critique undercuts the ground on which the proof of its validity must be based. This fundamental contradiction reappears in various forms in Nietzsche's disciples. It can be traced in Bataille, Lacan, and Foucault, who continue the critique of subject-centered reason through anthropological, psychological, and historical arguments. It can also be found in Heidegger and Derrida, who follow Nietzsche's attack on metaphysics and therefore want to return to pre-Socratic philosophy. The most radical questioning of philosophy, however, may well turn into a defense of the status quo. He uses the case of Heidegger to demonstrate the link between a radical critique of rationality and German fascism, and later he uses the case of Foucault to show the contradictions involved in a theory of power that borrows from Nietzsche. Within the context of this theory no critique of existing power structures can escape the argument that it is itself involved in claims for power. At the end of his chapter on Nietzsche, Habermas suggests that Heidegger at the same time continues and surpasses Nietzsche's critique of rationality. Heidegger takes over Nietzsche's aestheticism, the attempt to rescue philosophy by transforming it into art, but at the same time he wants to limit this program and moves toward a restitution of philosophy proper. Unlike Nietzsche, Heidegger does not appreciate the provocation of modernist art, its subversive function vis-à-vis a professionalized discourse of philosophy.

Here it is useful to provide a more detailed analysis of Habermas's criticism of Heidegger, because this polemic serves as the background for his reading of Derrida and the American deconstructionists. Heidegger and Bataille, as far as they follow Nietzsche's lead, face the same problem: they want to carry out a radical critique of reason which "attacks the roots of the critique itself" (*PD*, 101). In his presentation of Heidegger's philosophy, Habermas follows the traditional division between Heidegger's early thought, which was still under the impact of Edmund Husserl's philosophy of consciousness, and the late philosophy of the 1940s and 1950s. But he does not follow Heidegger's own interpretation of this development, which reads the later writings as a *Kehre* (turn) that reinterprets the problems and questions presented in *Being and Time* (1928). Habermas's resistance to the late Heidegger's humanism is clearly motivated by political considerations. More than once Habermas points to the dangerous political implication of Heidegger's position, that is, its closeness to fascism. This connection is not simply a matter of Heidegger's dubious personal decision; rather, it is Heidegger's very discourse that is involved in thought patterns and arguments that affirm the power of the National Socialists.

Still, Habermas's critique cannot be reduced to a narrow political polemic. His aim is to demonstrate the inherent connection between Heidegger's specific philosophical criticism of traditional metaphysics and the historical circumstances in which this discourse was developed. In other words, Habermas offers a radical historical reading of Heidegger, while Heidegger himself thought of his philosophy as being above historical events. This interpretation throws a different light on Heidegger's position. His critique of *Seinsverlassenheit* (abandonment of being) appears as a mystification—an empty shell that can be filled in different ways according to changing historical circumstances. Thus, while Heidegger's position in *Being and Time* does not yet actively support the doctrine of National Socialism, neither does it preclude it. This political problem is grounded in a philosophical argument. Habermas stresses again and again that Heidegger remained much closer to a philosophy of consciousness (*Subjektphilosophie*) than he was willing to admit. While the genesis of *Being and Time* has to be seen in the context of the neo-ontological movement of the 1920s, it is apparent that Heidegger could not return to pre-Kantian ontology. His own project grew out of neo-Kantian philosophy and the problems of *Lebensphilosophie* (philosophy of life). Thus, Habermas notes: "He [Heidegger] makes use of the vocabulary of the neo-ontological turn in order to further the dissolution of the concept of the transcendental subject; but even in this radicalization he holds on to the transcendental attitude of a reflective illumination of the conditions of the possibility of the being of the person as a being-in-the-world" (*PD*, 142). Not only are Heidegger's pro-fascist statements between 1933 and 1935 (when he still believed in the revolutionary power of the movement) compatible with the language of *Being and Time*, but so is his later critique of fascism, where he stresses the critique of technology.

Habermas presents Heidegger as a German intellectual whose biography and philosophy participated in the fascist movement. Such an involvement cannot be found in Heidegger's French disciples. Derrida's interest in Heidegger's critique of metaphysical thought, for instance, is clearly unrelated to Heidegger's 1933 political decision. What Derrida appreciates in Heidegger's position is the emphasis on the end of European history and the decline of traditional European philosophy. Thus, Derrida continues Heidegger's later writings, but at the same time he returns to Husserl's phenomenology, which he interprets as the final expression of European logocentricity. Habermas describes Derrida's project as an anarchist and subversive struggle that aims at undermining the foundations of Western metaphysics (*PD*, 161–62)—a strategy Habermas acknowledges as an important contribution, although he does not believe in its efficacy. According to Habermas, Derrida's critique of European metaphysics remains dependent on the very structures he wants to criticize. The attempt to explode the foundations of logocentric thinking only leads to the search for ever deeper foundations (*écriture*). This fundamentalism in reverse cannot, therefore, escape the structure of a philosophy of origin (*Ursprungsphilosophie*). Hence, Derrida is closer to Heidegger than he himself would admit.

What are Habermas's arguments, and what are their implications? In his chapter on Derrida, Habermas focuses his analysis on Derrida's critique of Husserl. From a critique of Husserl's theory of language and his thesis that an ultimate grounding of pure philosophy should be possible through intuitive *Anschauung* (perception), Derrida reaches a position that favors *écriture* rather than phonemes. As Derrida notes: "The rationality which governs a writing thus enlarged and radicalized, no longer issues from a logos. Further, it inaugurates the destruction, not the demolition but the desedimentation, the de-construction, of all significations that have their source in that [signification] of the logos. Particularly for the signification of truth" (*PD*, 164). Habermas traces the argument Derrida presents in *Speech and Phenomena* in detail; his strategy, in other words, aims at an immanent critique. The point of his reconstruction is to show that in Derrida *écriture* rather than Logos becomes the starting point. Habermas appears to be willing to follow Derrida's critique of presence and his insistence on difference. At the end of his argument he notes: "Thus, Derrida achieves an inversion of Husserlian foundationalism inasmuch as the originative transcendental power of creative subjectivity passes over into the anonymous history-making productivity of writing" (*PD*, 178).

This is where Habermas finally inserts his criticism. He understands Derrida's movement as a reversal rather than an overcoming of *Ursprungsphilosophie*. The history of Being is replaced by a complicated mirror image: the mirroring of a text in another one, which again is mirrored in a third one. Each text can only directly or indirectly point to the original text without ever reaching the *Urschrift* (original text). This search for the original text, however, which for Derrida takes the place of the search for the transcendental subject, is for Habermas both a continuation and a radicalization of Heidegger's program. "Against his will, he [Derrida] lays bare the inverted foundationalism of this thought by once again going beyond the ontological difference and Being to the differance proper to writing, which puts an origin already set in motion yet one level deeper" (*PD*, 181).

The weakness of Derrida's approach, Habermas argues, lies in its dependence on the very kind of *Ursprungsphilosophie* that Derrida means to criticize. Thus, Derrida ends up with a "formulalike avowal of some indeterminate authority" (*PD*, 181). It is obvious that Habermas does not expect Derrida's project to result in a viable political praxis. Strangely enough, however, he does not make this criticism explicit. Rather, when dealing with the sociopolitical consequences of Derrida's philosophy, Habermas emphasizes the positive value of deconstruction in comparison with Heidegger's endorsement of archaic Greek culture. Following Susan Handelman, Habermas argues that Derrida's approach has to be seen against the background of Jewish mysticism and its heretical hermeneutic theory.[4] Hence, Derrida's deconstruction belongs to a tradition

---

4. Susan Handelman, "Jacques Derrida and the Heretic Hermeneutic,"

that opposes the hegemony of Christian logos and its hermeneutics in Paul's teaching. The attempt to rescue writing from
the hegemony of the spirit suggests Derrida's proximity to Benjamin's anarchist philosophy of history. For Habermas this
comparison clearly implies both respect and distance. Habermas has never concealed his admiration for Benjamin; at the
same time he has made it clear that he does not believe in the
feasibility of Benjamin's project.[5]

In an extended footnote to a passage concerning the relation
between philosophy and literature (*PD*, 408–409) Habermas
makes a very important general point: he argues—not only
against Derrrida but also against Adorno and Benjamin—that
they read and write philosophy as if they were only one generation removed from Hegel. These critics, insofar as they see
themselves as disciples of Nietzsche, remain caught in those
universal problems they received from the philosophical tradition extending from Plato to Hegel. Habermas, on the other
hand, wants to remove philosophy from this need for an ultimate grounding (*Letztbegründungen*) and to limit its project.
According to him, the business of philosophy does not differ fundamentally from other disciplines—all results are fallible
in principle, they are grounded in praxis and history, and
therefore they have to be reconsidered under different circumstances. In this claim for a pragmatic position, Habermas is not
far from someone like Rorty, whom he explicitly mentions in
this context. This position, however, does not imply a repudiation of normative claims, as one might read the move against
Letztbegründungen. This is precisely the point where Habermas disagrees with Foucault, with whom he shares more common ground than with Derrida.

---

in *Displacement: Derrida and After*, ed. M. Krapnick (Bloomington, Ind.,
1983), 98–129.

5. See Jürgen Habermas, "Walter Benjamin: Consciousness-Raising or
Rescuing Critique," in his *Philosophical-Political Profiles* (London, 1983),
129–63.

Apparently Habermas was seeking a dialogue with Foucault before the latter unexpectedly died in 1984.[6] In his obituary, Habermas openly expressed a feeling of appreciation, without, however, suggesting at any point that he was in agreement with Foucault's theory. Habermas's proximity to Foucault's work, which also clearly comes through in the two chapters devoted to him in *The Philosophical Discourse of Modernity*, is grounded in the nature of the questions that Foucault would ask, especially in Habermas's interest in Foucault's critique of the philosophy of consciousness. Reading *The Order of Things* and *The Archeology of Knowledge*, Habermas could not fail to notice the similarity with (but, of course, also the difference from) his own attempts to overcome the transcendental approach (which was still dominant in *Knowledge and Human Interest*) by moving closer to the epistemology of systems theory. This comparison would also, however, reveal the similarities of Foucault's and Luhmann's positions with respect to fundamental methodological assumptions—for instance, their basic common antagonism to hermeneutics. Thus, Habermas's analysis of Foucault's work concentrates on two related aspects: the antihermeneutic attitude of archaeological and genealogical history and the move toward a general theory of power in Foucault's late writings. For Habermas this theory of power is the bold but ultimately unsuccessful attempt to establish a new kind of subject-decentered historiography without metaphysical foundations.

While the ninth chapter primarily introduces Foucault's theory, the tenth chapter, entitled "Aporias of a Theory of Power," presents Habermas's critique of Foucault's theory. Here, the focus will be on three questions: (1) what does Habermas mean by his claim that Foucault is undercutting the hermeneutic approach, (2) how does Foucault's general theory of power grow out of this antihermeneutic strategy, which replaces the con-

6. See Jürgen Habermas, "Mit dem Pfeil ins Herz getroffen," in his *Die neue Unübersichtlichkeit* (Frankfurt, 1985), 126–31.

cept of interpretation (*Verstehen*) with the concept of discourse, and (3) why does Habermas so emphatically object to the theory of power?

Foucault, so Habermas argues, wants to move away from the historical paradigm that favors the present (as the point of departure) and understands the writing of history as a form of self-understanding. This strategy also necessarily undercuts the hermeneutic approach. "Hermeneutical effort is aimed at the appropriation of meaning; in each document, it hunts out a voice reduced to silence that should be roused into life again. This idea of a *document* pregnant with meaning has to be called into question just as radically as the business of interpretation itself" (*PD*, 250). This implies that the perspective of the observer replaces the perspective of the participant. Closely connected with this stance are the attack on any totalizing form of history, which attempts to understand the process from a central concept, and the renunciation of expressive causality, which argues that the divergent phenomena of a given period can be related to a center containing the essential meaning of the period. Foucault replaces historical interpretation with the analysis of discourse—a method that deliberately keeps its distance from the material under consideration.

Readers familiar with Foucault will find little new in the ninth chapter. Yet, the reconstruction of the argument (as usual in Habermas) is no more than a preparation for the systematic discussion that follows in chapter 10. Again, Habermas begins his critique of Foucault's theory of power with a close reading of the text. Then Habermas suggests that discourse analysis is faced with a fundamental problem. "What then counts as fundamental are the rules (accessible to archeology) that make possible the ongoing discursive practice. However, these rules can make a discourse comprehensible only as regards its conditions of possibility; they do not suffice to explain the discursive practice in its actual functioning—for there are no rules that would govern their own application" (*PD*, 268).

Foucault is faced with the problem that a discursive practice controlled by its rules cannot determine the context in which it functions. Foucault responds to this problem with a general theory of power. The archaeology of knowledge is therefore subsumed by a genealogy of knowledge "that explains the emergence of knowledge from practices of power" (*PD*, 268). Still following Foucault's strategy Habermas acknowledges two advantages of this move in Foucault's theory. First, this strategy allows Foucault to distance himself from the philosophy of consciousness, and second, it provides the various discourses of knowledge with a common ground. The general theory of power is supposed to explain the operation of theoretical discourses. Habermas, however, argues that this strategy is doomed to failure; he holds that Foucault's theory of power does not escape the quandaries of subject-centered philosophy. According to Habermas, the theory of power itself is ambiguous because it is supposed to operate on two different levels. On the one hand, it is expected to analyze empirical power constellations; on the other hand, it has to function as a transcendental theory explaining the very possibility of theoretical discourses. As Habermas notes: "In his basic concept of power, Foucault has forced together the idealist notion of transcendental synthesis with the presuppositions of an empiricist ontology" (*PD*, 274). Consequently, Foucault faces the following aporia: If we assume with Foucault that the concept of truth is based on the concept of power (rather than the other way around, as idealism presupposes), then we cannot explain successful action, since successful action can be measured only in cognitive terms, that is, according to its adequacy vis-à-vis specific circumstances. Of course, in using this argument against Foucault, Habermas presupposes the priority of the acting subject—a subject that relates to the world either in terms of cognition or in terms of practice. Foucault, on the other hand, reverses this relationship: Subjectivity is the result of discourses grounded in power relations.

   Although Foucault and Habermas strive toward a similar goal, a critique of the philosophy of consciousness, their solutions to this problem differ significantly. While Foucault (following Nietzsche) treats normative considerations (*Geltungsansprüche*) as purely functional aspects and reduces them to power relations, Habermas insists that this strategy does serious harm to the definition of social praxis. Moreover, he claims that Foucault's theory rests on basic contradictions. The most fundamental one is this: genealogical historians must make a truth claim for their research and presentation. As soon as they apply the genealogical method to their own project, it leads to an unresolvable contradiction. Habermas distinguishes three aspects of this aporia (*PD*, 276): genealogical historians are part of a temporal context; an analysis of history grounded in a specific moment of history itself can make only relative truth claims; and genealogical historians, no matter how much they try to distance themselves from the material (documents, facts, and so on), remain partisans. Foucault's method suppresses the hermeneutic aspect of historical analysis In his early work Foucault simply does not reflect on the position of the cognitive subject, the perspective of the historian. In his later work, under the influence of Nietzsche, this objective stance results in general skepticism—an attitude Habermas somewhat viciously calls "professing irrationalism" (*PD*, 278). He observes: "The unmasking of the objectivist illusions of *any* will to knowledge leads to an agreement with a historiography that is narcissistically oriented toward the standpoint of the historian" (*PD*, 278). If we limit the concept of truth to the specific discourse in which it is used, if, in other words, we limit the category of truth to the impact it has within a specific discourse, then Foucault's theory cannot be universalized and would have no more than local relevance. This conclusion, however, frustrates Habermas because it takes Foucault's project seriously and supports his attempt to undermine any form of power (also those forms that dress up as scientific truth). Hence, Habermas insists (against Foucault) on a universal concept of truth that cannot be derived from power relations. (This claim, of course, does not exclude the possibility that concrete scientific projects may be motivated by considerations other than the search for truth). Clearly, for Habermas power and truth operate on different levels. Specifically, truth cannot be grounded in power. In the end, Habermas disagrees with Foucault's claim that all norms and standards are ultimately relative; he disagrees with the thesis that the historian must therefore refrain from value statements in order not to be affected by the influence and power of existing discourses. With good reasons, Habermas argues that this position cannot be carried out consistently. Foucault's discourse—as a radical critique of the humanities and social sciences (*Geisteswissenschaften*)—contains implicit value judgments. Habermas wants to show that Foucault, as much as he steers clear of an explicit statement, occasionally admits that normative criteria are unavoidable (*PD*, 284).

At this point Foucault and his disciples might ask Habermas, How do you explain these norms and values (in the social as well as in the scientific sphere)? Do you not fall back on a position that emphasizes the need for these values and covers up their origin in power relations? These questions would force Habermas to account for his own position and to examine the basis from which he launches his critique of poststructuralist theory. In the concluding chapters he tries to answer these questions by restating his own theory. Most of all, he wants to demonstrate that there is a third way—besides philosophy of consciousness and poststructuralism (chapter 11). Furthermore, he wants to illuminate why the project of modernity cannot simply be canceled (chapter 12).

As one would expect, in these final chapters Habermas basically refers back to his theory of communicative action. He considers this theory a realistic and pragmatic approach— equally distant from the dangers of logocentric philosophy of consciousness with its problems of *Letztbegründungen* and from the pure rejection of metaphysics in the work of Foucault, Derrida, and their disciples—a rejection that easily results in irrationalism. This claim also throws more light on Habermas's understanding of the project of modernity (*Aufklärung*). What he has in mind is not, contrary to what some of his critics have claimed, simply the continuation of the idealist tradition. Habermas thinks in terms of a third alternative that would avoid the dangers of logocentrism and deconstruction. In this search, he feels close to a philosopher like Rorty who tries to rewrite the history of philosophy in terms of a radical critique of modern philosophy and its development from Descartes to Heidegger. Habermas could hardly share this program fully because he would have to cut himself off from the tradition in which he was trained, but it is apparent that today he has more affinities with thinkers like Dewey or Mead than with German idealism or even with the philosophy of the early Marx. Like Foucault and Derrida, Habermas insists on a paradigm change because he concurs with them that the metaphysical tradition of European philosophy is exhausted. In his opinion, the old paradigm is to be replaced with the model of communicative action in which neither the subject nor factual relations are the basis. Instead, the point of departure is communicative interactions. In particular, Habermas wants to undercut the opposition of an empirical and a transcendental subject, an opposition that even the critics of logocentrism have retained in their attacks.

How can this program be grounded? How can it be defended against the criticism that it remains part of the old paradigm of subject philosophy (Lyotard's criticism)? Habermas decided to ground his theory in language theory, especially speech-act theory. In the eleventh chapter he restates his arguments for this approach. Habermas believes that language itself contains the premises for a theory of communicative action. In other words, the explication of speech acts is not only supposed to explain how actual human communication works, but it is also supposed to demonstrate why consensus and thereby human solidarity is possible at all. It is impossible here to discuss this theory in detail. The following will, rather, focus primarily on its implications for the understanding of modernity. Habermas argues that the linguistic approach allows a rereading of the project of the Enlightenment in a different light and thereby reappropriates its semantic content. This revisionist tendency in Habermas's interpretation of modernity has to be emphasized more strongly than usual. As Habermas notes, "By contrast, as soon as we conceive of knowledge as communicatively mediated, rationality is assessed in terms of the capacity of responsible participants in interaction to orient themselves in relation to validity claims [*Geltungsansprüche*] geared to intersubjective recognition. Communicative reason finds its criteria in the argumentative procedures for directly or indirectly redeeming claims to propositional truth, normative rightness, subjective truthfulness, and aesthetic harmony [*Stimmigkeit*]" (*PD*, 314). To put it differently: the use of reason is not conceived anymore in terms of an absolute origin; rather, it unfolds within the context of an intersubjective exchange of arguments, an exchange that will necessarily raise normative claims. But these claims are not absolute: they can be questioned at any given time.

Habermas's use of speech-act theory contains a descriptive and a normative aspect. On the one hand, the analysis of speech acts explains how human communication actually works. On the other hand, it is also used by Habermas to ground his social theory, which emphasizes human emancipation. Habermas has been accused by his critics of idealizing the actual use of language in human communication. This reproach, however, misses the real problem. The weak spot in Habermas's argument is the dual function of language. By pointing to the actual operation of linguistic and social communication, Habermas conceals that these empirical conditions are ultimately turned into a normative understanding of language. This dualism results in an aporetic situation, which, incidentally, is not very different from the contradictions in Foucault's theory of power—although with a different turn. By insisting that linguistic communication, as it functions in the real life-world, provides the basis for the new paradigm, Habermas distances himself from a transcendental argument. But this move has a price: the rigid equation of facts and norms. As Habermas notes: "Inasmuch as communicative agents reciprocally raise validity claims with their speech acts, they are relying on the potential of assailable grounds. Hence, a moment of *unconditionality* is built into *factual* processes of mutual understanding" (*PD*, 322). Those norms to which we have recourse in our everyday interaction are, as Habermas suggests, context-bound, but there is another important aspect, which "serves as the foundation of an existing consensus" (*PD*, 323). This thesis seems to be close to a transcendental argument. To put it differently: if we want to avoid the quasi-transcendental structure of the argument, it might be safer to drop the use of universal norms and favor a purely local, context-bound use of rationality. Obviously, Habermas is not inclined to draw this conclusion, since universal normative claims (*Geltungsansprüche*) are of great importance for the structure of his emancipatory social theory.

The last chapter, then, tries to make two points: it shows why Habermas in the final analysis refuses to subscribe to the presuppositions of poststructuralist theory, and it sketches the outline of an alternative theory. It becomes quite clear, incidentally, that Habermas does not speak out in favor of a continuation of classical Critical Theory. In fact, he sees the later work of Adorno, for instance *Negative Dialectics* and *Aesthetic Theory*, as part of a tendency from which he wants to distance himself. Why, then, does Habermas, after a full-scale analysis of its major texts, decide to draw a line between himself and French theory? He argues that the poststructuralist critique of reason reduces the concept of rationality to such an extent that significant distinctions become irrelevant. In particular, Habermas turns against the undialectical critique of subjectivity— the general attack on logocentricity. This polemic has reduced the ambiguity of modernity by stressing the negative elements without considering the positive side of the account. The frontal attack has thereby repressed the progressive potential of modernity. As Habermas observes:

> Not only the devastating consequences of an objectifying relation-to-self are condemned with this principle of modernity, but also the other connotations once associated with subjectivity as an unredeemed promise: the prospect of a self-conscious practice, in which the solidary self-determination of all was to be joined with the self-realization of each individual. What is thrown out is precisely what a modernity reassuring itself once meant by concepts of self-consciousness, self-determination, and self-realization. (*PD*, 337–38)

This statement clearly defines the direction of Habermas's program. It differs significantly from the project of his teachers (Horkheimer and Adorno) and also from those traditions within Marxist theory that want to reemphasize the category of human praxis. Unlike Horkheimer and Adorno, Habermas can positively relate to Max Weber's work. While *Dialectic of Enlightenment* reads modernity—through the eyes of the early Lukács—primarily as a process of increasing reification, Habermas sees Weber's description of modern history (a process of disenchantment) also as a positive and encouraging tendency. Since *Legitimation Crisis*, Habermas has maintained that modern society has developed through a process of *Ausdifferenzierungen* (differentiations), which results in a system consisting of relatively autonomous subsystems and spheres. Thus he writes about the cultural system: "These knowledge systems of art and criticism, science and philosophy, law and morality, have become the more split off from ordinary communication the more strictly and one-sidedly they each have to do with one linguistic function and one aspect of validity. But they should not be considered on account of this abstraction per se as the phenomena of decline symptomatic of subject-centered reason" (*PD*, 339). It is fairly obvious that this sentence also contains a critical indictment of Adorno's philosophy. For Habermas, the fundamental development on which his reflections on modern society are based is the difference between the life-world and system, as it begins to surface during the eighteenth century. In this context he encourages the rehabilitation of reason (*Vernunft*)—a project beset with problems, as Habermas knows so well. Hence, his defense of reason must chart its course most carefully in order not to succumb to the dangers of instrumental, or to the lure of "inclusive," reason—both of which have a totalitarian character.

It is precisely poststructuralist objections to the specter of a totalizing rationalist norm that, as one might have expected, have made *The Philosophical Discourse of Modernity* a highly controversial book in America, once it was available in English (1987).[7] The battle lines were predictable: they pretty much followed the division between the Critical Theory camp and the poststructuralist camp. Also predictably, the reception revealed a considerable amount of misunderstanding about Habermas's position, especially his conception of rationalism and his defense of modernity. To some extent, Habermas's earlier essay ("Modernity—an Incomplete Project")—with its strong indictment of implicit conservative tendencies within postmodernism/poststructuralism—blocked an adequate appropriation of Habermas's *Philosophical Discourse*, in which the epistemological problems figure much more prominently than the political ones. Among poststructuralists—John Rajchman for instance—it was simply assumed that Habermas extended his argument in order to reinforce his earlier position.[8]

There is no need to trace the details of this rather acrimonious debate, in which received opinions and stereotypes have overshadowed the discussion of the substantive issues. Instead, I hope to bring these issues more to the foreground by turning the tables on the prominent poststructuralist discourse in this

---

7. See esp. John Rajchman's review article "Habermas's Complaint," *New German Critique* 45 (Fall 1988): 163–91.
   8. Ibid.

country; rather than challenging Habermas on the basis of poststructuralist models of analysis, I would like to raise the question What can Habermas's theory contribute to the discourse on power and truth? Can the Habermasian version of Critical Theory throw light on poststructuralist positions? Further, considering the debate between Habermas and Foucault, another crucial issue is the distinction commonly made between normative and descriptive levels. If we accept this distinction as useful, how do we justify it and ground it theoretically? While Habermasian theory has tended to privilege the normative use of reason, Foucault's writings have strongly emphasized the descriptive level of particular historical analysis. This tension leads us to the core of the debate over Habermas's rationalism and his defense of modernity.

Once one has stripped away the polemical rhetoric, the question about norms is, I believe, at the bottom of the debate between John Rajchman and Richard Wolin.[9] Although I will not trace this discussion in detail, in general, the argument in favor of Foucault's (and against Habermas's) position can be presented in the following way: philosophical discourses, like all cultural discourses, are culture-bound and historical. Consequently, one can no longer theorize about modernity in the same manner as in the eighteenth century, when people were seeking for universal structures of knowledge. Habermas, since he continues to use the theoretical apparatus of the Enlightenment, fails to understand the historical end of the project of modernity, with its stress on teleological history (evolution). Once we grant that history is a construct rather than an actual (linear) process, we no longer have an Archimedian point from which to judge progress and reaction, good and bad. This situation necessitates a new approach (and a new definition of "critical"): instead of confronting "bad" reality with "good"

---

9. See Wolin's response to Rajchman's review essay (cited above), entitled "On Misunderstanding Habermas: A Response to Rajchman," as well as Rajchman's "Rejoinder to Richard Wolin," *New German Critique* 49 (Winter 1990).

norms in order to improve society, one "tries to explore what
we take for granted as necessary and fixed in our existence as
something that has been happening to us, and which we may
refuse to accept."[10] Foucault's theory wants to eliminate the
normative aspect of rationality because it tends to interfere
with our access to historical events (in their specific function).
Norms and standards are there to be questioned. Concepts like
justice must not be trusted; rather, a critical approach analyzes
actual discourses of justice to demonstrate how the use of this
concept depends on particular social practices. According to
Rajchman's account, Habermas fails to recognize Foucault's
project and therefore superimposes his own categories on Foucault's writings.

In the final analysis, for Foucault, reason and rational behavior are always defined in local terms: "there is no such thing
as Objectivity or Rationality in general."[11] Consequently, the
distinction between true and false statements relates only to
rules grounded in a specific discourse. Still—and this is where
I would locate the weakness in the Foucauldian argument—
the description and analysis of particular discursive practices,
which lead to a recognition of the plurality of discourses, always require a comparative rationality that in itself can never
be merely local. How do we make rational decisions when we
have to address competing and conflicting discourses, let us
say, of social justice? Habermas offers a solution by arguing
that there are formal universal norms available that can serve
as a guide for a rational discussion. The formal character of
these norms has to be underscored: they are not supposed to
deal with specific contents; rather, they are expected to map
the parameters and define the character of public communication. Hence it is possible to argue that the concerns and
problems of marginalized groups can be dealt with most successfully when rationality is restricted to principles of formal

10. Rajchman, "Habermas's Complaint," 174.
11. Rajchman, "Rejoinder to Richard Wolin," 158.

procedure. In other words, the distinction between universal and local aspects of reason, between generalizable norms and culture-bound questions of the good life, is necessary. For this reason, Habermas criticizes Foucault's attempt to reduce rationality to the level of a cultural context.

In his desire to overcome a relativistic position and to secure the possibility of rational discussion (but not through deductions from a priori knowledge, as some of his critics have maintained), Habermas tends, I feel, to underestimate the epistemological strength of local reason and, conversely, to overrate the need for overarching norms of rationality. Although Habermas agrees that most of the practical questions with which we are confronted in our life-worlds cannot be solved through demonstrative arguments, he tries to transcend an unstable pluralism, where individual needs and interests cancel each other, and wants to hold out the possibility of a normative and rational consensus that is stronger than a rationally negotiated, pluralist compromise. According to Habermas, this outcome can be achieved by separating formal procedure from substantive content. When we are faced with fundamental divergences in value orientation, however, this distinction tends to break down. The boundaries between procedural rationality and cultural rationality (concerning the "good life") are less stable than Habermasian theory assumes. To put it differently, demonstrative norms—even norms of formal procedure—that transcend specific cultural contexts are not available in the public sphere where political and social issues are debated. Yet this does not mean that there is no room for rational debate. Particular and local rationality does not claim to provide a conclusive mechanism for creating a consensus, but it offers a comparative analysis of needs and values so that a compromise can be reached. This means that rational debate does not have to be based on demonstrative universal norms. At the same time, we have to note that this argument does not eliminate the difference between the normative and the descriptive aspects of rationality, as Rajchman appears to assume; the move from a problematization of Habermas's claim for demonstrative norms to a rejection of norms and procedures is not persuasive. It is flawed because it makes the problematic assumption that these norms cannot be questioned, overlooking the fact that Habermas's formal notion of communicative norms stresses precisely the process of questioning and debate.

6   The Politicization of Aesthetic Theory: The Debate in Aesthetics since 1965

In West Germany the politicization of aesthetic theory and literary criticism began during the second half of the 1960s. If one were to describe everything that took place in the fifteen years between 1965 and 1979, the resulting recitation of names and projects would contribute little to our understanding of the matter.[1] I have therefore chosen to focus on themes and categories that can aid us in laying out the internal logic of the theoretical discussion. This approach assumes that one can organize the processes of theory formation into a historical pattern. As a consequence, the years between 1965 and 1979 are presented as comprising a unified epoch or phase that differs from the preceding and following years. The legitimacy of this assumption can be assessed only by critically examining the theoretical material itself. My approach thus relies on a schema whose validity can be demonstrated only by investigating its contents.

In 1969 Hans Robert Jauss alluded to Thomas Kuhn by speaking of a paradigm shift in literary criticism.[2] Jauss foresaw a new theoretical model emerging from reception aesthetics. As Jauss himself later admitted, this claim proved rash; yet, in the

---

1. Please consult the Postscript to this chapter for some remarks on the decade of the 1980s in Germany.

2. Hans Robert Jauss, "Paradigmawechsel in der Literaturwissenschaft," *Linguistische Berichte* 3 (1969): 44–56.

mid-1960s, significant changes do indeed begin to occur in West Germany.[3] Nevertheless, these changes do not so much take place because new theorems are developed; rather, they result more from a rediscovery of older, obscured approaches and positions. In retrospect, this turn can be characterized as a break with the modernist and avant-gardist aesthetics variously represented by Theodor W. Adorno and Gottfried Benn. This is not to claim that Adorno's theory played no role in influencing later developments. On the contrary, it is precisely his theory that became extraordinarily important to the debates and self-understanding of the 1970s. This initial break is instead a matter of rejecting particular elements of Adorno's thought: his attachment to the great names of modernism like Franz Kafka, James Joyce, and Samuel Beckett, and his conception of the social function of art as it is expressed in his essays on Jean-Paul Sartre, Georg Lukács, and Bertolt Brecht. Those who opposed the modernists' aesthetics concentrated on the defensive stance of postwar modernism vis-à-vis the contemporary social contradictions that became evident in West Germany with the formation of the Great Coalition in 1966. This division was a thoroughly painful and, for the most part, deeply traumatic event for both sides, for the student movement's theory of art was profoundly indebted to the crucial stimulus of Adorno's work.

I will not even attempt to sketch out Adorno's aesthetic theory here; it is enough to name those features of his theory that were received by the New Left and then wielded against him:

1. In contradistinction to traditional academic aesthetics, Adorno's theory is historically oriented, both in relation to its object and in respect to its own position. In each case, it ad-

3. Hans Robert Jauss, "Racine und Goethes *Iphigenie*—Mit einem Nachwort über die Partialität der rezeptionsästhetischen Methode," *Neue Hefte für Philosophie* 3 (1973): 1–46.

dresses the work of art only in the context of its historical emergence and reception.

2. We are not dealing with a historicist but an ideologically critical historical approach. This means that the encounter with the work of art that deserves the name of criticism interrogates the structure of the work of art by attending to the element of historical truth it contains.

3. Adorno is indebted to the Marxist analysis of commodities for crucial insights into the conditions of aesthetic reception and production under capitalism. The rubric of "culture industry" summarizes this approach, which ultimately relates the aesthetic to the economic sphere.

4. Lastly, Adorno formulates a theory of aesthetic autonomy that radically departs from the concept of the organic work of art and the notion of aesthetic reflection.

This extremely broad characterization nevertheless allows for a more precise delineation of the paradigm shift. Adorno's theory denies itself a political application of its own insights and negates the step from a contemplative to a practical attitude. This can in no way simply be attributed to personal idiosyncrasies. Adorno rejects the politicization of aesthetics, which would of course include his concept of art, because his social theory ruled out any essential transformation in the global system of organized capitalism. In the face of the proletariat's integration into existing society, the resistance of late Critical Theory was confined to the level of reflection. This political resignation dramatically affects the aesthetic sphere, which for Adorno becomes the sole realm in which freedom from and opposition to the omnipresent system can be articulated.

The theoretical kernel of this position is already formulated at an early stage in Adorno's thinking. In the essay "On the Fetish Character in Music" from the year 1938, which should be understood as a confrontation with Walter Benjamin's essay "The Work of Art in the Age of Mechanical Reproduction," Adorno resists his friend's attempt to draw political conclusions from the destruction of the aura—that is, of aesthetic autonomy.[4] Adorno expressly repudiates Benjamin's hope that the technical grounding of art as it was emerging in film might have progressive political implications. The theory of the culture industry anticipated here by Adorno is not interested in technology as a new force of production but in the exchange value of art, an exchange value that unswervingly guarantees art's degradation. This difference of opinion between Adorno and his older friend is not mentioned out of caprice, for precisely this conflict becomes a crucial catalyst in the confrontation between Adorno and the New Left. The rediscovery of Benjamin's later writings, which were only partially represented in the 1955 edition of his works overseen by Adorno, changed the emphasis of the debate with help from theories that had already been developed in the 1930s—most significantly by Benjamin and Brecht. The increasingly embittered 1967 debate between the Frankfurt School and the journal *alternative* over the authentic form of Benjamin's writings is symptomatic of the intensification of what I would like to designate as the political aesthetics of the 1960s.[5] It would certainly be precipitous at this point to trace back this materialist aesthetics, which clearly relies on Marx, exclusively to the rediscovery of Benjamin. The search for a materialist theory of art leads in the late 1960s to a series of different, to some extent conflicting, efforts that take issue with Critical Theory.

In a schematic way, one can distinguish between four different schools of thought. During the first phase of the movement, that is, between 1967 and 1969, Herbert Marcuse and his writings were particularly important for the self-understanding of the Left, for they directly met the demand for

4. Theodor W. Adorno, "On the Fetish Character in Music and the Regression in Listening," in *The Essential Frankfurt School Reader*, ed. Andrew Arato and Eike Gebhardt (New York, 1982), 270–99; Walter Benjamin, "The Work of Art in the Age of Mechanical Reproduction," in *Illuminations*, ed. Hannah Arendt (New York, 1969), 217–52.
5. See *alternative* 56/57 (Oct./Dec. 1967) and 59/60 (Apr./June 1969).

a political aesthetics. Marcuse answered the question In what way can art and literature play a role in transforming society? Although Marcuse's theories certainly receded into the background after 1969, they continued to exercise a considerable degree of influence in the 1970s, particularly among those who continued the tradition of Critical Theory. Nevertheless, after 1972—above all with his *Counterrevolution and Revolt* (1972)—Marcuse revised his thesis of the total transposition of art into praxis and spoke out against a desublimated praxis, thus preparing the way for the turn against political aesthetics. Christian Enzensberger's literary theory, for instance, which strictly separates political praxis and utopia, is deeply indebted to Marcuse's approach despite its polemic against Critical Theory.

Commodity aesthetics, which likewise arose from Critical Theory, took a different path. The commodity aesthetics developed by such authors as Wolfgang Fritz Haug, Hans Heinz Holz, and Friedrich Tomberg grappled with Horkheimer and Adorno's *Dialectic of Enlightenment*. At first, these efforts followed Adorno's use in his aesthetic theory of Marx's analysis of commodities; yet, over time, commodity aestheticians clearly distanced themselves more and more from the premises of the Frankfurt School in their stringent development of a materialist commodity aesthetics. By 1970 this process resulted in these theorists' seeing themselves in pronounced opposition to the Frankfurt School. The debate over commodity aesthetics dwindled away over the course of the 1970s after Hannelore Schlaffer contributed what she viewed as the critical conclusion to this debate, until W. Martin Lüdke renewed the discussion in 1977.[6] A similar process of rediscovery, in this

6. See Hannelore Schlaffer, "Kritik eines Klischees: 'Das Kunstwerk als Ware,' " in *Erweiterung der materialistischen Literaturtheorie durch Bestimmung ihrer Grenzen*, ed. Heinz Schlaffer, Literaturwissenschaft und Sozialwissenschaften 4 (Stuttgart, 1977), 264–87; and W. Martin Lüdke, "Der Kreis, das Bewusstsein und das Ding: Aktuell motivierte Anmerkungen zu der vergangenen Diskussion um den Warencharakter der

instance of Georg Lukács and Bertolt Brecht, encouraged the group around the journal *Argument* to draw closer to an orthodox Marxist position. This retrospective reflection on buried traditions, whose onset can be dated at about 1967, intensified theoretical discussion even as it simultaneously problematized anyone's claim already to possess a consistent materialist theory. The intensive appropriation of these materialist traditions necessarily led to the insight that an avant-gardist position, as it was represented by Benjamin and Brecht in the 1930s, could not be reconciled with the theory of Georg Lukács. The treatment of the expressionism debate and the later concern with the polemics of the *Linkskurve* made it evident that absolutely no consensus obtained in the Marxist camp about essential theoretical questions such as the problem of realism, the function of art, the assessment of specific artistic means, and so on. Helga Gallas's work *Marxistische Literaturtheorie* (1971) created a historical explanation, even as it deepened the conflict by taking up a pronounced Brechtian position while critically distancing itself from Georg Lukács and East German literary criticism.[7]

Thus, it is difficult to find a common denominator in the literary theory produced within the leftist camp during the 1970s. One does encounter fragments of and approaches to a materialist theory that clearly share a certain hostility to academic literary criticism and its aesthetics. This opposition was not least aimed at the Constance school, which fielded a phenomenologically grounded reception aesthetics as an innovative alternative to orthodox Marxism.[8] Otherwise, one can only

---

Kunst," in *Lesen, Literatur und Studentenbewegung*, ed. W. Martin Lüdke (Opladen, 1977), 124–57.

7. Helga Gallas, *Marxistische Literaturtheorie: Kontroversen im Bund proletarisch-revolutionärer Schriftsteller* (Neuwied, 1971).

8. For a summary of reception theory, see *Rezeptionsästhetik*, ed. Rainer Warning (Munich, 1975). For the Marxist position, see Bernd Jürgen Warneken, "Zu Hans Robert Jauss' Programm einer Rezeptionsäthetik," in *Sozialgeschichte und Wirkungsästhetik*, ed. Peter Uwe Hohendahl (Frankfurt, 1974), 290–96. For a discussion of reception theory in East

note the variety of opinions and viewpoints that were promulgated in such journals as *Kursbuch, alternative, Das Argument,* or *Aesthetik und Kommunikation.* One could make similar statements about the situation in France or the United States at the beginning of the 1970s. Yet when one carefully examines the period between 1965 and 1979 and compares the developments in the German debate with those taking place in French or American discussions, profound differences appear in the objects granted critical attention, the premises granted validity, and the methods that form the basis of discourse. If one wishes to grasp the aesthetic theory of the 1970s as a historical process, one must concentrate on the points where contradictions and oppositions become immediately apparent.

I begin with the political aesthetic that, primarily under the influence of Herbert Marcuse, radicalized the Frankfurt School's theory of art. Marcuse's earlier works, such as his famous 1937 essay on the affirmative character of culture, characteristically centered on a critique of ideology that opposed the concept of an autonomous culture transcending social pressures.[9] After his intensive study of Freud, however, Marcuse's interests began to focus on the utopian element of art. In *Eros and Civilization* (1955) Marcuse construes the opposition between art and reality found in classicism's aesthetic concept of autonomy in such a way that art comes to have an essential role in the emancipation of humanity. Art undermines the reality principle of analytical reason by advocating the principle of sensuousness. Marcuse develops the theory of a sensual liberation through aesthetic experience that prepares the way for political emancipation. What was chiefly a theoretical problem

---

Germany, see Peter Uwe Hohendahl, "Aesthetik und Sozialismus: Zur neueren Literaturtheorie der DDR," in *Literatur und Literaturtheorie in der DDR,* ed. Peter Uwe Hohendahl and Patricia Herminghouse (Frankfurt, 1976), 100–162.

9. Herbert Marcuse's famous essay, first published in the *Zeitschrift für Sozialforschung* in 1937, has been translated as "The Affirmative Character of Culture," in Herbert Marcuse, *Negations* (Boston, 1968), 88–133.

at the time *Eros and Civilization* first appeared became an immediate political problem in the late 1960s. In the preface to his *Essay on Liberation* (1969), Marcuse not only ascertains that his position accords with that of the radicals in France and the United States, he also emphasizes the utopian character of their demands: "The radical utopian character of their demands far surpasses the hypotheses of my essay; and yet, these demands were developed and formulated in the course of action itself; they are expressions of concrete political practice."[10] Marcuse achieves the transition from art to politics by attributing the character of social praxis to the new sensibility and aesthetic experience. The way in which Marcuse develops this thesis explains the initially surprising claim that the new sensibility itself already possesses the quality of praxis. Marcuse's gaze is no longer primarily directed at the artistic product, but at the moment of experience, which, as sensual reason, opposes instrumental reason. City planning, conservation, and ecological reforms are subsumed under the aesthetic sphere, which itself thereby becomes a political sphere. With Marcuse, aesthetics becomes political by freeing us from conventional politics. At the same time, this liberation embodies the sublimation of art. Art and reality coincide as soon as art gives up its autonomous status and becomes the daily practice of human beings. In 1969 Marcuse approaches Benjamin's conception of a postauratic art that belongs to the masses.

Among the German journals of the Left, the *Kursbuch* represented—at least temporarily—Marcuse's political aesthetics. Peter Schneider's 1969 essay "Die Phantasie im Spätkapitalismus und die Kulturrevolution" (Fantasy in late capitalism and the cultural revolution) exemplifies this tendency within the *Kursbuch*.[11] Writing under the influence of the failed May revolt in Paris, Schneider draws a distinction between the

10. Herbert Marcuse, *Essay on Liberation*, (Boston, 1969), ix.
11. Peter Schneider, "Die Phantasie im Spätkapitalismus und die Kulturrevolution," *Kursbuch* 16 (1969): 1–37; reprinted in Peter Schneider, *Atempause* (Reinbek, 1977), 127–61.

economic-political and the cultural revolution. He then follows Marcuse by concluding:

> Simultaneously, De Gaulle's tanks have shown what the economic-political revolution cannot do. It cannot beget the revolutionary consciousness which corresponds to the state of development of industrial productive forces; it cannot transform the emancipation of the oppressed class into the emancipation of the individual; it cannot develop the liberation of society from capital further into the liberation of fantasy from the performance principle; and it cannot win if it does not begin as a cultural revolution and become a cultural revolution once more.[12]

In this instance, the cultural and aesthetic sphere is designated the realm in which revolutionary praxis must develop if it is to shatter the organization of late capitalism, for this system is comprised not only of classes and organizations but also of elements of consciousness that serve oppression. Schneider thus views the cultural revolution as a culminating step: "After the demolition of the state apparatus and the socialization of the means of production, it [the cultural revolution] transforms the emancipation of society from private property into the practical supercession [*Aufhebung*] of all relations of servitude which are modifications and consequences of alienated labour."[13] Again, Marcuse's theory serves as a bridge between the repressive culture of capitalism and ultimate liberation.

The union of Marx and Freud proposed by Schneider in 1969 obviously relies on Marcuse. It is certainly remarkable how Schneider, who was probably not yet aware of the *Essay on Liberation*, politically hones the position of *Eros and Civilization*. Whereas in 1955 Marcuse had addressed the utopian moment of art as art's political dimension, Schneider sharply

12. Translated from Schneider, *Atempause*, 127. All translations from articles and books in German, here and throughout the chapter, are provided by Brian Urquhart unless otherwise noted.

13. Ibid., 128; first interpolation, mine.

separates these aspects and notes a contradiction between the practice-free utopia of bourgeois art and the revolutionary action upon which a political aesthetics should be founded. With this distinction, Schneider breaks with Marcuse, whom he accuses of formalism. It is evident that the step with which Schneider would like to surpass his predecessor is precisely the one Marcuse himself takes in 1969—the desublimation of art into social praxis. In the words of Schneider: "Under late capitalism, the progressive, usable phantasy is absolutely no longer at home in art; instead, it is at home where it seeks its satisfaction in the revolutionary, rather than imaginary, transformation of society." According to Schneider, both traditionalist and avant-gardist works of art have lost their revolutionary force in late capitalism. "Form in art no longer expresses the promise of a future realization of desires; on the contrary: form makes a kind of promise out of real suffering and the real destruction of desires by still allowing the promise to become an object of imagination."[14]

From this criticism of Adorno's and Marcuse's aesthetics, Schneider draws the conclusion that in the context of late capitalism, one can identify only two meaningful functions for art: the agitative and the propagandistic. This conclusion remains noteworthy for its theoretical grounding. Although Schneider's approach remains beholden to Marcuse and Critical Theory, his social theory relies more on an orthodox position, such as Lenin's or Paul Sweezy's theory of imperialism. This attempt to modify the aesthetic theory of the Frankfurt School and simultaneously provide it with a new theoretical foundation seems characteristic of the situation of the New Left after 1969.

The same holds true of commodity aesthetics, which does not proceed so much from political as from economic analysis. The first attempts to develop a materialist commmodity aesthetics link up with Critical Theory, namely, with Horkheimer and Adorno's *Dialectic of Enlightenment*. This is true of Wolf-

14. Ibid., 146, 152.

gang Fritz Haug's 1963 essay "Zur Aesthetik von Manipulation" (Toward an aesthetics of manipulation). Intent on providing an ideological critique, the essay tracks down the purpose and form of advertising in late capitalism: "The advertisement appears with the deceptive appearance of mediating universality," whereas in reality it only represents the interests of capital.[15] The use of aesthetic signs boils down to channeling the existing needs of the population in such a manner that they benefit consumption and, as a result, profit. Commodity aesthetics clearly became significant only in its second phase, when it departed from Critical Theory. In the 1970 preface to *Kritik der Warenästhetik* (Critique of commodity aesthetics), Haug settles accounts with the approach of the Frankfurt School by rebuking it for proceeding from surface phenomena and ignoring essential structures. According to Haug, this produces a speculative theory in which the particular and the whole are related to one another in an unmediated fashion. Nevertheless, the target of his critique is not the concept of totality, which Haug in no way relinquishes, but the ontologization of a particular phase of late capitalism by the Frankfurt School. The materialist grounding called for by Haug from that point on relies on the Marx of *Capital* and not on the Paris manuscripts of 1844, whose emphatic concept of alienation provided the basis for the project of Critical Theory. "The task which I set myself," commented Haug in 1970, "was therefore to derive the phenomena of commodity aesthetics economically and to develop and present their systematic connection."[16]

Haug's theory, which proceeds from Marx's analysis of commodities, can scarcely be considered a theory of art; the scope of the aesthetic realm is defined in much broader terms than is the case with Adorno. Haug uses the concept of the aesthetic

15. Wolfgang Fritz Haug, *Warenästhetik, Sexualität und Herrschaft* (Frankfurt, 1972), 32.
16. Wolfgan Fritz Haug, *Kritik der Warenästhetik* (Frankfurt, 1973), 11.

on the one hand to designate sensuous knowledge (as does Kant) and on the other hand to designate the realm of the beautiful. The subject matter is clearly not primarily works of art but commodities that use the semblance of the beautiful in order to sell themselves. Since works of art certainly have offered themselves on the market as commodities ever since the eighteenth century, however, the next obvious step would be to apply the aesthetics of the commodity to the work of art.

Hans Heinz Holz took this step by formulating an argument that closely resembles Benjamin's analysis of the aesthetic aura and its disappearance. He follows Benjamin in discerning a precapitalist phase in which the work of art appears above all as a cultic object. When the cultic value of the object vanishes and the work of art's new function centers on display, then the work of art approaches the commodity:

> The work of art become commodity now shares all features of the essence of the commodity: it participates in an art market which is subject to the play of supply and demand, and in which the sales practices are in principle no different than those found in the market dealing in commodities of utility [*Gebrauchsgüter*]. The sales strategy employed in the two markets differ only in that the art market does not claim that the commodities it offers possess an immediate use value, but a spiritual value for the purchaser.[17]

Yet, at the same time the reception of the work of art changes, so too does its form of production: that is, the artist must offer his or her works to an anonymous market in order to make his or her way. The artist becomes "constrained by a product form which is compatible with the market." For Holz, the essential significance of commodity aesthetics lies in its refusal to examine the work of art without reflecting on the context in which it is rooted. In his view, commodity aesthetics is concerned with "analyzing the structural determinants which lie

17. Hans Heinz Holz, *Vom Kunstwerk zur Ware* (Neuwied, 1972), 16.

in the relations of production and distribution." This analysis of art as a commodity does not lead to political aesthetics, since, like Critical Theory, Holz places great emphasis on the commercialization of art. Yet the concept of aesthetic autonomy familiar to Critical Theory no longer plays a decisive role for Holz. Under developed capitalism, loss of autonomy is the fate of works of art: "The degradation of the work of art to a commodity implies the loss of the particularity of the aesthetic: from now on, the aesthetic object can only be exalted above other, random objects of utility by a decisionistic act of arbitrariness."[18]

Evidently, Holz goes one step beyond Haug's position. Whereas Haug still attributes some significance to the aesthetic sphere—that is, the realm of art—Holz stresses that criticism may not stop at the level of the work of art. In other words, the theory of art will dissolve into art history and the sociology of art. "The relative autonomy of the aesthetic," he argues against Adorno, "is annulled [*aufgehoben*]; instead of serving as a medium of reflection, the aesthetic becomes a mere function of society, an ideological simulacrum."[19] According to Holz's definition of art's present crisis, art has lost its authentic function. Moreover, in contrast to Marcuse, Holz promises art no new function. Holz extends the scope of commodity aesthetics by denying any difference between works of art and objects of utility.

This all-inclusive identification, which could not draw on Adorno for support, becomes the main target of Hannelore Schlaffer's critique, mentioned above.[20] Her goal is to do away with commodity aesthetics by proving that the autonomy of art was left essentially untouched by the development of a capitalist market. According to Schlaffer, it was only in the area of distribution that the work of art was pulled into the

18. Ibid., 25, 27, 37.
19. Ibid., 10.
20. Schlaffer, "Kritik eines Klischees," 264–87.

market and transformed into a commodity. Indeed, neither production nor reception were substantially affected by these conditions: "A commodity is the union of exchange value and use value provided that it is transferred in the exchange between buyers. The artist and the purchaser only apparently enter into an exchange relation, for artistic value cannot be determined and clearly cannot be paid for."[21] Against commodity aesthetics, Schlaffer argues that artistic labor or aesthetic production is not socialized and therefore not subject to the laws of the market. Since aesthetic production is not alienated, the autonomy of the work of art is in principle secured. The commodity aspect is secondary. This argument, as Lüdke rightly objected, underestimates the social character of artistic production. Lüdke refers to the historically changing context influencing the work of the artist and his or her artifacts.[22]

Generally speaking, one must ask whether the opposition between aesthetic autonomy and social determination can be specified on an abstract level. Indeed, it would appear that this relationship must be understood as a historical one that changes qualitatively between the eighteenth century and the present. It matters less, then, that the work of art cannot become an object of utility because it is spiritual, than does the circumstance that the work of art's function—like its reception—changes over time. Hence the category of autonomy, which Schlaffer derives from the very nature of works of art, itself proves to be historical. In this respect, Holz appropriately grasps the present situation as a historical crisis that cannot simply be resolved on the level of theoretical reflection. Holz's argument nevertheless clearly lacks a careful distinction between material and aesthetic production. Schlaffer's much-needed objection to this form of commodity aesthetics critically questioned precipitous, globalizing judgments and theoretical clichés. Lüdke's contribution demonstrated that the

---

21. Ibid., 277.
22. Lüdke, "Der Kreis, das Bewusstsein und das Ding," 133.

discussion did not come to an end with Schlaffer; he not only summed up the debate, he also articulated the possibility of its theoretical solution.

With good reason, Lüdke stresses that, as a rule, earlier approaches apply categories from political economy too directly to the aesthetic realm and do not sufficiently take into account the process of reification. At this juncture, however, the discussion is referred back to its starting point, namely, the reification theory of the early Lukács, which supplies the basis for the Frankfurt School. Thanks to Lüdke's attentive reconstruction, Adorno's theory of art again becomes visible as the starting point of the debate. It appears that the polemical turn against the Frankfurt School did not necessarily overcome it; rather, it led to an elaboration of certain possibilities already present in Adorno's thought. Both the thesis that in late capitalism all art is degraded to the status of a commodity and the thesis that the autonomy of art is inalienable can be found in Adorno. Thus, the discussion returns to Adorno, where the original formulation of the problem could be found. Lüdke argues that the critique of commodity aesthetics cannot restrict itself to specific conclusions, such as those put forward in the thesis of the commercialization of art or its autonomy vis-à-vis the market. On the contrary, this critique must deal with the Marxian concept of the commodity and the reification theory derived from it: "The thesis of the commodity character of art only obtains its real explanatory value by relying upon the Marxian conception of the fetish-character of commodities. In the meantime, it has become problematic for the thesis of the commodification of art to draw upon a reification theory developed from the fetish-character of commodities."[23] Lüdke's critique here is directed against the hidden orthodoxy of Critical Theory. Considered systematically, commodity aesthetics rests upon the theory of reification, which in turn is

23. Ibid., 150.

derived from Marx's analysis of the commodity in *Capital*. As a result, any doubt about Marx's economic theory must correspondingly affect commodity aesthetics and the theory of reification.

Lüdke brings this critique to bear in his discussions of Habermas, Claus Offe, Wolfgang Pohrt, and Luhmann. Lüdke would like to fill the gap in the argument with a theory of pure aesthetic experience that "could break through the reified structures of contemporary experience"; but because Lüdke quite clearly perceives that aesthetic experience always is mediated socially, he cannot relinquish the category of reification he just repudiated.[24] This contradiction becomes clearer as soon as Lüdke outlines his program. He would like to avoid the rigid conclusions of a theory that can offer only the concepts of degradation or autonomy to aesthetic experience. In other words, he wants to develop a theory that does justice to immediate experience and the subjective aspect of social reality. "If need be, the agenda can be expressed in a formula: to attain a maximum of immediate experience with a minimum of instrumental mediation."[25] This formula nevertheless simply displaces the problem, since it refers to the opposition between subjective experience and positivistically formed objective concepts. The primary focus of commodity aesthetics, however, is on the "historical" dialectic in the relationship between material relations of production and aesthetic creations. This problem cannot be solved by recourse to the concept of immediate experience, the current feasibility of which would first have to be demonstrated. Lüdke's proposed solution ignores the social mediation of experience and thereby becomes not so much untheoretical as unhistorical.

Let me briefly summarize the outcome of the first phase of the theory discussion. About 1970 a consensus existed in the leftist camp on the inadequacy of the aesthetic theory of the

24. Ibid., 152.
25. Ibid., 153.

Frankfurt School. Furthermore, both political and commodity-
aesthetic theories were in agreement that the work of art as
an artifact no longer could remain the central object of aesthetic
theory. For both approaches, although for differing reasons, it
was no longer immediately evident that the work of art possesses a self-sufficient value. The discussion of the 1970s can
be grasped as a response to this zero-point situation. The assertion that the theory of art had to abandon the category of
the work of art turned out to be hasty; and the elimination of
Critical Theory proved to be easier to demand than to accom-
plish theoretically. The ensuing development certainly cannot
be understood as a mere restoration of an earlier state of affairs.
Instead, the unsolved problems of materialist aesthetics forced
a revision. This is above all true of the thesis that art can
continue to claim legitimacy only as propaganda or agitation.
I will use three examples to introduce the possibilities and
limits of the West German theoretical debates of the 1970s: in
the case of Thomas Metscher's theory I will discuss the recla-
mation of the concept of art under the aegis of Marxist orthodoxy; in connection with Christian Enzensberger's study I will
look at the critique of political aesthetics; and lastly, I will
examine the work of Peter Bürger, his historicization of Critical
Theory, and the problems it leaves unresolved.

Since Bürger's historicization of Critical Theory also encom-
passed Lukács's theory of art, a conflict between Metscher's
and Bürger's positions was unavoidable. I would like to begin
with this debate, which was carried out in 1975 in the journal
Das Argument. At the core of this debate stands the question
What approach should the aesthetic theory of the 1970s acknowledge as its legitimate theoretical predecessor? Metscher,
after turning away from Adorno, decides to fall back on Lenin's
reflection theory and from there develop a theory of the work
of art that is in close proximity to Lukács. Bürger, by contrast,
responds to the same set of circumstances by drawing the conclusion that only historical reflection—that is, the continuation and radicalization of Critical Theory—can resolve the

aporias of the situation. In his reply to Bürger's polemic, Metscher sums up the orthodox position and stands by the theory of reflection and an aesthetics of realism.[26] Relying on the reception theory of East Germany, Metscher argues that the Leninist theory of reflection embraces both productive and reproductive aspects of society and, as a result, takes into account more than Peter Bürger admits. Art production based on reflection has an effect on reality through its product—the work of art. This concession to reception theory's arguments does not prevent Metscher from subsequently expounding his position without responding in any greater depth to the core of Bürger's objections. The argument that aesthetic theory is tied to certain historical preconditions and that, as Bürger asserts, it is finished as a normative theory is not accessible to Metscher because his conceptual apparatus is produced deductively and lays claim to logical correctness. This does not mean that Metscher is not aware of his historical situation—on the contrary, he understands the return to reflection theory as part of a strategy that is important for West Germany in particular; even so, this political task cannot simply be assigned to a theory that derives from general epistemological principles rather than reflection upon a specific historical situation.

Metscher's designedly abstract approach is indicative of his theory's systematic character: "The epistemological approach necessitates a procedure which in the first instance proceeds not historically but systematically. Since it remains largely abstract, it may be capable of breaking through to the concrete only sporadically.... The epistemological principles of Marxism-Leninism possess a degree of generality which continually stands in need of concretization." Metscher integrates the theory of art into the general theory of reflection by conceptualizing aesthetic production as a "cognitive act," that is,

---

26. Thomas Metscher, "Aesthetische Erkenntnis und realistische Kunst," in *Das Argument* 90 (May 1975): 239–58; reprinted in his *Kunst als sozialer Prozess* (Cologne, 1977), 221–57.

as a particular form of knowledge—the aesthetic.[27] The tradition of Hegelian aesthetics is perceptible here: like Hegel, Metscher places his emphasis on the truth content of works of art. In Metscher's own formulation: "According to Hegel, in beauty the idea is actualized in the form of appearance [*Schein*] as the 'concrete intuition' [*Anschauung*]—that is, a sensuously objective appearance in which, as Lenin said, the 'entire wealth of the world' is enclosed." Lenin's materialist reinterpretation of the Hegelian idea allows Metscher a definition of art that finds the essential preserved in the representation reflecting reality. "Art is therefore not—in the Platonic sense—a copy reproducing empirical phenomena but an articulation of the concrete 'concept' constituting the world of the empirical; art is the sensuous manifestation of the lawfulness of social processes."[28] In short, the truth content of works of art does not refer to empirical objects but to the totality of reality. Metscher's aesthetic theory of reflection is unmistakably close to Lukács's theory of realism, even though it does not follow Lukács rigorously.

Metscher expressly supports Lukács against Ernst Bloch and the objections of radical leftists while he also, as might be expected, strictly defends Lukács's use of the category of totality. Metscher's critique of Lukács commences at the point where Lukács conceptualizes totality as something closed. For Metscher, Lukács's inability to do justice to the work of Brecht marks the one-sidedness of his theory, which does not sufficiently take into account the active role of consciousness. Certainly, one should not overlook Metscher's tendency to integrate Brecht's theory in a harmonizing rather than critical manner into his own theory, which is more influenced by Lukács. As a result, Metscher ends up taking the bite out of

27. Thomas Metscher, "Aesthetik als Abbildungstheorie," in his *Kunst als sozialer Prozess*, 150–52, 156.
28. Ibid., 160, 161.

Brecht's polemic against Lukács. Since Metscher commits himself to Leninist reflection theory and passes it off as the logical continuation of Marxian theory, the dialectic of being and consciousness is brought to a standstill. Theory ossifies into a doctrinal edifice from which one then makes deductions. In the following formulation, Metscher collapses art and historical praxis, imitation, and activity: "Art is a concretion of social experience, of historical praxis in the form of a sensual copy, whereby the particular structure of this copy is primarily determined by the structure of the duplicated reality."[29] It is noteworthy that Metscher places more value on the structural homology than on the act of producing. As a result, for Metscher the objective dialectic of a specific social situation becomes decisive for the representation (*Darstellung*). Without wanting to, Metscher here inherits Lukács's objectivism.

Bürger's critique of this position is above all directed against its deductive approach, which in his view must repress problems essential to present-day aesthetic theory. "Preliminary decisions [*Vorentscheidungen*] are arrived at which are not secured by historical investigation, but legitimated solely through the appeal to Leninism."[30] The neoorthodox theory of art suffers from simply appropriating the classics rather than taking up a historical-hermeneutic—and therefore critical—stance. For Bürger, in contrast, the evolution of art is itself the historical precondition upon which every theory must reflect: "An aesthetic theory which does not reflect this radical change [brought about by the modernists and the avant-garde] in its categories, cuts off its access to its object from the very start." Furthermore, concludes Bürger, such a theory is not in a position to orient itself in the present. Bürger then criticizes Metscher as follows: "What is missing from Metscher's dis-

29. Ibid., 202.
30. Peter Bürger, "Was leistet der Wiederspiegelungsbegriff in der Literaturwissenschaft?" *Das Argument* 90 (May 1975): 227.

cussion is a precisely articulated standpoint in the present."[31]
What is at stake in this debate is the Marxist legacy. While
Metscher takes the classical texts as his models and renovates
them for the present day, Bürger deprives them of their unquestioned normative status by consistently following his
historical-hermeneutical approach. For Bürger, who thereby
radicalizes the method of Critical Theory, historical reflexivity
also applies to theory itself. Theory is therefore precluded from
having recourse to older positions in its search for a materialist
aesthetics. Bürger finds historical reflection lacking already in
Lukács's invocation of the authority of reflection theory to
denounce modernism and the avant-garde as decadent. The
struggle between historical critique and normative aesthetics,
which in Lukács is ultimately resolved in favor of the latter,
is nonetheless—as Bürger rightly points out—the central problem of every aesthetic theory that directly or indirectly rests
on Hegel. Historical criticism must object to Lukács's theory
on the grounds that the historical logic of art had to lead, not
to realism, but to the emergence of new forms and the transformation of the function of art altogether.

Like many aesthetic theories in the 1970s, Bürger's own attempt to resolve the problems of the materialist theory of art
starts out from a critique of Adorno's aesthetics. This critique
develops the approach of Critical Theory up to the point where
Adorno's philosophy of art proves to be just as historical as
that of Lukács. Since Adorno's theory is considered the appropriate theory for the avant-garde, it simultaneously takes on
the role of a theory whose validity is historically determined
and qualified. Adorno puts forward a theory of the nonorganic,
avant-gardist work of art that does not yet take into account
the obsolescent character of the avant-garde: "The debate between Lukács and Adorno concerning the legitimacy of avant-
gardiste art is confined to the sphere of artistic means and the
change in the kind of work this involves (organic versus avant-

31. Ibid., 220 (my interpolation), 221.

gardiste). Yet the two authors do not thematize the attack that the historical avant-garde movements launched against art as an institution."[32] In other words, Adorno upholds a normative aesthetics no less insistently than Lukács and does not carry out the historicization of the theory of art that begins with Hegel to its logical conclusion. This is precisely what Bürger attempts to do when he reduces theoretical conflicts to outdated, dogmatic struggles and incorporates them into the history of the institution "art."

The decisive step in this historical argument is the following: the avant-gardist movements of the early twentieth century did not simply radicalize the demand for aesthetic autonomy; rather, they furnished a self-critique of art and urged the sublimation of the traditional division between art and life-practice. Bürger concludes, "But once the historical avant-garde movements revealed art as an institution as a solution to the mystery of the effectiveness or ineffectiveness of art, no form could any longer claim that it alone had either eternal or temporally limited validity." The legacy of Hegel's and Marx's philosophies of history liquidates the possibility of a normative aesthetic theory: "the normative examination is replaced by a functional analysis, the object of whose investigation would be the social effect (function) of a work, which is the result of the coming together of stimuli inside the work and a sociologically definable public within an already existing institutional frame."[33]

Bürger's historicization of aesthetic theory changes the character of the discussion vis-à-vis the 1960s. In the first and second phases of the student movement, the search for a materialist aesthetics was carried out in the form of a polemical confrontation between certain given positions (Adorno, Lukács, Brecht, Benjamin), while in the third phase—which has

32. Peter Bürger, *Theory of the Avant-Garde*, trans. Michael Shaw (Minneapolis, 1984), 86.
33. Ibid., 86, 87.

been exemplified in this essay by Bürger's *Theory of the Avant-Garde*—one encounters an increasingly pronounced consciousness of the contemporary historical situation and, as a result, a growing distance from the earlier models. Bürger warns, for example, against the unmediated appropriation of Brecht's theory.[34] It is clear that neoorthodox theory did not take this warning to heart. It ended up paying a dear price for this disregard. Neoorthodox theory disengaged from the specific literary and political situation in West Germany and displayed features of a certain alexandrine hermeticism absent even from East German theory once it had parted company with Lukács.

Ultimately, as the example of Christian Enzensberger's *Literatur und Interesse* (Literature and interest, 1977) makes clear, this revision also takes hold of the political aesthetics of the student movement. The central thesis of political aesthetics held that belles lettres had lost the socially critical function that Adorno imputed to it and that it therefore had to be replaced by an agitational literature that could exercise direct political influence. Enzensberger's theory can be understood only against the background of this thesis. In contrast to Marxist orthodoxy, Enzensberger's theory reflects West German circumstances much more concretely. The unnamed starting point of this theory is the failed leftist cultural revolution. Enzensberger did not embark on the privatization of literature under way at that point, but instead—and in this respect he became the consummate successor to Critical Theory—examined the aporias of political aesthetics: the failure of literature to induce social change and the rigid instrumentalization of literature for the class struggle. Marcuse had already repudiated the radical desublimation of art into social praxis and returned to the concept of the work of art in his 1972 book *Counterrevolution and Revolt*. Enzensberger expands this skepticism into a general theory by making the category of lack of meaning (*Sinndefizit*) into the starting point of aesthetic

34. Ibid., 88.

production. According to Enzensberger, all known societies manifesting division of labor and social differentiation suffer from lack of meaning. The unequal distribution of resources and opportunities leads to inadequacies that then, in order to appear meaningful, demand legitimation. "The lack of meaning consequently remains; it derives from social shortcomings, cannot be eliminated by ideology, and fundamentally asks for redress."[35] At least deficiencies can be overcome in fantasy. As the product of fantasy's activity, literature has the function for Enzensberger—as for Freud—of compensating for inadequacies. This compensation theory is obviously at odds with the tradition of Critical Theory, particularly with Adorno's philosophy of art, since it essentially disputes the claim of purposelessness. For Enzensberger, aesthetic production is always already and primarily responding to an unsatisfactory state of affairs. It is therefore part of the ideological consciousness that serves to legitimize this condition. Furthermore, where the Frankfurt School continued to maintain the oppositional power of the authentic work of art, Enzensberger views the aesthetic coherence of the work of art as more of an argument for its affirmative character. The opposition between art and reality typically found in Critical Theory is reinterpreted in such a way that art furnishes what reality withholds. In Enzensberger the beautiful appearance becomes deception: the emergence of literature begins with a need for deception about reality. Ineluctably harnessed to this set of relations, literature serves privileged interests. The core of this theory is the function of art; for this reason, Enzensberger's theory is fundamentally concerned with the question of reception, even if he completely repudiates the reception aesthetics of the Constance school. The act of reading or seeing (in the theater) is for Enzensberger always an act of identification: the reader sympathizes with the heroes, takes on their points of view, and in this way

---

35. Christian Enzensberger, *Literatur und Interesse* (Munich, 1977), 1:52.

achieves gratification. The intention of this description of reception is to prove that literature can have no real effect. Contrary to the assumptions made by political aesthetics or
reception aesthetics, since literature appeals to needs that demand immediate satisfaction, the recipient's consciousness remains unchanged.

This pessimistic conclusion may correspond with what came
to be known in the West German discussion as the *Tenden-
zwende* (change in tendency or commitment). Yet Enzensberger does not limit himself to recanting political aesthetics. He
simultaneously attempts to redefine the social contribution of
aesthetics and thereby continues to follow the model of Critical
Theory in spite of himself. Nevertheless, this is done with the
help of new methodological instruments. Enzensberger relies
on phenomenology in order to illuminate and clarify the concept of meaning (*Sinn*). By drawing a distinction between the
category of meaning and the concept of interest, Enzensberger
creates a utopian realm where art reposes: "Art shares the structure of utopia and the redeemed relation of meaning, but not
their content."[36] As would be expected, this constellation has
crucial consequences for the definition of the work of art and
the beautiful in art. In conspicuous proximity to classical aesthetics, Enzensberger defines the work of art as a self-
referential, self-contained organism. Part and whole stand in a
necessary relation to one another. The language of literature
does not refer to reality in a traditional way and does not fulfill
any pragmatic function, while the work of art is removed from
any historical referent.

What Enzensberger refers to as the utopian structure of art
is, as aesthetic autonomy, thoroughly familiar to aesthetic theory. Because it is elevated above social history and the realm
of interest, the work of art manifests its negation of lack (*Man-
gel*) as a fictitious fulfillment of meaning. The question then
arises, what separates Enzensberger's theory from Schiller or

36. Ibid., 131.

Herbert Marcuse? Enzensberger reproaches utopian idealism for being largely determined by class interests. While this argument can be used against Schiller because in his case his social agenda and his aesthetic theory do not coincide, the same can hardly be said for Marcuse. What separates Enzensberger from Schiller and Marcuse is, upon closer inspection, not so much the different definition of utopia as the oppositional function of the utopian moment in literature. Enzensberger conceptualizes the contents of literature as basically ideological; they are replicas of the bad status quo. "Art is there to superscribe the bad status quo with utopias." Only aesthetic structure allows one to understand the experience of living a life which has a consistent meaning. "Aesthetic mimesis is not in the first instance concerned with the objects, but with the structural imitation of social utopia."[37] Enzensberger thus concludes that art is free from ideology only when it is pure structure, form, or figure. By way of contrast, the transfiguration of contents necessarily proves ideological because there the received elements of reality are idealized until the contradictions disappear.

It is evident that Enzensberger cannot be interested in the real effects of literature. They have no place in his theory. It is precisely the utopian structure that is the reason for literature's "profound indifference toward current politics."[38] Literary theory in this instance manifestly reflects on its own task: it criticizes the demand it had articulated during the 1960s. Enzensberger renounces political aesthetics as well as ideology critique and withdraws to a metahistorical theory that is first developed in purely phenomenological terms and only subsequently applied to history. The result of this move is an irresolvable contradiction: from a systematic philosophical perspective, the abolition (*Aufhebung*) of aesthetic autonomy cannot take place simply because works of art in principle cannot

---

37. Ibid., 145, 147.
38. Ibid., 150.

be assimilated to life-practice. Yet, in the conclusion of the theoretical section of his work this is precisely the move that Enzensberger heralds as the political solution to the aesthetic problem. In his view, the revolt of the Parisian students in May of 1968 completed what had only been anticipated in trivial literature: "Art and life have become one and the same." These historical reflections, which bear on the manifestations of crisis in art during the 1960s, burst the systematic framework of Enzensberger's theory. As a result, one encounters the following comment: "Art has become boring, and ideology hackneyed."[39] Art's traditional social function—to demand that the social lack of meaning be remedied—has lost its power of conviction. Yet for Enzensberger, in contrast to Adorno, this disappearance of art (*Entkunstung*) is not a regression but the sign of a positive societal turn. For, through its decline, art at the same time loses something of its complicity with hegemonic consciousness.

Was there a common denominator in West German theories of art at the conclusion of the 1970s? As one can see from the examples discussed above, this was certainly not the case at the doctrinal level. There is no new aesthetic theory that occupies the same central position as the theories of Lukács and Adorno did during the 1950s and early 1960s. It is more relevant to speculate on why the kind of philosophy of art represented by Lukács, Bloch, Adorno, and Marcuse—who all inherit the legacy of Hegelian aesthetics—became exhausted. With reference to Adorno's *Aesthetische Theorie*, Otto K. Werckmeister speaks of subjective conceptual studies that are no longer capable of asserting a general claim to validity.[40] In other words, theory decays to the level of private confessions. With the use of a concept from Adorno, Dieter Wellershoff described the situation more generally as the de-aestheticization of art (*Ent-*

39. Ibid., 178, 179.
40. Otto K. Werckmeister, "Das Kunstwerk als Negation: Zur geschichtlichen Bestimmung der Kunsttheorie," in his *Ende der Aesthetik* (Frankfurt, 1971).

kunstung der Kunst): "The posture of the consumer is the subjective correlate of the untrammeled character of art arising from the disappearance of any normative expectation which would limit the expansion of production. The last phase of this production is to dismiss the prerogative of art itself."[41] Wellershoff allows the various positions to pass review once more (Bloch's utopianism, Marcuse's philosophy of praxis, and Adorno's theory of autonomy), without expecting a breakthrough from any of them. For Wellershoff, this means the end of the aesthetics informed by the philosophy of history, the aesthetics that always assumed, regardless of the approach it took, that the work of art—to borrow Adorno's metaphor—is the sundial of history. Although neither Lukács nor Adorno wants to admit it, art has shifted to the periphery; its emphatic significance has diminished along with the cultural traditions (religion, morality) that customarily nourished it. It was only in the course of the 1970s that these problems of aesthetic theory turned out to be the significant ones. At the end of the 1970s it was no longer a matter—as it was for Lukács and Adorno—of the structure of the work of art under the conditions of progressing capitalism, but a matter of taking stock of the crumbling or already lost cultural traditions that gave rise to art in the first place.

This point of view first gained primacy in Habermas's 1972 essay on Walter Benjamin.[42] Upon its appearance this essay was wrongly read as a defense of Adorno's position against a materialist interpretation of Benjamin. If one scrutinizes Habermas's comments on Adorno more closely, however, it is impossible to overlook the fact that Habermas no longer sees any future for Adorno's theory of art. For Habermas, Adorno's theory belongs to an earlier epoch by reason of its pessimistic

41. Dieter Wellershoff, *Die Auflösung des Kunstbegriffs* (Frankfurt, 1976), 81.

42. Jürgen Habermas, "Walter Benjamin: Consciousness-Raising or Rescuing Critique," in his *Philosophical-Political Profiles*, trans. Frederick G. Lawrence (Cambridge, Mass., 1983), 129–64.

esotericism. It offers nothing that could help confront the problems arising from the radical loss of tradition in late capitalist societies. Philip Brewster and Carl Howard Buchner have rightly pointed out that the Benjamin essay must be regarded as preparing the way for Habermas's theory of legitimation crisis.[43] To the extent that Habermas distances himself from the Marxian concept of praxis and distinguishes more clearly between labor and communication, the problem of language advances into the foreground. And in this connection, Benjamin's contribution becomes important for Habermas by virtue of precisely that element of Benjamin's thought that does not fit into the orthodoxy of the Frankfurt School.

Both Lukács and Adorno, to a certain degree, still assumed the bourgeois legacy in the concept of culture as a matter of course. Culture must be critically examined insofar as it drags along false consciousness; however, the authentic core of culture can in each case be reconstructed in the autonomous work of art. The ties to the aesthetic theory of idealism have not yet been severed. Within the framework of his crisis theory, Habermas throws open an issue whose radical nature was not anticipated in the classical form of Critical Theory: the achievement of conditions under which cultural traditions in late capitalist social systems can no longer renew themselves. In light of this situation, not only traditional hermeneutics but also the classical critique of ideology turn out to be ways of appropriating cultural tradition. "To this extent, critique is no less a form of appropriating tradition than hermeneutics. In both cases appropriated cultural contents retain their imperative force, that is, they secure the continuity of a history through which individuals and groups can identify with themselves and with one another." Habermas compares this situation to others in which culture is either strategically-

43. Philip Brewster and Carl Howard Buchner, "Language and Critique: Jürgen Habermas on Walter Benjamin," *New German Critique* 17 (Spring 1979): 15–29.

functionally organized or historically-objectively refashioned. The conclusion thus presents itself: "Apparently traditions can retain their legitimizing force as long as they are not torn out of interpretive systems that guarantee continuity and identity."[44]

Yet this process of extraction occurs when the state systematically intervenes in the cultural realm by subjecting long-standing traditional relations to rational planning. A lack of meaning arises which cannot be compensated for. Habermas maintains the thesis that capitalist societies were "always dependent on marginal cultural circumstances" and that bourgeois culture "was never able to reproduce itself from itself."[45] Bourgeois culture is not completely compatible with the capitalist system—it is, on the contrary, largely tied to traditionalistic worldviews. This interpretation puts Habermas markedly closer to Benjamin than to Adorno, whose theory of modernity highlights its correspondence to the capitalist market. According to Habermas, who in this instance follows Arnold Hauser as well as Benjamin, the radicalization of aesthetic autonomy in the theory and praxis of modernity leads to the division between the bourgeoisie and the avant-garde. "Under the sign 'art for art's sake,' the autonomy of art is carried to the extreme. The truth thereby comes to light that in bourgeois society art expresses not the promises but the irretrievable sacrifice of bourgeois rationalization, the plainly incompatible experiences and not the esoteric fulfillment of withheld, but merely deferred, gratifications."[46]

With this sentence Habermas definitively parts company with Adorno's and Marcuse's theories of art, which adhered to art's esoteric promise despite the prevailing deprivation. Like Benjamin, Habermas assumes that the art of the avant-garde has lost the aura and forfeited its autonomous status. "Modern

44. Jürgen Habermas, *Legitimation Crisis*, trans. Thomas McCarthy (Boston, 1973), 70, 71.
45. Ibid., 77, 76 (translation modified).
46. Ibid., 85 (translation modified).

art had already shed the aura of classical bourgeois art by making the process of production evident and presenting itself as something that was produced. But art infiltrates the ensemble of use values only when it surrenders its autonomous status."[47] Without slavishly committing himself to it, Habermas absorbs essential elements of Benjamin's theory, particularly the connection between avant-garde movements and the decay of the aura, which Habermas interprets as an important aspect of the motivation crisis of the late capitalists. This occurs not least of all because Habermas in some degree appropriates the critique of the cultural heritage Benjamin had advanced in the "Theses on the Philosophy of History." Habermas not only makes use of the critique of historicism—one could also find this in the works of Horkheimer and Adorno—he also brings to bear Benjamin's critique of tradition as the conception of historical continuity.

Habermas conceives of the liquidation of autonomy as a consequence of the societal process of rationalization Max Weber had described. Naturally, Habermas is aware of the fact that Adorno never accepted this step when Benjamin took it. Habermas sums up Adorno's position once again so that he can append the following comment: "In contrast, for arts received collectively—architecture, theatre, painting—just as for popular literature and music, which have become dependent on electronic media, there are indications of a development that points beyond mere culture industry and does not *a fortiori* invalidate Benjamin's hope for a generalized secular illumination."[48] Habermas concludes from Benjamin's theory that postautonomous art harbors within it the possibility that the experience of happiness residing in mimetic behavior can become exoteric and universal. In the context of this essay, the question of whether Habermas's solution is sound is not under discussion; it is much more significant that here, in confront-

47. Ibid., 86.
48. Habermas, "Walter Benjamin," 142.

ing Walter Benjamin, the theory of postautonomous art is recognized as the central theme of the 1960s, and indeed, not simply as a continuation of the discussion about the de-aestheticization of art (*Entkunstung der Kunst*)—as Wellershoff would have it—but as an articulation of contemporary possibilities.

Postscript

When I assessed the development of German aesthetic theory in 1979, the question of politics was being raised mainly within the Marxist tradition. Hence the discussion took place among various Marxist positions while traditional criticism (historicism or formalism) maintained its distance from political questions. Even reception aesthetics (Jauss, Iser, and the Constance school), after initially competing with Marxist theory, soon relegated these issues to the background and focused on the "implied reader," that is, the relationship between textual structures and reading processes. In doing so, reception theory formalized the critical moment of the art work at the level of individual reader consciousness. Already during the early 1970s, Jauss's theory took an anthropological turn that deemphasized his partial sympathy with Adornian theory, and consequently turned away too from attention to a historical grounding of aesthetics.[49] On the whole, reception aesthetics, after claiming a radical position during the late 1960s (as both a response to the student movement and an antidote to Marxism), returned to a more moderate position, a stance that acknowledges its indebtedness to the hermeneutical tradition.

Looking back at the theoretical debates of the late 1970s and 1980s, it seems to me that, by and large, they did not follow and develop the discussions of the previous decade. Much of radical Marxist theory (orthodox as well as neo-Marxist) dis-

49. See Hans Robert Jauss, *Aesthetic Experience and Literary Hermeneutics* (Minneapolis, 1982).

appeared without leaving many traces in the current discourse. The exception is Critical Theory, especially the work of Jürgen Habermas, which tends to overshadow the other disciples of Horkheimer and Adorno. Yet Habermas, particularly during the 1980s, has been more interested in problems of moral and political philosophy than aesthetic theory. As a result, the discussion about the political meaning of aesthetic theory has not advanced significantly among his students. The recent resurgent interest in Adorno's theory, on the other hand, has shifted its emphasis more toward the problems of grounding and epistemology at the clear expense of social questions, which stood at the center of the debate between 1965 and 1975. The return to Adorno, in other words, has to be seen in the context of the influx of a poststructuralist discourse from France, beginning in the late 1970s and gaining some momentum during the mid-1980s. In the context of this new discourse, the political question has resurfaced in a different form: whereas the previous debate centered on the political implications of the art work and then searched for the appropriate theoretical articulation of the problem, the discussions of the 1980s focused on the political character of theory itself, bringing into the foreground not only the politics of theory (the political position of a specific theory) but also the political meaning of the internal structure of theories.

This became particularly apparent in the Habermas/Foucault debate in which Habermas took initially the position that poststructuralist theory implicitly supported the conservative forces by embracing a postmodernist stance.[50] While the exchange between Habermas and Lyotard or Derrida received a great deal of attention also in this country, both its political and its philosophical contexts have not been fully understood, since the theoretical and political configuration in West Ger-

---

50. Jürgen Habermas, "Modernity—An Incomplete Project," in *The Anti-Aesthetic: Essays on Postmodern Culture*, ed. Hal Foster (Port Townsend, Wash., 1983), 3–15.

many only partly overlaps with the American situation. What has to be taken into consideration here is the growing tension among the disciples of Adorno and Horkheimer, on the one hand, and the emergence of a poststructuralist camp, on the other. The political debate of the 1980s has occurred primarily between Habermasian theory and a Foucauldian position, as it was developed by critics like Friedrich A. Kittler, Heinrich Fink-Ertel, and Harro Müller. This discussion was certainly not limited to the status of art and literature; in fact, these traditional questions played a relatively minor role. Even for the hermeneutic camp, which had been almost invisible during the early 1970s, the theory of interpretation did not focus primarily on the work of art. The involvement of post-Gadamerian hermeneutics in Germany with poststructuralist theory—in the work of Manfred Frank, for instance—clearly radicalized the hermeneutic project in various ways, though not always in clear alignment with the main debate as it was carried out between Habermasians and Foucauldians.[51]

As these few remarks indicate, the discursive map of West Germany has changed so radically during the 1980s that the positions of the 1960s and early 1970s can hardly be recognized anymore, even within Critical Theory. Most obvious is the lack of an orthodox Marxist position. To some extent, this is the result of external forces—namely the purge of German universities of radicals after 1972. *Berufsverbot* certainly helped to marginalize orthodox Marxism (Leninist or Maoist). On the whole (and this assessment includes the New Left), the Marxist paradigm, which so clearly shaped the debates of the 1960s, lost its momentum after 1980. A good indication of this phenomenon is the fate of social history in German literary criticism. The idea of politicizing literary history through the paradigm of social history, leading to a number of major mul-

51. See Manfred Frank, *Das individuelle Allgemeine: Textstrukturierung und -interpretation nach Schleiermacher* (Frankfurt, 1977); and his *Das Sagbare und das Unsagbare: Studien zur neuesten französischen Hermeneutik und Texttheorie* (Frankfurt, 1980).

tivolume projects, came under increasing criticism from various sides when the first volumes appeared.[52] By 1985, there was almost a consensus that the project had failed because of its problematic theoretical core. Progressive literary history collapsed under a critique coming from two theoretical positions, namely Foucauldian discourse analysis and post-Gadamerian hermeneutics. In both cases, the central categories of the project—historical evolution, social totality, classes, mediation, and so on,—came under attack. In the field of literary criticism, these scattered debates were, I think, more important than the exchange between Habermas and French post-structuralists.

The most crucial development in the political dimensions of literary theory, however, and therefore a good starting point for an overview of the 1980s in West Germany, is the appropriation of Foucault's work, which began in the late 1970s: the reception of Foucault rather quickly changed the parameters of the debate and with it the nature of the political. Helga Gallas's work can serve as a good example of this transition. While her early work, especially her discussion of German Marxist criticism of the 1920s and 1930s, drew on the authority of Karl Korsch and Brecht (in opposition to Lukács), her later readings of Heinrich von Kleist retreat from traditional political issues, focusing instead on the nature of writing and the subject in the text.[53] In this transition, the former commitment to Marxist theory seems to disappear, or is even replaced by hos-

52. A number of prominent publishing houses, among them Hanser, C. H. Beck, and Metzler, planned multivolume literary histories. None of these was completed. The best example of this type would be the volume edited by Rolf Grimminger, *Deutsche Aufklärung bis zur Französischen Revolution 1680–1789*, vol. 3 of *Hansers Sozialgeschichte der deutschen Literatur*, 11 vols. (Munich, 1980). For a detailed analysis, see Peter Uwe Hohendahl, "Bürgerlichkeit und Bürgertum als Problem der Literatursoziologie," *German Quarterly* 61 (Spring 1988): 264–83.

53. See Helga Gallas, *Marxistische Literaturtheorie: Kontroversen im Bund proletarisch-revolutionärer Schriftsteller* (Neuwied, 1971); and her *Das Textbegehren des "Michael Kolhaas": Die Sprache des Unbewussten und der Sinn der Literatur* (Reinbek, 1981).

tility toward historical criticism. This gesture of rejection is equally strong in the early writings of critics like Horst Turk and Friedrich A. Kittler in their attempt to establish a counterdiscourse in German criticism.[54] To a large extent, their energy went into deconstructing the critical models of the previous decade. This critique would also include the concept of the political, as it was used by the New Left or orthodox Marxists. Much of the leftist polemic against the West German state was now discarded as merely "utopian."

This anti-utopian element has shaped the understanding of political issues, both on the level of academic politics (political position of camps or groups) and the level of theoretical models. It is primarily the concept of discourse analysis, taken over from Foucault, that informs the critical debate of the 1980s. Exemplary is the introduction of Jürgen Fohrmann and Harro Müller to the volume *Diskurstheorien und Literaturwissenschaft* (1988), which defines the agenda of the collection of essays by a critique of Hans Robert Jauss's reception model, one version of the post-Gadamerian hermeneutic approach. In defining the Jaussian model (they could have used Iser's model as well) as "Sinn-Bildungsprozess," that is, as a model in which reading is supposed to create *meaning*, they link it to the hermeneutic tradition that dominated the nineteenth and early twentieth centuries.[55] Its goal, Fohrmann and Müller argue, is to make the text speak, to answer the questions of the inquiring critic. Hence critical reading results in a commentary that claims to be a reconfirmation of the text. Fohrmann and Müller intend to deconstruct this model, first, by linking it with a dialogical model grounded in a traditional concept of the subject and, second, by questioning the viability of this concept of the subject (invoking Luhmann's systems theory).

54. See *Austreibung des Geistes aus den Geisteswissenschaften: Programme des Poststrukturalismus*, ed. Friedrich A. Kittler (Paderborn, 1980).

55. Jürgen Fohrmann and Harro Müller, eds., *Diskurstheorien und Literaturwissenschaft* (Frankfurt, 1988), 9.

The reduction of the subject to the level of an element in the social process has significant implications. It tends to deflate, for instance, the political rhetoric of the New Left that emphasized subjectivity as the core of political praxis. Yet, this new political stance is also directed against the Habermasian version of Critical Theory, in particular its assumption that society can be defined in terms of communicative interaction. The attack on the "autonomous subject," legitimized by the authority of Lacan, Derrida, Foucault, and Luhmann, undermines the terms of the theoretical discourse of the 1960s and 1970s.

The American reader will find most of this familiar. Fohrmann's and Müller's introduction sums up and repeats many of the theoretical developments that took place in the United States in the 1970s. More interesting and important than this parallel, however, is the question How does this paradigmatic leap affect the conception of the political? One would look in vain for an explicit answer. For Fohrmann and Müller, there is no reason to believe in the oppositional force of the art work itself, nor is it plausible to have faith in the impact of the work (Jauss, Iser), not to mention the critical force of the author (Sartre, Lukács) or the critical community (Habermas). What remains is *Diskursanalyse* (discourse analysis): "This entry ticket into discourse analysis conceives of constellations and hence also of texts as *constructed* and *artificially* closed-off, dispersed unities, which arise out of differences. In this sense, one can speak of the plurality of a text, which is always constituted out of the judgment-statements [*Aussagen*] of various discourses, and even in its solitary existence always already attests to *intertextuality* or *interdiscursivity*."[56]

In other words, textual analysis can be identified as part of the social process but not used as a lever to engage in political action. In fact, Fohrmann and Müller do not offer a political agenda; their questions are concerned primarily with the in-

56. Ibid., 16.

ternal structure of the discourse model (definition of rules and relations). It is not accidental that among the contributors both Manfred Frank, as the proponent of hermeneutics, and Peter Bürger, as a critic close to the Frankfurt School, directed their polemic against the category of *discourse*. Frank, after examining Foucault's concept of the discourse, tries to show that the elimination of the subject is the result of a restrictive methodology, a repressive act that confronts Foucault with a considerable contradiction: on the one hand, Foucault declares discourses to be *unhintergehbar* (something one cannot "get behind"); on the other, he asks for an enlightened critique of these discourses in spite of the fact that this critique cannot be grounded (without a subject).[57] Bürger is even more explicit in his critique: Foucault's decentered theory is constructed in such a way that it creates its own center. In the attempt to break away from transcendental philosophy Foucault is bound to return to his premises.[58]

Obviously, in this exchange the focus of the political debate has shifted: since the beginning of the 1980s, that is, after the impact of poststructuralism, political issues have been articulated as *epistemological* issues or, conversely, epistemological problems have been treated as political questions. This modification occurred not only in the poststructuralist discourse; it is equally noticeable in the post-Gadamerian hermeneutic debate, where the conservative celebration of tradition (as a pre- and postsubjective position) has been replaced by a radical examination of the subject and/or individual.

It was especially Manfred Frank, a student of Gadamer, who defined the new task of literary criticism already in 1977 as a dialogue between the hermeneutic tradition (coming from Schleiermacher) and the semiotic tradition (following Saussure). What makes this dialogue important and meaningful for

57. Manfred Frank, "Zum Diskursbegriff bei Foucault," in ibid., 25–44.
58. Peter Bürger, "Die Wiederkehr der Analogie: Aesthetik als Fluchtpunkt in Foucaults *Die Ordnung der Dinge*," in Fohrmann and Müller, *Diskurstheorien*, 45–52.

Frank is the challenge of the structuralists and poststructuralists, their polemical stance toward the hermeneutic tradition. Yet, Frank—and this is noteworthy—refuses to perceive this exchange as a conflict between conservative and radical (progressive) forces; rather, in *Das individuelle Allgemeine* (1977) these political terms are cautiously avoided, since Frank wants to underscore the dialectic link between hermeneutics and semiotics. For this reason, Frank carefully outlines the contemporary debate before he returns to Schleiermacher's theory, emphasizing the intrinsic connections between positions that have been described as incompatible. In any case, the epistemological discussions remain completely abstract. It was only almost a decade later that Manfred Frank, in his lectures *Was ist Neostrukturalismus?* (1984), more explicitly put the political implications of the debate between "French" and "German" theory into the foreground. In 1984, Frank claimed for the hermeneutic tradition "critical and utopian potentials," which had left their traces on the radical students of 1968.[59] Also, Frank at least alludes to the Frankfurt School and its oppositional character. He suggests that only a combination of existential-ontological hermeneutics (Heidegger) and Critical Theory could articulate a progressive political critique of the contemporary situation. The dialectical treatment that Frank offered in his lectures is supposed to overcome the humanism/antihumanism opposition that defined the theoretical and political agenda of the 1980s. In this respect, but only in this, Frank's introduction is comparable to the agenda of the New Historicism—an attempt to bring together and integrate structuralist and hermeneutic approaches, clearly not by adding their elements but, rather, through a historical critique of the conflicting positions.

What remains unsaid and unexamined in this articulation of the task is its exclusion of theoretical positions that were central during the 1960s and 1970s. While the orthodox Marxist

---

59. Manfred Frank, *Was ist Neostrukturalismus?* (Frankfurt, 1984), 9.

tradition has disappeared almost entirely in Manfred Frank's program, Critical Theory is allowed to survive as a marginal position through its connection with hermeneutics (Karl Otto Apel, Habermas). Even those West German critics (like Kittler) who would strongly disagree with Frank's agenda (the structure/subject relationship) would share Frank's chart of the contemporary debate, marked by the surprising absence of Marx. In other words, the critical discourse has returned to its philosophical beginnings, articulating a strong preference for epistemological issues over social problems.

The notable exception would be the feminist movement(s) in West Germany, although even here the nature of the political involvement, as inside observers have noted, has undergone considerable changes. Still, compared with the general discourse of literary criticism, feminist approaches have retained a more explicit political agenda, ranging from the struggle against section 218 (the law against abortion) to poststructuralist criticism, in which the work of leading French feminists (Hélène Cixous, Luce Irigaray, Julia Kristeva) has been appropriated. The political impetus of the West German women's movement expressed itself both in the peace movement and the ecological movement (the Greens), where it reached larger segments of the population. At the same time, the project of emancipation, as it was formulated during the late 1960s and early 1970s by leftist women's groups, has lost its impact. In a recent essay, Cornelia Klinger concludes that a theory of emancipation and human progress has been relegated to the past.[60] Klinger, who is ready to defend such a project—at least up to a point—considers herself as somewhat "old-fashioned," since this defense entails also a defense of the subject and subjectivity—precisely the categories that have come under attack.

60. Cornelia Klinger, "Abschied von der Emanzipationslogik: Die Gründe, ihn zu fordern, zu feiern oder zu fürchten," in *Autonome Frauen: Schlüsseltexte der Neuen Frauenbewegung seit 1968*, ed. Ann Anders (Frankfurt, 1988), 293–329.

Reappraisals

The continuing politicization of German feminism thus owes its force to a new agenda in which Critical Theory plays only a marginal role. Aesthetic theory in particular, the legacy of Adorno and Benjamin, is no longer central to the political debate.[61] To some extent—and here we see a clear parallel to the general discourse in literary criticism—poststructuralist theory has taken its place and simultaneously redefined the meaning of the political. Among other things, this approach has resulted in a far-reaching critique of the concept of emancipation as it was used by the New Left. Under the influence of Gilles Deleuze and Félix Guattari, Lyotard, and Lacan, the notion of the subject has come under attack; also, with the growing impact of Lacan and Foucault, the question of power has been revised in a different way and with it the definition of women's political struggle.[62] In this new constellation, the question of power refers to knowledge, its acquisition and dissemination, rather than traditional political conflicts, which were carried out under the banner of equality. Since poststructuralist theory, especially through its critique of the subject, is not compatible with more traditional women's demands based on the idea of emancipation and since these demands have not been fulfilled in West Germany, the German women's movement has witnessed considerable tensions about the nature of the political struggle during the 1980s.

In this context, aesthetic theory in its post-Adornian form has contributed to the subversion of conventional politics, but

61. This distance is due, to some extent, to the initial rejection of the male-dominated New Left in 1968, which was very much under the influence of the Frankfurt School. The gap has never quite closed again. As a result, the fruitful elements in Critical Theory, for instance, the Odysseus excursus in *Dialectic of Enlightenment*, were never appropriated. For an account of the feminists' rejection of the Sozialistischer Deutscher Studentenbund, see Helke Sander, "Rede des Aktionsrechts zur Begründung der Frauen," in Anders, *Autonome Frauen*, 35–47.

62. See, for instance, Marianne Schuller, "Vorgabe des Wissens. Notizen zum Verhältnis von 'weiblicher Intellektualität' und Macht," in Anders, *Autonome Frauen*, 174–99.

the general relation of aesthetics and politics as it was conceived in Critical Theory stands in an uncertain position. It remains to be seen whether the new political criticism—whether in its feminist, its Habermasian, its Foucauldian, or its poststructuralist form—will continue its heavily epistemological course, or if different questions about art and late capitalist society will reopen the central issues in Critical Theory.

7   Reappraisals of Critical Theory:
     The Legacy of the Frankfurt
     School in America

The participants in any discussion about Critical Theory in the
United States have to keep in mind that Critical Theory is not
identical with the Frankfurt School, at least not with the work
of Horkheimer and Adorno or their disciples in postwar Germany. In this country, Critical Theory, particularly during the
1950s and early 1960s, was primarily associated with Herbert
Marcuse, Erich Fromm, and Leo Lowenthal, originally members of the Institute for Social Research, who decided to stay
in America after World War II. Clearly, the American New Left
was informed and shaped by the work of Herbert Marcuse,
rather than that of Adorno or Walter Benjamin. Of course, it
is also true that Marcuse's *Eros and Civilization* and *One-
Dimensional Man* prepared the way for the reception of Adorno's and Benjamin's more complex and demanding oeuvres
during the 1970s. As Martin Jay has shown, the reception and
integration of Adorno's work was a slow and uneven process,
which, with good reasons, can be called incomplete even today.[1] Much of Adorno's and Benjamin's writings are not yet
available in English and are still waiting to be discovered by
American critics. Still, it would be misleading to argue that

1. Martin Jay, "Adorno and America," in his *Permanent Exiles: Essays
on the Intellectual Migration from Germany to America* (New York,
1986), 120–37.

the theory of the Frankfurt School is not known in the English-speaking world. English editions, especially of Jürgen Habermas's writings, and numerous critical studies attest to its visibility. In fact, during the last decade, the presence of the "German" brand of the Frankfurt School has to some extent eclipsed the "American"contribution of Marcuse and Lowenthal, because the work of Adorno, Benjamin, and Habermas participates more openly in present theoretical discourse. This presence today clearly transcends the level of primarily historical interest, which had guided Martin Jay's first attempt to map the ideas and concepts of the Frankfurt School in *Dialectical Imagination* (1973) and Susan Buck-Morss's intricate analysis of the early Adorno in her book *The Origin of Negative Dialectics* (1977).[2]

Today, we have to assess the presence of Critical Theory in different ways. We have to appraise its function within the contemporary configuration, which has radically changed since the initial reception of the Frankfurt School during the late 1960s. At that time, the work of Adorno, Benjamin, and the early Habermas was integrated into the American discussion as a way of reinforcing the project of Western Marxism. The oppositional and critical force of these writers was directed against the formalist preferences of the New Critics and liberal social theory, for instance, the theories of Talcott Parsons and his students. The emphasis was clearly placed on the aspect of radical intervention to be carried out by marginal social groups. In *Marxism and Form* (1971), Fredric Jameson articulated this concern by bringing together the voices of Adorno and Benjamin with those of Lukács and Sartre. Jameson's attempt at a synthesis underscored the refunctioning of Critical Theory in the American context. While the Frankfurt School in Germany was quite unwilling to join with Lukács, in the United States,

2. See Martin Jay, *The Dialectical Imagination: A History of the Frankfurt School and the Institute of Social Research, 1923–1950* (Boston, 1973); and Susan Buck-Morss, *The Origin of Negative Dialectics: Theodor W. Adorno, Walter Benjamin, and the Frankfurt Institute* (New York, 1979).

Critical Theory was brought in as a supplement to more traditional Marxist theory. This supplemental role—in the case of Jameson ultimately predicated on a Lukácsian model—had two strategic functions: first, Critical Theory was expected to provide Marxist literary criticism with a more refined model in which the mediation between social and aesthetic forces would be worked out in a more satisfactory manner; second, the influx of Critical Theory was expected to counter the growing influence of structuralist Althusserian Marxism, whose most visible proponent became Terry Eagleton.

It would suffice to glance at the reviewer section of *Telos*, on the one hand, and that of *New Left Review*, on the other, to get an impression of the ongoing struggle within the leftist camp. The relentless polemic of *Telos's* contributors against the new "orthodoxy" under the disguise of French structuralism relied implicitly and occasionally explicitly on the rhetoric of the Frankfurt School against orthodox Marxism. For the *Telos* circle, Marx could be rescued from the dead weight of the Third International only through the rigorous emphasis on the critical and subversive moment in his works. In this context, Critical Theory served as a weapon to undermine the structure of reified dogma. Yet even the Frankfurt School was not critical enough; the writings of its members too had to be purged of hidden orthodox elements. In his introduction to the *Essential Frankfurt School Reader* (1978), Paul Piccone outlined what he considered the essential aspects of the Frankfurt School. More important, Piccone underscored the need for a critique of Critical Theory in its own spirit. He argued: "Contrary to Left conventional wisdom, according to which the quandaries of critical theory are the result of its having jettisoned fundamental Marxist assumptions, the real problem was the exact opposite: the unwarranted retention of too much traditional Marxist baggage."[3] This indictment, apart from the question

3. Paul Piccone, "General Introduction," in *The Essential Frankfurt*

of its historical truth, reflects a very specific moment in the history of the New Left, namely the realization that its project had failed. The struggle for political and social emancipation was now perceived as a myth that had to be exploded—with the help of Critical Theory, especially Adorno's micrological criticism. At this juncture, Piccone resolutely rejected Marcuse's attempts at theorizing on a macrological level, which he saw as confirming, at least implicitly, the Lukácsian project of *History and Class Consciousness*. From this vantage point, the failure of Critical Theory has to do with the central flaw of *Dialectic of Enlightenment*, its inability to articulate the dialectic of advanced capitalist societies in specific historical terms. As a result of this inability, "the dialectic becomes dehistoricized to cover the whole of Western civilization as the genesis of the domination of the concept. Consequently, critical theory does not even attempt to prefigure the future by elaborating the mediations necessary to bring it about, and becomes purely defensive: it ultimately retreats to defend particularity, autonomy and nonidentity against an allegedly totally administered society where thinking itself appears as a dispensable luxury."[4]

Piccone's critique focuses precisely on those moments that would resurface in the debate of the 1980s: subjectivity, autonomy, and nonidentity. What Piccone holds against Adorno is the unchallenged presence of a concept of totality that would necessarily marginalize nonidentity. In the totally planned society, resistance is antiquated from the beginning. Piccone's attempt to recuperate Critical Theory emphasizes oppositional impetus at the expense of content. For Piccone, the future of Critical Theory lies in its radically undogmatic rethinking of advanced capitalist societies, especially their political and cul-

School Reader, ed. Andrew Arato and Eike Gebhardt (New York, 1978), v, xv.

    4. Ibid., xvi.

tural systems. This radical critique includes the Adornian category of negativity, since the characteristic of postwar state capitalism is its ability to create and tolerate its own opposition. In this context, *Telos* for many years gave its support to the Habermasian version of Critical Theory, since *Legitimation Crisis* (1973) seemed to offer the kind of analysis that Piccone had sketched out in his introduction. The journal's more recent return to Adorno, and its simultaneous growing hostility toward Habermas, reflects yet another turn in the definition of "Critical Theory," a turn that articulates the interface of Critical Theory and poststructuralism.[5] Within the theoretical discourse of the 1980s, a new configuration has begun to emerge. Perhaps the crucial aspect of this new constellation is the breakup of Critical Theory, particularly the separation made between Habermas, on the one hand, and Adorno and Benjamin, on the other. Hence, the work of these theorists, despite the common background they share, has functioned in rather different ways.

The most obvious case is the theory of Jürgen Habermas, which in some quarters has been identified with Critical Theory. It is interesting to note, however, that its reception during the 1980s, highly controversial as it was, took a separate path from the Frankfurt School. Not only did Habermas's work address problems of social and political theory that the older generation had not articulated, but it also redefined the parameters in such a way that it opened a dialogue with theorists who would not have responded to Horkheimer's and Adorno's writings. The American discourse of the 1980s locates Habermas, and quite justly so, as a consistent defender of modernity. It is not accidental, therefore, that Thomas McCarthy's introduction to *The Theory of Communicative Action* (1984) invokes the modernity/antimodernity opposition in order to outline the Habermasian project. The defense of reason must

5. See Robert Hullot-Kentor, "Back to Adorno," *Telos* 81 (Fall 1989): 5–29.

articulate itself as a critique of reason. More specifically, McCarthy situates this project and its relevance in the context of a post-Heideggerian and post-Wittgensteinian age that has thoroughly deconstructed the categories of the Western tradition.[6] While the details of McCarthy's introduction are of no particular importance in this context, the crucial question for someone who wants to introduce a theory based on linguistic consensus is its locus in the American discussion. For McCarthy, Habermasian theory indeed corrected and superseded the older Frankfurt School by exposing the decisionism of Max Weber's sociological model, which Horkheimer and Adorno took over too uncritically. Therefore, McCarthy suggests that Habermas was right to criticize Western Marxism, including the Frankfurt School, and replace it with a system/subsystem model. "He seeks to demonstrate that this model can make good the failure of orthodox Marxism to comprehend central features of advanced capitalism—in particular, government interventionism, mass democracy, and the social-welfare state." McCarthy concurs with Habermas's premise that the problems of modernity are not "rooted in rationalization as such" but are connected with failures of institutionalization, in particular with the colonization of the life-world by instrumental rationality.[7]

It is interesting to note that McCarthy's introduction to Habermas's *Theory of Communicative Action* refers only in passing to Habermas's earlier work. By contrast, Richard J. Bernstein's introduction to *Habermas and Modernity* (1985) offers a much broader historical perspective, beginning with the philosopher's early experience. Yet his account also places the emphasis on the "mature" work and the question of rationality/modernity (the Weberian connection). Not unlike McCarthy, Bernstein argues that the unresolved problem of

6. Thomas McCarthy, "Translator's Introduction," in Jürgen Habermas, *The Theory of Communicative Action*, vol. 1: *Reason and the Rationalization of Society* (Boston, 1984), viii.

7. Ibid., xxxiii, xxxvii.

rationality (the Weberian cage of modern society), as it resurfaces in Lukács and later in Horkheimer and Adorno, propelled Habermas beyond the frame of the old Frankfurt School toward a better solution. This solution would overcome the aporias of *Dialectic of Enlightenment*. Clearly, the Habermas debate of the 1980s gravitates toward *his Theory of Communicative Action*, his *Philosophical Discourse of Modernity* (English edition, 1987), and his writings on moral theory; this tendency pushes his early work toward the background. In keeping with this trend, Bernstein criticizes *Knowledge and Human Interest* (1969) as a flawed transitional work whose unresolved problems forced Habermas radically to reconceptualize his theory. The quasi-transcendental grounding of his theory clearly invoked criticism from the analytical and the poststructuralist camp. In 1969 Habermas's theory was still rooted in the tradition of a philosophy of consciousness (Descartes). What Bernstein observes and supports in Habermas's more recent work is a reworking of the older concerns with a system of human interests on the basis of a theory of universal pragmatics. Most important, however, as Bernstein points out, Habermas has left the realm of a philosophy of consciousness and turned to a dialogical model. For Bernstein and the Habermasians in North America—among them Thomas McCarthy and Seyla Benhabib—the rational defense of reason and modernity is possible and clearly desirable. By the same token, Critical Theory is wedded to a conception of rationality that clearly transcends instrumental reason.

Hence, in the Habermas debate of the 1980s it is generally taken for granted that the theory of communicative action supersedes negative dialectics. Even those who invoke the work of Adorno and Horkheimer, like Albrecht Wellmer and Martin Jay, by and large do not call for a return to the Frankfurt School. As a result, in the American discussion Critical Theory has become polarized. Its Habermasian version, certainly more prominent among social scientists and philosophers, speaks to a community with rather different concerns than the first gen-

eration of the Frankfurt School. Thus, the critics of Habermasian theory are not necessarily the critics of Benjamin or
Adorno, as we will see later. Their objections have little in
common with the orthodox Marxist critique of the Frankfurt
School (even that of the praxis group) or the polemic of empirical sociology, as it was articulated by Karl Popper in the
Positivismusstreit of the early 1960s. The criticisms of Thomas
Lukes or Richard Rorty bring categories to bear on Habermas's
work that would hardly be applicable to either Adorno or Benjamin.[8] Both of them draw on the Anglo-American philosophical tradition in their critical discussion of Habermasian social
theory. What is characteristic for their ongoing debate is that
its participants (we can add the names of Nancy Fraser, Seyla
Benhabib, and Thomas McCarthy) are basically sympathetic to
the Habermasian project, although they are in many instances
not satisfied with its arguments and therefore highly critical
of its results. By and large they share with Habermas a skeptical
attitude toward poststructuralist models and approaches.

In this respect, Richard Rorty's contribution stands out, since
it makes an explicit attempt to bring Habermas into the orbit
of French theory and the postmodernism debate. Rorty summarizes the controversy between Habermas and Lyotard in the
following way: "So we find French critics of Habermas ready
to abandon liberal politics in order to avoid universalistic philosophy, and Habermas trying to hang on to universalistic philosophy, with all its problems, in order to support liberal
politics."[9] Habermas's reluctance to give up metanarrative as
a form of legitimation, Rorty feels, is related to his aversion to
a form of social and political criticism that is "context-
dependent" (instead of generalizable). Vis-à-vis these two pos-
itives, he argues—and more recently McCarthy has presented

8. Richard Rorty, "Habermas and Lyotard on Postmodernity," and An-
thony Giddens, "Reason without Revolution? Habermas's *Theorie des
kommunikativen Handelns*," in *Habermas and Modernity*, ed. Richard
J. Bernstein (Cambridge, Mass., 1985), 161–76, 95–124.
9. Rorty, "Habermas and Lyotard," 162.

similar arguments—that there is no need for a metanarrative, that the legitimation crisis of the modern age resulted from Kant's interpretation, especially his move to split "high culture up into science, morality, and art."[10] Rorty strongly opposes this interpretation, since it valorizes a metanarrative of modernity that is too narrow (German) and too pessimistic. What is more important, however, than Rorty's cultural evaluation of Habermas's tradition is his insight that French poststructuralism—for instance, Foucault's theory—shares some of Habermas's problems insofar as it buys into the Kantian definition of modernity and therefore also into the Habermasian agenda (although of course not into his solutions). Hence his critique addresses both Lyotard (and Foucault) and Habermas, insisting on a new canon without subject philosophy and metanarrative but with a strong commitment to liberal (Habermasian) politics.

In terms of its historical significance, Rorty's essay helped to clarify not only Habermas's position vis-à-vis the continental philosophical tradition but also to map the fundamental conflict of the postmodernism debate that was initiated by Habermas's 1980 essay "Modernity versus Postmodernity" and later fueled by his *Philosophical Discourse of Modernity* (1987). Since Habermas includes Horkheimer and Adorno in his fundamental critique, this debate has had an impact on the recent reception of Adorno as well. It was not entirely accidental that Rorty suggested a return to Adorno and Horkheimer as one way of getting away from metanarratives. On the other hand, it would be difficult to see Adorno outside the continental philosophical tradition that Rorty wants to cancel. For that reason, a philosophical alliance between Adorno and Rorty's pragmatism is unlikely—except for isolated points, such as the avoidance of dogmatic metanarratives and the need for mi-

10. Rorty, "Habermas and Lyotard," 166; Thomas McCarthy, "Practical Discourse and the Relations between Morality and Politics" (Paper read at a Habermas conference at the University of North Carolina, Chapel Hill, Oct. 1989).

crological criticism. Much of recent Adorno criticism has used similar issues in order to recover aspects of Critical Theory that were lost or repressed in Habermasian consensus theory.

Of significant import in this context is Joel Whitebook's attempt to reconstruct the contribution of Freud and psychoanalysis to Critical Theory.[11] While the primary interest of his essay is the reworking of psychological aspects of Critical Theory in Habermas's work, Whitebook resists the tendency of much recent Habermas criticism simply to discard the older Frankfurt School as "superseded" by Habermasian theory. To be sure, Whitebook's reconstruction of the Freudian components of Critical Theory is anything but uncritical. It points, among other things, to the limitations of id theory, as it was favored by Adorno and Marcuse, and to the somewhat pessimistic tone of id psychology. Whitebook specifically relates the "pessimism" of *Dialectic of Enlightenment* to the authors' inability to come to terms with and integrate ego psychology. Yet, at the same time, he underscores the importance of the original agenda of the Frankfurt School by pointing out that Habermas, in his attempt to overcome the theoretical impasse of the early Critical Theory, also tends to shortchange the initial project.

Whitebook criticizes the Habermasian project for its neglect of the central concern of Adorno and Benjamin with happiness, a concern not grounded in abstract norms but linked to the concept of mimesis. As a consequence of its "linguistic turn," Habermasian theory of communicative action loses the sense of an "inner foreign territory," which defines Freudian theory and also its appropriation by Marcuse and Adorno. Hence for Habermas the category of alienation becomes less central and the problem of happiness a secondary one. His systematic distinction between happiness and social justice allows him to

11. Joel Whitebook, "Reason and Happiness: Some Psychoanalytic Themes in Critical Theory," in Bernstein, *Habermas and Modernity*, 140–60.

place in the foreground a notion of progress in the realm of morality, possibly at the expense of happiness. We should note that Whitebook acknowledges the theoretical advances of Habermasian theory over the older Frankfurt School, but he also wants to discuss the price for this gain. His critique boils down to the question of external reality and, more specifically, the question of the body. Thus he concludes: "we cannot defend the project of modernity—which must be defended—at the price of sacrificing the naturalistic tradition that runs from Feuerbach throughout the young Marx and Freud to the early Frankfurt School."[12]

Much of the recent discussion of Critical Theory has focused on the question Whitebook brings up in his assessment of Habermas's theory: Can one assume (with Bernstein, McCarthy, and others) that the theory of communicative action canceled older Critical Theory, or is there a need for a return to Adorno and Benjamin? To some extent, this question itself reflects the limited reception of post-Adornian Critical Theory in this country, for within the context of the German discussion it would not be plausible to perceive Habermas as the only heir to the Frankfurt School. Under these circumstances, resistance toward Habermasian theory can easily take the form of a "return" to older models, just as the dissatisfaction of the second generation of the Frankfurt School in West Germany articulated itself as a "return" to the Marxist origins of the Frankfurt School in the 1930s. This strategy of going back to the roots is sometimes linked to another move: the suggestion that the essence of Critical Theory is closely related to theoretical positions such as deconstruction or New Historicism. In this case, Adorno and Benjamin can be played out as potential allies against the Habermasian version of Critical Theory, or, on the other hand, Adorno can be framed—as in Bernstein's account—as a crypto-Heideggerian.

It may be appropriate at this point to examine the stakes of

12. Ibid., 160.

the debate. It goes without saying that the request for a return to Adorno and Benjamin has little to do with the historical moment of their writings. The contributors to *Telos*—where the call for a return has been most consistent in recent years— are not ultimately interested in a historical reconstruction of the Frankfurt School, for instance, its program of the 1930s and its evolution during the 1940s and 1950s. The core of the agenda involves a rejection of Habermasian theory, of its definition of progress, modernity, and social justice. In other words, the politics of Habermasian theory, its function within the American academy, has aroused the suspicion of the Left. By the same token, the decidedly more positive evaluation of Habermas in the writings of Perry Anderson (at Adorno's expense) reflects a significant change in the configuration of British Marxism.[13] Here it is deconstruction that serves as the negative force for the reevaluation. In both cases, the reappraisal of Critical Theory also involves reconfigurations in the understanding of oppositions and alliances. The political agenda, however, is rarely spelled out; typically, it is couched in epistemological and methodological terms. Unlike the 1960s and early 1970s, when theoretical issues were frequently reduced to political ones, during the 1980s we find a tendency to discuss political conflicts under the disguise of theoretical models. For this reason the contemporary contribution of Critical Theory is best assessed in the context of specific themes and issues.

My own discussion will focus on three areas, namely, conceptions of culture, the postmodernism debate, and the theoretical articulation of feminism. Obviously, these thematic concerns are interrelated, though they operate on different levels: among them, it is primarily the theory of culture that serves as a metalevel for the discussion of the other two, feminism and postmodernism. In its more differentiated conception of culture, Critical Theory is said to have made major gains in

13. Perry Anderson, *In the Tracks of Historical Materialism* (Chicago, 1984).

comparison with traditional Marxism. In different ways, Benjamin, Adorno, and Marcuse criticized reductive base/superstructure models. For Habermas, a return to a traditional model was never in question; at the same time, however, from his early work on, his conceptualization of culture differs significantly from Adorno's attempts. These differences have left their traces in the American debate of the 1980s—not only in the encounter between Critical Theory and poststructuralist approaches but also in the less pronounced dialogue with Cultural Marxism and the New Historicism.

In certain ways both Marcuse's and Adorno's definitions of culture stayed very close to a rather narrow traditional conception of high culture (*Kultur*). Their work can positively invoke "culture" as the canonical tradition in literature or music. When Adorno practiced his method of close reading, the typical focus remained masterpieces of the high-culture tradition, for instance, Beethoven's late sonatas or Goethe's *Iphigenie*. Needless to say, this exclusive definition of culture, with its close proximity to a conservative understanding of culture as an autonomous aesthetic realm, has not attracted much attention lately. More important are two aspects of Adorno's theory that have informed the discourse of the New Left and more recently seem to resurface in the work of the New Historians. First, the autonomy of culture is not absolute but mediated through social conventions and institutions. Such a conviction rejects as ideology the abstract concept of culture and considers the cultural criticism based on such an abstract notion dogmatic and uncritical. Second, the relationship between high culture and mass culture must not be understood as an opposition but rather as a dialectical relationship that has to be examined as part of the social formation. It was precisely this aspect of Adorno's theory of mass culture that was not fully understood in the American mass-culture debate of the 1940s and 1950s, since this debate treated the opposition as an abstract dichotomy. The Frankfurt School's critique of mass culture not only undermined this dichotomy but, in doing so, also broadened the concept of culture, bringing into prominence aspects that traditional criticism had constantly excluded from critical scrutiny. The recent canon debate is clearly indebted to Critical Theory, although the connection is rarely explicit, since the immediate impetus for the discussion frequently comes from studies of ethnic subcultures and women's studies.

Obviously, it would be misleading to describe the critical discourse of the 1980s as a straight continuation or even modified extension of the Frankfurt School—or of Western Marxism, for that matter. What current critical approaches have retained, however, is a sense of the intrinsic relation between cultural interpretation and social theory. In fact, in the present debate, the classical distinction between them, which still informed the work of the older Frankfurt School, has vanished. Cultural theory has subsumed social theory, primarily under the rubric of cultural practices. Conversely, forms of domination and coercive practices are no longer exclusively or primarily located at the level of the social system. The concept of affirmative culture, introduced by Herbert Marcuse in 1937, captures part of this shift but not all of it. His own work, as well as that of Adorno, remained linked to the category of the autonomous art work as the bearer of oppositional and utopian forces and thus could not embrace a broad anthropological concept of culture. For Marcuse and Adorno the "core" of culture, the advanced art work, escapes cultural hegemony through its own formal structure, which articulates the opposition against the social relations in which it is embedded.

For the ongoing critical debate in the United States, the differentiated concept of culture of the Frankfurt School has been fruitful, yet by no means binding. Classical Critical Theory becomes one of a number of voices; frequently it is used—for instance, in John Brenkman's *Culture and Domination* (1987)—as a critical force for the discussion of thematic problems. For Brenkman, a critical definition of culture has to hark back to the writings of Marx and Engels. In this historical unfolding of the cultural problematic, the contribution of the

Frankfurt School becomes a significant moment (but no more than that) in the history of Western Marxism. Moreover, on a critical note, Brenkman suggests that Western Marxism (and the Frankfurt School) remains bound to the tradition of scientific Marxism, that is, to "the reduction of culture to consciousness and of social relations to relations of production."[14] As a result, culture becomes eclipsed and depoliticized.

While this assessment is useful in the case of Adorno, it certainly misses the core of Benjamin's later writings, which are precisely concerned with the political moment in culture. Brenkman, however, is certainly justified in underscoring the need for a political definition of culture. Of course, in this statement not only is the concept of culture at stake, but so also is the concept of the political. The typical dismissal of Adorno's philosophy of art during the 1970s as quietistic was predicated on a notion of politics as radical opposition rather than self-reflexive subversion. In more recent definitions of the political, the micrological aspect of culture and the literary text—favored in Adorno's approach—plays a more important role. It is not accidental, therefore, that Brenkman in his reading of Blake's poetry comes back to the notion of internal contradictions and language practice. Where he turns away from Adorno is the latter's understanding of the art work as an autonomous construct. Instead, he wants to focus on the double movement of a reading that responds to overdetermined and multivalent poetic language. By invoking Freudian interpretation, he wants to stress the suspended or floating attention of Blake's reader. But this strategy of reading and situating the literary text is much closer to Adorno than Brenkman seems to realize. Where he does indeed transcend the Adornian scope of criticism is in his notion that interpretation, even in its ideal form, always contains a moment of resistance, that the ideal reader is always engaged in social practices that codetermine the act of reading.

14. John Brenkman, *Culture and Domination* (Ithaca, 1985), 100.

What emerges in Brenkman's discussion is a fundamental dissatisfaction with the social theory of the older Frankfurt School. Indeed, for Brenkman the most apparent weakness of Adorno's later theory stems from the fact that he and Horkheimer failed to develop a more flexible model of capitalist societies after 1944. While Adorno considerably refined his aesthetic theory and criticism during the 1950s and 1960s, his concept of the advanced capitalist society as a totally administered society froze and did not take in later developments. The moment of reification becomes the final word for all social practices. Therefore, the subjective moment, unable to express itself socially, moves into the art work. This, however, means that the true locus of Adorno's late social theory is his aesthetic theory. The definition of the art work as a monad contains more than Adorno's explicit formulations of the relationship between society and art; it is the core of Adorno's theory, namely, the complete entwinement of the social and the aesthetic. To this we have to add the political aspect. The work of art is the site of political resistance. Still, Brenkman's critique addresses an important point. In Adorno's later theory the social agent is underprivileged; or, to put it differently, the social structure dominates the individual and his or her social practice. By harking back to Raymond Williams and British Cultural Marxism, Brenkman means to insert a different understanding of cultural practice, which undercuts the society/ art dichotomy. The political significance of this strategy deserves attention. Its intent is to mobilize the interaction between poetry and society as an interaction between two discursive practices in such a way that the outcome is not already predetermined. In order to reestablish the political thrust of the Marxist tradition, Brenkman abandons Adorno's social theory as well as the premises of his micrological analysis, turning to a psychoanalytical approach instead.

If the political aspect of culture is at the center of the recent debate (and the case for this emphasis can be made), the legacy of Critical Theory comes into play in various and contradictory forms. Different strands and phases can and have been played out against each other. Clearly, the concept of the political in Benjamin's criticism figures differently from that in Habermas's theory, for instance. But in spite of considerable differences of emphasis and outspoken disagreement about the legacy of Critical Theory, one is struck by a common element in more recent essays and books. Whereas the tenor of the discussion in the 1970s stressed the distance toward the older Frankfurt School for political reasons, the critical discussion of the 1980s has recuperated the political force of Critical Theory, especially in the writings of Benjamin, but also, more surprisingly, in the work of Adorno. For example, in *Modern Culture and Critical Theory* (1989), Russell A. Berman argues that Horkheimer and Adorno's *Dialectic of Enlightenment* contains a political message that speaks to the contemporary situation, though mediated through a historical analysis of the mid-1940s. The radical move, Berman suggests, consists of educating the individual for autonomy. "For critical theory, autonomy is the project of the subject who has not yet escaped heteronomous determination but who might do so, a potential indicative of the openness of history not closed off by the idealism of an epistemic logic of genealogy."[15] We should note that the target of this polemical formulation is no longer a conservative defense of freedom or an orthodox Marxist conception of class struggle but Foucault's concept of genealogy with its stress on power. What Berman wants to bring into the foreground are the different political implications of two positions that seemingly concur in their critique of the Enlightenment. The point of this comparison is that Critical Theory, unlike Foucauldian genealogy, is not satisfied with a pessimistic account of structures of domination. Instead, it marks the moment of freedom in the resistance of the victim. This

15. Russell A. Berman, *Modern Culture and Critical Theory: Art, Politics, and the Legacy of the Frankfurt School* (Madison, Wis., 1989), 15.

reading of Adorno stands in clear although unacknowledged opposition to that of Habermas in the *Philosophical Discourse of Modernity*, notwithstanding that it shares the turn against genealogy. Clearly, the attempt to revitalize Adorno, particularly in the area of cultural criticism, has created a division in the appropriation of Critical Theory. This strain becomes more visible in the postmodernism debate—a debate that has been labeled as an exchange between "German" and "French" theory, represented by Habermas and Foucault.

This is not the place to review the entire debate.[16] My observations will focus on the role of Critical Theory as a force in the definition of postmodernism. In this context, it is important to remind ourselves that Critical Theory is not identical with Habermasian theory. This is especially true in regard to the analysis and evaluation of modernity. The voices of the Frankfurt School have to be carefully distinguished. The intervention of Jürgen Habermas in 1980, which has made for a great deal of agitation in various camps, must also be understood as part of an ongoing debate within the Frankfurt School about the Enlightenment and its implications. It was prefigured already in the controversy between Benjamin and Adorno about the loss of aura and the function of mass culture and the new media (film).

For a number of reasons it is not entirely surprising that the response to Habermas's project has been ambiguous and strained among American critics, who are fundamentally sympathetic to Critical Theory. Moreover, from the vantage point of the American discourse on postmodernism, the contribution of Habermas came at a rather late stage of the debate. As Andreas Huyssen points out in his essay "Mapping the Postmodern," the debate about the end of modernism emerged in the

16. Two recent contributions questioning postmodernism in a Marxist frame are David Harvey, *The Condition of Postmodernity* (Oxford, 1989), and Douglas Vellner, ed., *Postmodernism/Jameson/Critique* (Washington, D.C., 1989).

United States during the 1960s.[17] Critics like Leslie Fiedler and Ihab Hassan introduced the term to examine contemporary literature. It was only during the late 1970s that the concept of postmodernism surfaced in France and Germany, where it took on a much broader meaning. The initial discussion dealt with the fate of the avant-garde after World War II and focused on the expansion of the literary and artistic opposition during the 1950s. The postmodernism debate of the 1980s, on the other hand, fueled by the contributions of Lyotard and Habermas, addressed a much larger issue, for the opposition modernism/ postmodernism was now linked to another opposition, namely, modernity/postmodernity.

In his by now notorious essay "Modernity—an Incomplete Project," Habermas boldly subsumed the aesthetic debate under the historical debate about the post-Enlightenment age.[18] In doing so, he implicitly invoked the entire trajectory of Western Marxism from the early Lukács to the late Adorno, since in all its stages Western Marxism had to respond to the central problem: how do we understand and evaluate the transition that occurred during the eighteenth century? Clearly, through the amalgamation of modernism and modernity on the one hand, and of postmodernism and postmodernity on the other, the stakes became much higher—as did also the ensuing confusion. While Peter Bürger's *Theory of the Avant-Garde* (1974) conceptualized the problem of the end of the (classical) avant-garde in terms of a linear development from modernism to the avant-garde and its historical demise during the 1930s, thereby historicizing both Adorno and Lukács, the expansion of the debate during the 1980s has undermined the very teleology on which Bürger's argument was predicated.[19] As a result, the his-

---

17. Andreas Huyssen, *After the Great Divide* (Bloomington, Ind., 1986), 179–221.

18. This famous essay originally appeared in *New German Critique* 22 (Winter 1981) and was reprinted in *The Anti-Aesthetic: Essays on Postmodern Culture*, ed. Hal Foster (Port Townsend, Wash., 1983), 3–15.

19. Bürger's important work came out in Germany in 1974. See Peter

toricization of Adorno, which Bürger had emphasized, became again an open question. Similarly, Leslie Fiedler's strident attack on the ideology of High Modernism, which certainly included the position of Adorno, in a curious way supported the very distinction it wanted to undermine by reversing the traditional evaluation.[20] This reception of the Frankfurt School's cultural politics had to be exploded before a new appropriation could occur.

In the American configuration of the 1980s, some of the most interesting contributions to the problem of postmodernism and postmodernity have come from those critics who follow neither Habermas's line of argument nor the chorus of Foucauldian and Derridian counterattacks. Hal Foster's volume *The Anti-Aesthetic* (1983) and the fifth issue of *Cultural Critique* (1986/87) can be understood as attempts of the American Left to respond to the ambiguous shift in the discussion brought about by Habermas and Lyotard. In this context, Fredric Jameson's essay "Postmodernism and Consumer Society" is a key to the interface between the American Left and Critical Theory. On one level, Jameson's analysis of postmodernism stays close to the thesis of *Dialectic of Enlightenment*, which links modern mass culture to advanced capitalism. Jameson views postmodernist culture as an extension of that logic: postmodernism corresponds to a change in postwar capitalism. "The 1960s are in many ways the key transitional period, a period in which the new international order (neocolonialism, the Green Revolution, computerization and electronic information) is at one and the same time set in place and is swept and shaken by its own internal contradictions and by external resistance."[21] In

---

Bürger, *Theorie der Avantgarde* (Frankfurt, 1974). It was not translated into English until ten years later. See Peter Bürger, *Theory of the Avant-Garde*, trans. Michael Shaw (Minneapolis, 1984).

20. Leslie Fiedler, "Cross the Border—Close the Gap," in *A Fiedler Reader* (New York, 1977), 170–94.

21. Fredric Jameson, "Postmodernism and Consumer Society," in Foster, *The Anti-Aesthetic*, 113.

the immediate context, the question whether Jameson's assessment is plausible is not important; what matters is the clear connection of his position with the Frankfurt School. On another level, however, Jameson breaks away from a notion of autonomous art that Adorno never gave up. By defining the postmodernist style as pastiche, as a repetition without authenticity, he undercuts the avant-garde/mass-culture opposition on which Adorno's theory was predicated. From Adorno's point of view, this would mean that the moment of resistance in culture, which for him was inevitably coupled with the advanced art work, had vanished. The consequence would be complete despair, since hope, as Adorno tells us at the end of *Negative Dialectics* (1966), is linked to the nonconceptual particular, especially to the work of art.

Interestingly enough, Adorno's "pessimism," which overshadowed the German debate of the 1970s, has not had a major impact on the American postmodernism discussion of the 1980s. As Andreas Huyssen observed in 1981, the absence of a perceived downturn after the Second World War, as well as the absence of an indigenous American avant-garde (in the radical sense of the term), provided a dynamic to the postwar years that was missing in Europe. Thus he labels American art of the 1960s as the "colorful death mask of a classical avant-garde."[22] Yet the American endgame of the avant-garde, defining itself as postmodernism, is played out as rejection of high modernism and nostalgia for the historical avant-garde. While Huyssen, very much in the tradition of Critical Theory, points to the potentially affirmative character of postmodernism (for instance, its delight in pop culture), he carefully refrains from the Adornian tendency to view the end of the avant-garde as a complete closure of history. Rather, he concludes by underscoring the need for regaining a sense of history (beyond a notion of triviality) and a conception of cultural identity. At the same time, he does not advocate a return to the classical

22. Huyssen, *After the Great Divide*, 168.

avant-garde, whose claims to cultural and social regeneration have lost their validity.

This evaluation of postmodernism takes issue with the Adornian "pessimism" but also with Habermas's defense of modernity and (by implication) modernism. Huyssen's critique of Habermas, more suggested than strictly argued, stresses two points: the need for a more differentiated and dialectical account of the modern age than Habermas offers, and a strong suspicion against a theoretical project that relies on a totalizing view of history. These suggestions, clearly formulated against the background of poststructuralist theory, can be taken as an indication that the issue of postmodernism has encouraged a reorientation within the appropriation of Critical Theory. This reorientation often involves a more or less critical turn back to Adorno, as well as a (sometimes only implicit) distancing from the Habermasian "project of modernity." A good example of this complex move is the reading of Adorno in Russell Berman's recent work, *Modern Culture and Critical Theory*. Writing in a somewhat different context from Huyssen, Berman nevertheless provides (like Huyssen) a version of the Frankfurt School legacy that does not follow the Habermasian line in responding to postmodernism.

Berman develops his position by defending aesthetic autonomy (as Adorno's theory defined it) against Peter Bürger's critique. What Berman objects to in Bürger's theory of the avant-garde is Bürger's strong claim about the necessary linear development leading toward postautonomous art. Berman considers that Bürger's model overemphasizes "the predominance of a single aesthetic model within an institutional phase."[23] He argues that Bürger's central thesis about the failure of the avant-garde (and the consequent lapse into postautonomy) is based on the problematic assumption that the avant-garde constituted the hegemonic art form of the early twentieth century. Against this, Berman contends that the avant-garde was only

23. Berman, *Modern Culture and Critical Theory*, 49.

one strand in the configuration of modernism, and that it has maintained its critical position apart from the historical logic of monopoly capitalism. Consequently, Berman can valorize the avant-garde and its critical function, thereby opposing both postautonomous decline and postmodernist indifference. This argument rescues Adornian aesthetic theory without burying itself in the mood of despair that tinges much of Adorno's later writing.

In no way do I want to imply that Huyssen's and Berman's approaches to the problematic of postmodernism are identical. In fact, they clearly disagree. While Huyssen underlines the moment of subversion in postmodernist pluralism, Berman, more in the spirit of Adorno, tends to dismiss postmodernism as affirmative eclecticism. "The cultural theory of postmodernism provides the affirmative description of that which is merely given. Although it may carefully sketch power structures and practical strategies, its rejection of emancipatory autonomy precludes any systematic critical project."[24] What they do share, however—and this is the crucial point—is a sense of resistance to theoretical constructs of the kind that Habermas's later theory offers.

Obviously, the issue of postmodernism has not only divided the American Left, it has also brought about different and conflicting receptions of Critical Theory, ranging from an acknowledgment of postmodernist pluralism to a critique of its affirmative character based either on Adorno's idea of aesthetic truth or Habermas's notion of a loss of rational criticism. Similarly, there are also different emphases in the explicit or implicit political agenda connected with these positions—though these differences seem to be less pronounced than the theoretical ones. During the 1980s, the appropriation of Critical Theory in the United States, through its contact with other theoretical traditions, has (successfully, I believe) resituated the Left within the American discourse. While the theoretical

24. Ibid., 51.

interface has not necessarily changed the epistemological models, it has clearly redefined the political position of the Left, in particular its understanding of the theory/practice relation. What the question of postmodernism has helped to clarify for Critical Theory in this country is the inadequacy of the revolutionary models of the 1960s and the need for a broader definition of cultural practice, a conception in which the cultural and political are seen as complements rather than oppositions.

In even more dramatic ways than postmodernism, feminism has challenged received conceptions of culture and politics. In the case of West Germany (East Germany followed a different path altogether), it has led to a split between Critical Theory and feminist theory, since the cultural criticism of the Frankfurt School did not address the concerns of women. As far as the United States is concerned, the major strands of feminist theory that have dominated the discourse of the 1970s and 1980s—American feminism, represented by such critics as Susan Gubar, Sandra Gilbert, and Elaine Showalter, and French poststructuralist feminism (Hélène Cixous and Julia Kristeva)—followed different epistemological and methodological trajectories.[25] Only more recently has Critical Theory become a distinct voice. In the feminist debate, however, the locus of Critical Theory appears to be rather different from that of the postmodernist debate. Its critical edge has turned, to a large extent, against the "French" poststructuralist version of feminism. Hence its position is by and large closer to, but clearly not identical with, more traditional versions of Marxist theory emphasizing the *historical* nature of women's issues.[26] In this somewhat ambivalent alliance, the work of Jürgen Habermas, frequently attacked in the cultural debate, has become a focal point for a number of important questions.

25. See Toril Moi, *Sexual/Textual Politics: Feminist Literary Theory* (London, 1985).
26. See Sara Lennox's article, "Feminist Scholarship and *Germanistik*," in *German Quarterly* 62 (Spring 1989): 158–70.

In her essay "What's Critical about Critical Theory? The Case of Habermas and Gender" (1985), Nancy Fraser squarely addresses the problem of conceptualizing gender differences in the theory of communicative action.[27] The question of gender rarely surfaced in Adorno's work and was linked with the question of revolutionary movements in Marcuse's late writings only in a very general way, but Fraser rightly insists that Habermasian theory, because of its universal claims, has to respond to feminist issues on a number of levels, namely thematic, methodological, and epistemological. One obvious difficulty for a feminist appropriation is Habermas's silence on the specific social and cultural problems of women. One possible strategy to overcome this drawback would be to mobilize the distinction between labor and communication in Habermas for a critique of the bias in traditional Marxist theory toward male-dominated production, but one has to grant that, in terms of the structure of Habermasian theory, the male/female opposition does not fit easily into the difference between labor and symbolic action. Thus, Fraser suggests a more "structural" approach to the question of women's work, grafted onto the distinction between system-integrated and socially integrated (symbolic) actions. Furthermore, Fraser refers to the Habermasian division between life-world and system (typical for modern societies) in order to mark the difference between the private and the public sphere. In short, Fraser takes over major parts of Habermas's social theory for her own project, yet with the proviso that they have to be reworked for the articulation of feminist concerns.

From the feminist point of view, the private/public distinction mirrors the distribution between "productive" work and family. By putting the category to an empirical test, Fraser tries to show that the Habermasian distinction misses the mark,

27. Nancy Fraser, "What's Critical about Critical Theory? The Case of Habermas and Gender," *New German Critique* 35 (Spring/Summer 1985): 130.

that it especially does not adequately reflect the function of the family and the role of women in it. From a normative point of view, according to Fraser, the public/private distinction equally fails to address the imbalance of the traditional family structure. Specifically, Fraser notes a contradiction between the idea of social progress in Habermas's theory (which is expressed in terms of differentiation) and the norm of social justice. While social progress is linked to a process of differentiation in which the modern family and, with it, women are limited to the private realm, the idea of social justice cannot, as Habermas would agree, tolerate gender difference. To some extent, this critique misses the tension within the Habermasian concept of the public sphere, the tension between its factual and its normative aspect, by conflating these levels in Habermas's theory. What is more important, however, is the more general charge of gender blindness of the theoretical model that has defined Habermas's work since the mid-1970s. Fraser contends that his blindspot can be traced to the "categorical opposition between system and lifeworld institutions," which contains a bias toward a male-oriented society.[28] This critique simultaneously rescues other parts of Habermasian theory, however, among them the cultural interpretation of needs and the dialogical process of satisfying them.[29] For Fraser, the reception of Critical Theory is conceived as a selective and critical appropriation in which feminist concerns define the boundaries of acceptance.

Fraser's pragmatic strategy, with its somewhat understated understanding of the common ground, addresses primarily social problems but does not take up the larger issue of cultural difference that has defined the direction of feminist literary criticism. In this context, the question of the public sphere would take on a somewhat different meaning. Using Haber-

28. Ibid., 131 (also see esp. n. 47).
29. Rita Felski, *Beyond Feminist Aesthetics: Feminist Literature and Social Change* (Cambridge, Mass., 1989), 171.

mas's *Strukturwandel der Oeffentlichkeit* (Structural transformation of the public sphere), Rita Felski has argued that the
women's movement has created an important counter–public
sphere within a male-defined society.[30] In her emphasis on the
division within the public space and the possibility of undermining the hegemonic public discourse, Felski clearly extends
Habermas's conception in a direction that moves her close to
the position of Negt and Kluge.[31] The point Felski wants to
make is that a feminist public sphere opens up new spaces of
resistance that could and should be occupied by a variety of
approaches and theories. "Given the complex interpretations
of state and society in late capitalism, one can no longer pos-
tulate the ideal of a public sphere which can function outside
existing commercial and state institutions and at the same time
claim an influential and representative function as a forum for
oppositional activity and debate."[32] By stressing the need for a
discussion arena, she moves the reception of Habermas to the
level of metatheory, a move that allows her to integrate Critical
Theory in a more general way. Felski does not limit her discussion of feminist theory to specific doctrines of the Frankfurt
School; rather, she underscores a critical perspective on the
recent American conceptualization of women's studies. In particular, her approach raises the question of how feminist studies in the field of literature affect social and political structures.
Felski rightly calls attention to the situation of late capitalist
countries where the differentiation of the cultural and the po-

30. Ibid., 27.
31. See the introduction to this book for a discussion of Negt and Kluge.
The position to which I refer here is developed in their book, *Oeffentlichkeit und Erfahrung: Zur Organizationsanalyse von bürgerlicher und pro-
letarianischer Oeffentlichkeit* (Frankfurt, 1971). Negt and Kluge stress the
class-based notion of a counter–public sphere, but this argument is clearly
analogous to Felski's gender-based version of resistance. Both positions
arise directly out of the critique of Habermas's more univocal account of
the public sphere.
32. Felski, *Beyond Feminist Aesthetics*, 171.

litical spheres does not encourage the immediate impact of one sphere on the other.

Unlike Fraser, who is looking for a positive social model for the application of women's concerns, Felski stresses the "Adornian" aspect of Critical Theory, that is, its mode of critical reflection, as it engages theoretical positions. Again, it is the level of metatheory that becomes relevant for feminism, for instance, in a critique of feminist aesthetics both in American and French theory. Felski's metatheoretical method is especially telling in view of attempts to construct transhistorical modes of feminist writings. Within the American discourse, this project has frequently assumed a distinctive female sensibility grounded in a gendered experience. Yet, as Felski argues, this project is open to serious criticism because it overlooks significant social and cultural differences. "There are, moreover, obvious problems with a theoretical position which enshrines existing ideologies of sexual difference through reference to the supposedly intuitive and emotional quality of female consciousness, thereby merely reaffirming rather than questioning the authority of existing gender stereotypes."[33] Coming from Critical Theory, Felski argues that the lack of a sophisticated theory of ideology has typically trapped American feminism in an undifferentiated male/female dichotomy.

Whereas Felski's criticism of American feminism targets especially its reliance on ahistorical conceptions, her objections to French theory make a very different use of Critical Theory. Here she places in the foreground the similarities with Adorno's aesthetic theory, pointing to the problems involved in a modernist aesthetics. This critique builds on the post-Adornian concept of the avant-garde (Hans Magnus Enzensberger, Bürger), which has radically deconstructed the logical connection between the political and the aesthetic avant-garde. Like

33. Ibid., 27.

this critique, an advanced feminist position also has to question assumptions about a necessary connection between "avant-garde" fragmentary writing and political subversion. Making use of Mary Jacobus's critique of Hélène Cixous, Felski argues against any attempt to ground feminist criticism in the gendered nature of language.[34] For her this construct must fail because it dogmatically separates the feminine question from the social question and thereby "reiterates and is easily assimilated into a long-standing cultural symbolization of woman in Western society."[35] If Elaine Marks's statement, "Reading becomes the subversive act par excellence," is programmatic, the proximity to Adorno's aesthetic theory is indeed of crucial importance for a critical reading of *écriture féminine* (female writing or discourse).[36] Clearly, in this respect Felski tends to side with a Habermasian position that deflates the political claims of immanent criticism and, by extension, fragmentary, subversive writing. This critique emphasizes the need for contextualization: only the specific historico-social context allows the feminist critic to make political use of negativity. This leads to a method of reading that consistently deontologizes the feminist project, deconstructing the notion of an absolute distinction between the writing of males and females. The politics of writing and reading is not predetermined by fixed gender differences, rather, they have to be negotiated in the public sphere. Furthermore, the social and political function of a literary text has to be established within the context of the actual appropriation, that is to say, its subversive moment does not mechanically translate into political opposition.

Given the centrality of the concept of the public sphere for Felski's argument, it is not surprising that she turns to Habermas's *Strukturwandel*. We have to note, however, that her

34. Mary Jacobus, "The Question of Language: Men of Maxims and *The Mill on the Floss*," in *Writing and Sexual Difference*, ed. Elizabeth Abil (Brighton, 1982).
35. Felski, *Beyond Feminist Aesthetics*, 37.
36. Quoted in ibid., 39.

appropriation of Habermas's work, like that of Nancy Fraser, is selective. She clearly does not subscribe to the entire project of the early Habermas, which was not particularly sensitive to women's issues. Instead, she integrates those aspects of the Habermasian theory of the public sphere that help her to articulate the resistance of patriarchal societies to the needs of women. It is in this context that she examines the claims of feminist aesthetics and argues that there "remains, then, both an interaction and an inevitable tension between the spheres of 'feminism' and 'aesthetics.' "[37] It is a tension that cannot be resolved in either direction. The critical edge of literary analysis has to question the autonomy of the literary text as much as the social and political ideologies that determine the institution of literature. Again, this claim is rather close to Critical Theory in its general approach, even where Felski disagrees with specific theorists.

When Eugene Lunn examined the interface between Marxism and modernism in *Marxism and Modernism* (1982), he could still safely assume that the project of Western Marxism was more or less intact. Hence his own analysis traced the trajectory of German Marxism from Lukács to Adorno and Benjamin as part of the larger project of Western Marxism. In his conclusion, he (cautiously) affirmed Adorno's position on the avant-garde and mass culture while, at the same time, leaving some space for a Brechtian or Benjaminian position. Such an affirmation is, I feel, no longer possible. During the last decade, the meaning of the four theorists whom Lunn examined (Lukács, Brecht, Benjamin, Adorno) has changed in a major way. This does not mean that their work can be discarded. The question is its appropriation. It seems that the construct "Western Marxism" has lost some of its usefulness for the present debate. For one thing, Critical Theory, even in its traditional definition, does not easily fit this term anymore. Jürgen Habermas cannot be called a Western Marxist. Furthermore, Crit-

37. Ibid., 179.

ical Theory has opened up and moved in various directions by interfacing with different theoretical traditions. As a result, the conception of critical theory itself has altered. Boundaries that used to be stable have collapsed and new borderlines have emerged. This revisionism has been most visibly carried out by the New Historicists—theoretically speaking, a blend of the neo-Marxists (Frankfurt School), poststructuralists (Foucault), and cultural anthropologists (Clifford Geertz)—but it also appears, as I have tried to show, in the postmodernism debate. There is an obvious danger in this eclectic blending—the loss of the oppositional force, the "mainstreaming" of Critical Theory. The New Historicists have not always avoided this danger. But, on the other hand, there are considerable gains. To refuse the opening, to insist on the traditional boundaries, means to get caught in the past and to close off the future. The survival of Critical Theory depends on a self-critical reappraisal of its own tradition and of its locus within different cultural and political configurations. This ongoing process implies a different attitude toward its past, namely a nonlinear view of its own development and an acknowledgment of complex theoretical constellations. Of course, the early Frankfurt School, especially Horkheimer, was striving toward an interdisciplinary project in which the Marxist model was expected to be hegemonic. Forty years later and under very different circumstances, Jürgen Habermas made another attempt using a linguistic model. Both projects failed in their desire to favor a particular model. It seems that during the 1980s Critical Theory has been most effective as a local theory in a dialogical situation with different approaches and methods, receiving its strength from concrete social conflicts and struggles.

Index

Index

Index

231

Index

Index

Haberman, Jürgen (*cont.*)
  86 (*see also under* Adorno, Theodor W.)
  and "autonomous subject," 192
  and Benjamin, 105, 141, 183–87, 208
  and Bürger on Adorno, 96
  and communicative action, 102, 107, 109, 118, 121–22, 123, 146, 147–49, 204
  on critical reflection, 111
  and Critical Theory, 11, 12, 15, 17, 19–20, 100–101, 149, 215; de-emphasis of early Critical Theory, 7; and *Philosophical Discourse of Modernity*, 151–52; redefinition of Critical Theory, 9; in U.S., 15, 202–9; Whitebook on, 208
  on culture, 123, 184–86; and Derrida, 139–41
  English editions of, 199
  and Enlightenment, 11, 114–15, 131, 132, 147–48 (*see also under* Enlightenment)
  and feminism, 221–24
  and Foucault, 117–20, 132, 133, 134, 136, 141–47, 148, 152–54, 188–89, 215
  and Frankfurt School, 11, 100–102, 103, 106, 107, 110, 113, 117, 202, 203–4, 207, 215
  and French theory, 3, 132–33, 134, 149
  and Heidegger, 132, 136–38; and Derrida, 138–39, 140
  and Horkheimer, 10, 101–4, 106–8, 150 (*see also under* Horkheimer, Max)
  on ideology, 114–15, 116
  on "Left fascism," 9–10
  on life-world, 123–24, 125–30, 151, 203; and critical theory, 111

linguistic turn of, 4, 102, 207, 228 (*see also under* Communicative action)
  and Lüdke, 171
  on Lukács, 106, 117–18
  and Marxism, 2, 9, 12, 16–17, 101, 102, 117, 150, 210, 227
  and modernism, 133–34, 219
  and modernity, 11, 107–8, 121, 131, 134, 146–50 (*see also under* Modernity)
  and Negt/Kluge, 13, 14
  and New Left, 9–10, 14–15
  and Nietzsche, 102, 114–19, 132, 134–37, 141
  and postmodernism, 215, 216, 217, 219
  and poststructuralists, 3, 17, 132, 146, 149 (*see also under* Poststructuralist theory)
  on public sphere, 12–13, 14, 99–100, 154
  and rationality, 10, 102, 105, 107, 117, 119, 148, 149, 154, 204
  and systems theory, 16, 121, 122–24, 126, 142, 151, 203
Hallische Jahrbücher (Lukács), 28
Handelman, Susan, 140
Hardenberg, Friedrich von. *See* Novalis
Hassan, Ihab, 216
Haug, Wolfgang Fritz, 160, 165–66, 168
Hauser, Arnold, 185
Haym, Rudolf, 28
Hegel, G. W. F.
  and Adorno, 58–59, 68, 80–81, 82, 86, 89, 91, 92, 93, 97, 98
  and aesthetics, 174, 176, 177
  and Frankfurt School/Critical Theory, vii

Index

Index

Index

Index

Library of Congress Cataloging-in-Publication Data

Hohendahl, Peter Uwe.
    Reappraisals : shifting alignments in postwar critical theory / by
Peter Uwe Hohendahl.
        p.   cm.
    Includes index.
    ISBN 0-8014-2455-0 (alk. paper). — ISBN 0-8014-9708-x (pbk. :
alk. paper)
    1. Criticism.   2. Critical theory.   I. Title.
PN98.S6H6   1991
801'.95'09045—dc20   91-10127